citronila

18 buckle Kerr

185 Maroon Societies

184 memories of
Underdevelopment

186 087

178

179

184 Pilon Padella

183

180 Vrannio

181

178

177 Carpenter

183 Casa de

172 Releaser

173

187

The Voice of the Masters

Latin American Monographs, no. 64
Institute of Latin American Studies
The University of Texas at Austin

THE VOICE OF THE MASTERS
Writing and Authority in Modern
Latin American Literature

By Roberto González Echevarría

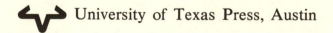 University of Texas Press, Austin

First Edition, 1985

Requests for permission to reproduce material from
this work should be sent to:
  Permissions
  University of Texas Press
  P.O. Box 7819
  Austin, Texas 78713

Library of Congress Cataloging in Publication Data

González Echevarría, Roberto.
  The voice of the masters.

  (Latin American monographs/Institute of Latin American
Studies, the University of Texas at Austin; no. 64)
  Bibliography : p.
  Includes index.
  1. Spanish American literature—20th century—History and criticism—Addresses,
essays, lectures. 2. Authoritarianism in literature—Addresses, essays, lectures.
3. Authority in literature—Addresses, essays, lectures. I. Title. II. Series: Latin
American monographs (University of Texas at Austin. Institute of Latin American
Studies); no. 64.
PQ7081.G638   1985   860'.9'98   85-644
ISBN0-292-78716-2

Para Severo y François

Contents

Acknowledgments

Various friends were present when this book was conceived a number of years ago as a graduate seminar at Cornell University. Two stand out in particular: Carlos Alonso and Rubéen Ríos Avila, now of Wesleyan University and The University of Puerto Rico, respectively. Their questions and comments at the very outset of the project were invaluable. The themes and ideas in the book later developed as a summer seminar sponsored by the National Endowment for the Humanities in 1979. Many were the contributions made by the colleagues attending the seminar. I would like to name here Fernando García Núñez of the University of Texas at El Paso, Alicia Andreu of Middlebury College, Gwen Kirkpatrick of Berkeley, John Incledon of Albright College, and Emilio Bejel of the University of Florida. The last in particular is a longtime friend with whom I have often discussed the ideas in the book. I have also benefited from discussions with very good friends and colleagues at Yale, whose points of view clearly are not reflected in the book. I am particularly indebted to Harold Bloom, Emir Rodríguez Monegal (whose private library is a treasure he generously puts at my disposal), Robert Stepto, Nicolás Shumway, Carlos Díaz Alejandro, and Marcelo Cavarozzi. I am responsible for the distortions of their valuable advice and they for the many good ideas I did not heed.

Editorial help was often provided by friends like Michelle Stepto, who revised my translation of "Meta-Final," and Nicolás Shumway, who read several pieces and made valuable suggestions. Frederick Luciani, now of Columbia University, was my research assistant during the 1981-1982 academic year, under the sponsorship of the National Endowment for the Humanities. He provided a first English draft of the paper on *Doña Bárbara*, which I had originally written in Spanish, and made many helpful suggestions, not to mention his priceless help in checking sources and tracking down old translations. His friendship and companionship during the year when this book was being finished were a source of inspiration and good cheer. Isabel Gómez, my wife, cleared the way so that I could devote my time to writing and research and answered many a question about spelling and usage.

Research funds were provided by the Social Science Research Council, and by Yale University's Griswold Fund and Councilium for International and Area Studies. The staff of the Latin American Studies program, which I chair, helped in all aspects of the preparation of the manuscript. I would like to thank Mrs. Ann Carter, administrative assistant to the program, for her aid in various important matters concerning finance, and Mrs. Mae Sanzone, who typed a sizeable portion of the manuscript. It is doubtful that, without their help, I would have been able to finish the book while burdened with the responsibilities of the program.

Among the writers whose friendship and conversation I cherished while writing this book about them, I must mention Alejo Carpentier, Miguel Barnet, Julio Cortázar, Gabriel García Márquez, and Guillermo Cabrera Infante. In the five days that he spent at Yale, a year before his death, Carpentier was generous with his vast erudition and good humor. Severo Sarduy and François Wahl, to whom this book is dedicated, have always provided warmth and hospitality in my visits to Paris and Saint Léonard. Making me feel at home has also meant making me part of their constant dialogue about literature and criticism, a dialogue devoid of pedantry and always enriching.

The Voice of the Masters

Latin American literature not only is an expression of our reality, or the invention of another reality. It is also a question about the reality of those realities. A question and at times a judgment. The constant presence of critical thought in the poetry and fiction of our America is not accidental: it is a feature of all modern literature in the West. . . . In this sense our literatures are modern. And they are so in a way that is more radical than our social and political systems, which ignore criticism and nearly always persecute it. —Octavio Paz

What makes a reading more or less true is simply the predictability, the necessity of its occurrence, regardless of the reader or of the author's wishes. "Es ereignet sich aber das Wahre" (not die Wahrheit) *says Hölderlin, which can be freely translated, "What is true is what is bound to take place." And, in the case of the reading of a text, what takes place is a necessary understanding. What marks the truth of such an understanding is not some abstract universal but the fact that it has to occur regardless of other considerations. It depends, in other words, on the rigor of the reading as argument. Reading is an argument (which is not necessarily the same as polemic) because it has to go against the grain of what one would want to happen in the name of what has to happen; this is the same as saying that understanding is an epistemological event prior to being an ethical or aesthetic value. This does not mean that there can be a true reading, but that no reading is conceivable in which the question of its truth or falsehood is not primarily involved.* —Paul de Man

Preamble

Contaminated, spurred on, we suffer here in America from the romantic urgency of expression.
—P. Henríquez Ureña

Authority and authoritarianism are concepts bandied about today by social scientists who study Latin America as well as by politicians who wish to justify policies that are often genocidal. Authoritarianism, to be sure, is a sad political reality in Latin America, affecting right-wing and left-wing regimes alike. Although the avowed aim of their policies may differ, authoritarian leaders in Latin America vary little, regardless of the political doctrines they profess: they are male, militaristic, and wield almost absolute personal power. Social scientists and historians are making decisive contributions to our knowledge of such figures, and one hopes, perhaps vainly, that these insights will prevent future politicians from supporting any regime that, in the name of concrete economic factors or abstract political doctrines, enthrones authority, privilege, and abuse.

Latin American writers have always been fascinated with authoritarian rulers. Unamuno, for instance, once remarked that Sarmiento must have loved Rosas, and Darío traveled through Central America with the support of local tyrants. Today, García Márquez, who was close to Omar Torrijos, is a friend of Fidel Castro. Although there is a fascination with power in all of modern literature, and although there are figures like Hugo, for example, who must be viewed as the literary counterparts of political dictators, Latin America's compelling historical and ideological circumstances strengthen the magnetism that draws language to politics and vice versa. It is not simply a matter of arguing that, since there have been and still are dictators in Latin America, its literature ought to reflect that fact. In my view, both the dictators and the language in which their image is cast start simultaneously, issuing from the same historical circumstances. As Carpentier, in *Reasons of State* (1974), has made very clear, both power and rhetoric are generated together and cannot exist independently of each other. In Carpentier's novel, academics and poets provide the appropriate rhetoric to help legitimize political power as some sort of autochthonous, telluric force. It is the metaphoric foundation of this rhetoric of power that recent dictator-novels have sought to undermine.

The outward manifestations of this rhetoric are many and pervasive, and as Julio Cortázar, a supporter of "progressive" causes in Latin America, has recently remarked, the rhetoric of power in Latin America knows no political doctrine:

I feel very pained when I go to a country like Nicaragua or Cuba and read the articles that are being published. I listen to the speeches and I discover that theirs is the same old rhetoric. A fairly obsolete language continues to be used, with words that are devoid of meaning and that have lost their sense. I spoke about this when I went to Madrid a few months ago. I told the young that no renovating, revolutionary work could be carried out if it was not first carried out in one's own head, in one's brain. One has to analyze and self-criticize the way we use words. People say "democracy," "freedom," "motherland" in the same way as our adversaries. That is to say, there is no search for a new language, a language that could really express the living experiences of socialism. The result is that both sides use the same language; with differing intentions, but the same language, the language of the Right, the language of a rotten world that is falling to pieces. The capitalist world has its language and can have no other, but the language of the Left, socialist language, cannot be the same. It has to wipe off all that drool, and that is a job that writers and readers, intellectuals, have to do in the first place.[1]

For doing just what Cortázar recommends, not a few Latin American writers have been jailed or forced to leave their countries, whether the authoritarian regime was right- or left-wing. The recent exit from Cuba of Reinaldo Arenas, Antonio Benítez Rojo, César Leante, José Triana, Belkis Cuza Malé, and Herberto Padilla is a good example. But Cortázar's point is well taken: the rhetoric of power in Latin America penetrates, is coterminous with, power itself.

The essays in this collection analyze how authority and rhetoric are dismantled in modern Latin American literature. My assumption throughout has been that there is a correlation between closure and authority, brought about by the same ideology on which the rhetoric of power is based. By "closure," I mean a perfect correlation between language and meaning, a seamless fusion of form and content that covers the struggle within language itself and the inherently misleading quality of rhetoric. In terms of immediate political action, there is no illusion on my part as to the effectiveness of this process of deconstruction both in literature and in criticism, but at the same time I am convinced, with Cortázar, that it has to be carried out.

Although I believe, as does Michael Ryan in his passionate book, that deconstruction has potential as political critique, I am not so sure that it can still productively be referred to as deconstruction at that level.[2] But there is no doubt in my mind that, for instance, the debunking of male authority in the dictator-novel is a healthy political therapy, or that the critique of language as a vehicle of proprietary rights in *Doña Bárbara* is a way of demonstrating the arbitrariness of certain forms of economic power in Latin America. Like Ryan, I would like to think that the sort of deconstruction I practice does not privilege literature, in the sense that I do not consider literature a realm free of political and ideological investments. As I endeavor to show throughout this book, literature is the equivalent of critical thought in Latin America, and critical thought most certainly includes politics. To speak of *lo literario* as an independent category is as banal as it is perverse to try to turn literature into propaganda for any political doctrine.

My indebtedness to the work of Jacques Derrida and Paul de Man should be as obvious as my departures from their theories. Though I have learned much from them, as well as from others, like Roland Barthes, I would like to think that I have learned even more from reading Borges, Carpentier, and Sarduy. I believe neither in critical orthodoxies nor in fixed critical categories subject to school-boy definitions. In my view, critical categories are dynamic and evolve through critical practice, and the fact that the object of our study is unavoidably cast in the same medium as our instrument of interpretation prevents steadfast definitions. What counts, as de Man says in one of the epigraphs to this book, is reading as argument. In this sense, the system that holds together and makes meaningful the language of criticism is akin to the process by which a fictional text is generated, a system that is far from being homogeneous or static.

My departure from both Derrida and de Man is perhaps most obvious in my attempt to place in a historical context delusions and tropes relating to voice and truth, as well as to writing as an inherently deconstructive activity. I could easily stake out my position in relative terms by saying that, although these may be imminent features of thought or language, they are peculiarly prominent in modern Latin American literature. But I would go beyond such a strategic position. To my mind, the awareness of the question of language as posited by Derrida is typically postromantic, whether such questions have existed in Western thought since the time of the pre-Socratics or not. I would go even farther and say that Derrida's position vis-à-vis these questions is eccentric in the same way that modern Latin American literature is eccentric, which would explain Derrida's penchant for quoting Borges.

In my version, deconstructive criticism is above all indiscreet in the strongest sense—that is, it does not respect the limitations its object claims for itself, but transgresses them and, indeed, seeks to uncover the meaning of the limitations themselves. It looks not only for what a text says, but especially for what it does not say, or for how it also says the opposite. The origins of this practice can be found in Marxism and psychoanalysis. As in the study of ideologies, deconstructive criticism tries to find that *camera obscura* in which perceptions are inverted; as in psychoanalysis, it examines exterior symptoms in an effort to uncover the repressed motive. But deconstruction is not a demystifying sort of criticism; it endeavors to demonstrate that constant presence of mystification and delusion, the existence of what I call a "mythology of writing," constituted by a series of contradictory figures. This is not an act of demystification, because demystifying presupposes the existence of a critical discourse capable of freeing itself from mystification and self-delusion. Deconstruction does not posit this possibility, and so it has often dwelled on the study of critical discourse itself. Deconstructive criticism's indiscretion, like charity, begins at home, since in practice it self-deconstructs as it deconstructs. If in this it resembles fiction—which not only narrates, but tells us how—such a resemblance is not accidental. I am not unaware that such a position implicitly reintroduces an authoritative claim; it invents a supercritical consciousness that winds up the mechanism and leaves it ticking, apparently on its own. This may well be the blind spot of deconstructive criticism, but, as we shall see, it is one that it shares with postmodern literature.

By modern Latin American literature I mean quite simply Latin American literature since its inception in the romantic period. Modernity as a crisis is a romantic anxiety of origins whose sources are romantic. There is a Latin American literature even before the romantics, but this is only so because it was conceived retrospectively by romantic thought. Literature as a concept and Latin America as an entity are both creations of modernity. In this book I hold that both were conceived in Latin America as a metaphoric field whose ground is nature, if I may avail myself of the same kinds of metaphors. Nature, the landscape, created through its own uniqueness and originality a new and original being who expressed himself or herself in the form of a new and different literature. This ideological safety net lasted up to the work of Borges and Carpentier, more specifically up to *The Lost Steps* (1953), a novel by the Cuban who had undoubtedly been a reader of the Argentinian.[3] The products of the deconstruction of that ideology compose what I call "postmodern" literature, which includes the so-called Boom and the dictator-novels studied here.

It seems inevitable to draw a historical parallel to the emergence of the Cuban Revolution, even if the latter eventually reinstated authoritarianism. The main trope in postmodern Latin American literature is the same supercritical consciousness mentioned with regard to deconstructive criticism. The most advanced work in that direction, initiated probably by Borges, is Severo Sarduy's narratives. What this postmodern literature is attempting to dismantle is nothing less than the central romantic trope, irony, and it does so by abolishing the individual self, whose quest for absolute knowledge is thwarted by the infinity of knowledge. What emerges out of the abolition of that self is the correlative figure of a Super Negator. It is doubtful, however, that this superconsciousness could express itself save through stories; that is, it does not have access to the language of knowledge necessary for it to become invested with power, hence the deconstructor's need to appeal to fiction, and not only to its style, but above all to its tropes.

Are these critical gyrations in both literature and criticism political? Or do they answer to a different need, one that still resides within the ideology it purports to deconstruct? I believe that they are political in a symbolic sense that satisfies needs beyond pragmatic political action. Political acts are often symbolic in the same sense. A good example perhaps is the way in which General Anastasio Somoza was assassinated in Asunción, Paraguay. The description in the *New York Times* of 19 September 1980 deserves quoting:

A Chevrolet pickup truck, possibly with as many as three people inside, followed General Somoza's Mercedes-Benz. As the Mercedes approached a two-story ranch style home, the truck either passed the car or pulled up close behind. The occupants of the truck began pouring automatic weapon fire into the car.

Others on the street also began firing automatic weapons. Then, from the front porch of the house, a man with a rocket launcher fired a projectile that hit the car broadside, blowing off the roof and the two front doors. The body of the driver, César Gallardo, a Nicaraguan, was blown onto the street.

The car came to a stop several yards away, the badly mauled bodies of General Somoza and his adviser in the back seat.

Clearly, blowing the dictator to bits with a rocket is an act that goes beyond political pragmatism. The kind of self-wounding both deconstructive criticism and postmodern literature carry out often has the same excessive, symbolic character. Killing Somoza after he was already deposed was a useless act, at least on the surface, but perhaps just as necessary symbolically. Modern Latin American literature may be useless in the same way. I do not pretend to know what its usefulness will be, if indeed it can be useful in any pragmatic sense, but it seems to be inevitable, much as the foregoing incident.

This book eschews a programmatic introduction or conclusion to remain faithful to its conception of the language of Latin American literature. In my view, that language is lodged in that literature's own process of revealing the self-eluding mechanisms of authority, in the stories literature tells about its own propriety and legitimacy. It is not a matter of finding what is strictly literary, whatever that may be, but of persistently questioning the authority of language to declare its own inner and outer boundaries.

I have tried to discover some of those stories by allowing the dialectical heterogeneity of language to work itself out over and over again. I have often been aided in this process by a seeming obstacle: my having to use English translations of the texts quoted and analyzed. By observing how a text was translated, or mistranslated, I have been able to see one or several instances of its dynamics as a generator of readings. It seemed appropriate, for this reason, to wind up this book with my own annotated translation of a text in which all of these issues are at stake. Needless to say, the stories that Latin American literature tells about its own legitimacy, as retold here, are not to be taken as the only ones, though they aspire to be a significant sample drawn from a new way of reading Latin American literature.

To sum up, the book is a collection of essays, not because of any whimsical desire to bring together a number of pieces written over the past few years, but as part of the book's main argument and critical stance. My basic argument is that there is implicit in modern Latin American literature an ideology through which both literature and criticism identify what Latin American literature is and how it ought to be read. Journalistic criticism repeats the surface manifestations of this ideology, be it through readings that docilely follow expository texts written by the major writers, or by creating on the social and political level groups that identify with the presumed tenets of the ideology. In literature, however, this ideology is constantly subjected to a radical critique within each work; this critique renders the ideology productive, and in a sense is what constitutes the work. In most criticism the ideology merely serves as support for an authoritative discourse that consistently misrepresents Latin American literature.

My effort in this book is to lay bare the productive activity of such an ideology in literary works, along with a number of seminal works of criticism. To have written a sustained, expository book on the subject would have led me to make the same kind of critical error that I attribute to most criticism of Latin American literature. In so doing, I would have naïvely assumed an authoritative voice while attempting a critique of precisely that critical gesture. This book, instead, tries to uncover the workings of modern Latin American literature through independent readings of major texts in the tradition, with an overarching set of philosophical and methodological preoccupations concerning both Latin American literature and critical theory. In addition to the reasons already given, I end the book with an annotated translation of a recent Latin American story as a way of underlining what I take to be my chief contribution as a reader of Latin American texts in a North American context: to be a bilingual reader, as it were, whose critical activity consists precisely in transferring a text from one code to another to sift out in that process what holds it together. Rather than explain a critical method and define a given literature, I hope to display a process of reading and defining.

I am well aware that there are notorious political discrepancies among the writers studied here, and that many major writers and even whole genres have been left out. Concerning the first, I do not believe that Latin American literature should be diminished by pitting Reinaldo Arenas against Miguel Barnet, or Guillermo Cabrera Infante against Julio Cortázar. Such a superficial approach is a view from within current squabbles that ought to be left to the press and to political entrepreneurs who pander to writers' whims in order to survive. Literature is made up of currents and cross-currents that transcend such polemics. As for the second possible objection, my aim is not to be comprehensive, but theoretical and synthetic, to search for a discourse rather than for the myriad individual manifestations of a given literature. Exclusions are not to be taken in this book as signs of a negative judgment, nor inclusions as invitations to an exclusive club. If all major figures had to be considered, I would have had to include essays on Paz, Borges, Guillén, Guimarães Rosa, and so on. The dazzling richness of Latin American literature would make such an enterprise, were it desirable, impossible. My contention is that the texts discussed here contain the main issues present in those produced by the many important writers left out.

1. The Case of the Speaking Statue: *Ariel* and the Magisterial Rhetoric of the Latin American Essay

1

Navegando en aguas de origen y ceniza
—Pablo Neruda

The essays in this book center on the relationship between the concept of culture and the idea of literature in modern Latin America. The main argument implicit or explicit in these pages is that the concept of culture has served as an ideology that gives meaning to Latin American literature, whereas modern Latin American literature emerges as it labors to unsettle that relationship, even in the texts that most openly appear to promote it. My contention is that the concept of culture in modern Latin America—from Sarmiento to Fernández Retamar, approximately—is made up of a cluster of tropes that attempt to hold down and control Latin American texts by attaching them to a set of given meanings. Although the breadth of this tropological cluster is considerable and its outward manifestations evolve throughout history, its structural role as a reliable repository of signification remains constant. As a reservoir of meaning, the concept of culture has consequently been a source of authority on various levels, ranging from pronouncements by cultural institutions supported by governments of the most varied political hues, to the work of the most revered essayists, critics, and scholars concerned with the issue of both national and continental identity. I am interested here in the function of the concept of culture in the elaboration of literature, in the conceptualization and practice of an idea of literature, not in the other institutions mentioned, though it seems to me that a study of cultural institutions in Latin America would be a fruitful one. In the functioning of literature as an institution the concept of culture is a key element. Remove the concept of culture and its corollary of national identity from the language of Latin American literature and that literature becomes nearly silent.

Yet Latin American literature, instead of contributing to the elaboration of a concept of culture, takes shape as it attempts to dismantle that concept in a contrary, negative structure that becomes its most salient and positive characteristic. It is my hope that this book will show how this subversive, paradoxically self-annihilating process has been taking place. I wish to show how the expository texts in the modern Latin American tradition formulate the uniqueness of Latin American literature in a way that literature denies, and how what is truly peculiar and unique in Latin American literature emerges from this complex and rather contradictory process. I intend to allow ideologically grounded notions of what Latin American literature is or should be to break into this process to release a phantasmagoria of figures and a struggle among them that issues from what is a dialectical self-affirmation and self-negation.

At its most descriptive, my project is based on an idea of Latin American literature that may be outlined as follows. A specific social class conceives of Latin American literature as a way of building up and implanting its beliefs and making them predominant. With regard to literature, these founding beliefs are, on the one hand, the existence of the individual self as a unity that seeks to establish its uniqueness and express it through the symbols it creates for itself, and, on the other, the collective presence of a given set of codes through which those symbols, that language of the self, can articulate themselves and communicate with others. One cannot describe this social class as the bourgeoisie in European terms, but it would be safe to say that the founding beliefs of that class are operational in Latin America and are at the base of its ideology.[1] The self and the codes are creations of that class and they often appear cloaked as spirit and nature, spirit being a sort of universal intelligence the individual possesses that allows him or her to interpret the world, and nature, a given system of signs whose propriety is ensured by the collectivity. There is an inherent circularity here that should not be evaded in attempting to comprehend the process. A class creates these concepts to invent its own way of being and implanting itself. Some of these inventions are blatantly political, as when natural law is invoked to ensure property rights, but they involve more than politics in the usual sense of the term, because they also attempt to regulate and codify sexual relations and even metaphysics.

Latin American literature draws from Latin American history—a history that should be read as a discourse elaborated by literature itself—a number of what I would call "themes." These themes all deal with the issue of Latin American literature's own legitimacy and uniqueness, that is to say, with the very possibility of a Latin American literature. They are elaborated on the basis of the two main beliefs I mentioned before: the self and culture. I call them "themes" because they are potentialities preceding practice. Once they are deployed in a work of literature, they turn into what I call "literary myths." As opposed to themes, myths are critical by virtue of the fact that their manifestation is made possible within contradiction, ambiguity, and self-denial. Important literary works in Latin America—those discussed in this book as well as a few others—are part of these myths, which I shall mention in more detail below. Second-rate works merely contain the themes; they mobilize a descriptive language that leaves untouched the various clashing elements that spark the themes into becoming a "mythology of writing," that is, texts belonging to the main current of Latin American literary discourse.

My hope is to set up a number of the myths that compose Latin American literature in analogy to the topics that Curtius discovered as constituting late classical and medieval literature. Needless to say, the differences between what I propose to do here and Curtius's enormous achievement are substantial. To begin with, the literature he analyzed was not beset by the desire for newness or originality, whereas modern literature, particularly modern Latin American literature, is propelled by the anxiety to be new and original. In addition, Curtius's topics were a sort of thematics, drawn from a storehouse of generally accepted, nonproblematic knowledge, whereas what I seek to lay out is a series of figures generated by the very problematic of knowledge and its relation to literature. My intention is to find a hidden unity in Latin American literature, a key to its various articulations, which is rendered visible only as the initial unity is discarded and stories are yielded by the dialectical process of denial and affirmation.

I study in this book several of the myths derived from the two basic ones about self and collectivity: the figure of the *maestro*, who is the possessor and transmitter of knowledge about culture; the figure of the dictator, who wields absolute power and is a hypostasis of the author; the figure of the author himself or herself, who can filter the voice of a "primitive," inarticulate other and turn it into an intelligible text that is paradoxically endowed with authority by the inarticulate other (e. g., Johnny and Manuel Montejo, in "The Pursuer" and *Biografía de un cimarrón*, respectively); the myth of nature, more specifically, the earth, as source of meaning and authority, and its correlative myth of exile, a separation from the earth that, through the ordeal of distance and return, presumably grants one a truer vision. By their very nature, these myths are not static and subject to descriptive analysis, but dynamic and instrumental in their own processes of self-analysis. Ours is, so to speak, a hermeneutic instrument that appears useful only in practice, not in display. It is a hermeneutic tool that dismantles that which it pretends to interpret. It suggests that the interpretive process itself is its meaning. One could logically say that Latin American culture, as it emerges in literature, is this process of simultaneous dismantling and self-constitution.

I am not arguing, of course, that Latin America has no culture of its own, and much less that there is no significant relationship between that culture and Latin American literature. What I am saying is that culture and literature create each other as necessary elements in a process of ideological formation. Even if by "culture" one simply means the systems of signs by which a given community organizes and communicates its values and beliefs at a given time in history, it should be evident to anyone traveling in Latin America or certain parts of the Hispanic United States that she or he is not in Saint-Germain-des-Prés or Washington Square.

I *am* arguing, though, that the concept of culture modern Latin American literature provides to encompass the Latin American world is more a part of a process of literary self-constitution than a reflection of the social and political realities of the various Latin American countries. Latin America is made up of a variety of different cultures, many of which have nothing to do with literature, neither as producers nor as consumers. A social scientist would be hard pressed to consider as belonging to the same social group an impoverished *mojado* from the southwestern United States and a cultivated dweller of Buenos Aires, even though their native language is the same. Many and quite radical are the class differences in Latin America, and to pretend that they can be smoothed over by appealing to an overall abstraction based on philology is at best a quaint academic quirk, if not an act of political bad faith. Nevertheless, and because literature consists of many acts of bad faith as well as not a few self-deceptions, Latin American literature has needed to conceive a unity of culture from the very beginning, or has wished for such a unity to come into being.

The reason for such persistence is historical: Latin America as a concept and as a political reality was created at the outset of modernity, that is to say, at the historical juncture that also brought into being the question of cultural existence, both as a question and as a conceptual need. There is no origin but that question itself, and literature returns to it constantly in order to bring about a closure.

The tenacity of this literary mystification can be attributed in part to the relations between literature and the institutions of power within Latin American society. In this sense, literature reflects society. The nationalistic ideology that has supported Latin American regimes since independence, institutions of learning charged with lending support to such ideologies, the most commonly held beliefs about the bonds established by the commonality of language, all rest on the assumption that there is a solid link between language, literature, and culture. There can be little doubt that nationalism as a founding ideology is a characteristic peculiar to marginal and dependent societies. Plundered since the nineteenth century by modern imperial powers, marginal societies create fables about their own originality modeled after those of the dominant societies on which they depend and from which they wish to defend and distance themselves. The search for national and cultural identity becomes an issue in countries where the nascent local bourgeoisie has the power, but not the distinctiveness, of its European counterpart and where traditional values and practices are replaced pell-mell by the effluvia of industrialized societies. One need not profess a Marxist ideology to realize this fact. The only convincing, sustained study of one such case in Latin America is in my view Manuel Moreno Fraginals's *The Sugarmill*. No serious study of this kind has been devoted to literature itself and its relation to power(less) and mimetic Latin American elites, though there are some in progress that might succeed if they manage to distance themselves from the verbiage and the rituals peculiar to much of Latin American Marxism.

My contention here is that in the beginning there is a causal link between the issue of national identity and the dependency relationship between the emerging Latin American bourgeoisie and Europe. The idea of literature is a Western, bourgeois idea. Why does there have to be a literature in the way that it exists in Europe if Latin America is different and unique, as the ideologists of culture insist? My assumption is that the drama at the core of Latin American literature results from the impossibility of answering this question satisfactorily. The new self that must express itself must do so in a language that is already burdened with old concepts and stories. The new self and the new literature are that struggle, not its desired result. I also assume that the figures that emerge in the process of Latin America's working this issue out have as a source the specific history of Latin America. The ceremonies and iconography of nationalism at its most visible level are particularly garish where nationalism is the central ideology supporting the state. Literature draws from such rituals and icons in order to put this ideology to a severe test. The recent dictator-novels in Latin America are the best example of this process, as is "Right of Sanctuary," a story by Carpentier in which the process of symbol formation in a nationalistic society is displayed and related to literature.

I contend, however, that the critical energy that Latin American literature directs against such a founding ideology is part of a larger mechanism implicit in all of modern literature, and it is in this sense that literature from Latin America is both modern and "universal." It is so, however, in a self-denying way that is much more poignant and dramatic than in many other parts of the world. The concept of culture is made up of a set of beliefs whose twin pillars are, as we have seen, national or collective identity and self-identity, and whose elaboration depends on philology, no matter how diffuse this typically nineteenth-century science becomes in the actual texts.

The main theme of Latin American thought has been the question of identity. A whole essayistic tradition, aptly studied by Martin S. Stabb, Peter Earle, and Robert Mead has set itself the task of defining what Latin America is, who Latin Americans are, and how literature both reveals and reflects that identity.[2] The principal texts in that tradition, from *Facundo* (1845) to *Calibán* (1968), have always taken literature into account, because the specificity and difference of Latin American literature are keys in determining the existence and authenticity of a Latin American identity. The orientation of these essays is varied, ranging from a sort of neo-Kantian idealism through existentialism and Marxism, without any of them ever threatening to become an independent philosophical system. The more powerful texts in that tradition, however, are fraught with contradiction and insistently take recourse to a highly figurative language. In short, they elaborate, as part of their own constitution, what I would like to call a "mythology of writing." This mythology of writing is an alternative founding fable in which the apparent doctrinaire core of a text is subverted, as in a sort of Oedipal nightmare. Identity, collective or personal, has been a major theme in modern fiction and poetry with similarly ambiguous results; that is to say, it has created a similar mythology.

In addition to the historical reasons mentioned, however, there is a basic fact: the whole quest-for-identity enterprise is rooted in language and, as such, is subject to the peculiar intricacies of the medium. The concept of culture is inevitably cast in the language of literature, where not only is it prey to ideological distortion, but cast in signs that lead not to synthesis and self-revelation, but to dispersion, concealment, indirection, and self-delusion. It is here that a certain criticism, which longs to ally itself with the social sciences and likes to think of itself as Marxist, often fails and winds up inveighing against Latin American authors out of the resentment of the dull-witted, or from misguided, if at times sincere, political fervor. The simplistic and colonialist belief of many of these critics is that Latin American literature should conform to their own specifications; above all they insist that it should be direct, deal with a certain predetermined subject matter, and, most important, bypass the entrapments of language. But Latin American literature persists in its indirection and continues to deal obsessively with identity in terms of sexuality rather than class, with language in terms of the mass media instead of philology, with individual personality in terms of pathological violence instead of class war; it seems to be more interested in the fate of the *macho* than in that of the *guerrillero*. It deals more with the past and its weight on the present than with the present as a harbinger of the future. Violent, perverse, bent on demolishing authority without dutifully offering viable alternatives of order, Latin American literature refuses to endorse pieties about the future or to project a programmatic sense of optimism.

Culture is memory, and memory is rooted in language. The only way to gain access to a Latin American literary mythology is through the very language of literature, but the price to pay for that journey is the acceptance of the inherently subversive nature of that language, in which the most cherished pieties are bound to be unsettled and the dearest argument is going to be contradicted. Literature issues from that hell where the dark figures of negation and transformation deface concepts predicated on authority and tradition. My aim is to peek into that hell. When and if the utopian heaven of naïve criticism finally arrives and language is divested of its devilish power of mediation, perhaps one will be able to stroll along the charred ruins of that hell with one's eyes safely open. Until then all versions of that underground are necessarily perversions. I have chosen to call those versions a mythology of writing because they always involve a fable about the origins of writing and are fraught with contradiction, violence, and symbolic figures, much like fairy tales. So, despite the historical precision that I wish to obtain, despite the knowledge I also hope to produce, my criticism engages these texts qua texts, hoping to allow that deconstruction to manifest itself in my own writing. In this sense, a programmatic eclecticism, in tune with that of literature itself, is at the core of my approach.

In one of the essays contained here I propose that among the founding stories in that mythology of writing is the one that makes an association between author, authority, and the figure of the dictator. I attempt to show in that essay that the emergence of the figure of the writer, who can bear no authority except that of negation, pries apart the relationship between authority and voice. The mythology of writing involving the dictator is one in which the link between identity and literature is undone. The specificity of Latin American culture and literature comes in the back way, as it were, in the form of the character embodying authority: the toppled dictator/author.

The historical and linguistic associations of the figure with Hispanic *machismo* are too obvious to explain here. Reaching all the way back to Arabigo-Germanic Spain, through the *caudillos, comandantes en jefe,* and *generales* of today's Latin America, the dictator figure clearly embodies paternal authority. This authority is the same as that which supports the essayistic tradition. After all, the dictator, being the embodiment of voice and power, is an analogon to language and culture, the fields of action of the essay. By this I mean that voice is the bearer of knowledge through the peculiarity of language, the latter being the object of philology, which in turn is the scientific foundation of such knowledge and the discourse that legitimizes authority by relating it to origins and sources.

In the essayistic tradition the voice of power and authority does not don the mask of the dictator. The figure that emerges to preside over the essay is the *maestro*, the teacher whose task is to plumb the depths of language and history in order to render the voice of culture articulate and apt for dissemination, in short, to turn this voice—pure, autochthonous—into a source of authority. It is no accident, of course, that many authors in the essayistic tradition were or are teachers, and that, in some cases, as in Sarmiento's, they had a significant influence on the actual foundation and organization of the educational systems in their countries. (Of the authors studied in this book, two not only were influential educators, but eventually became presidents of their respective countries: Sarmiento, of Argentina, and Gallegos, of Venezuela.) José Martí, José Enrique Rodó, Alfonso Reyes, Pedro Henríquez Ureña, Mariano Picón Salas, Roberto Fernández Retamar, and many other essayists were or are educators and pedagogues. Even a poet-essayist like Octavio Paz has often been a professor, and José Lezama Lima's *La expresión americana* was initially a lecture course. The same academic background can be found in other writers, like Cintio Vitier, René Marqués, Jorge Mañach, and many more. Vitier's *Lo cubano en la poesía*, for instance, was also a lecture course originally. The essay dealing with the issue of cultural definition has been much more in touch with the state and its educational institutions than has poetry or the novel. Some of the essays, such as those by Rodó and Henríquez Ureña, have had a direct and telling impact on education. The essay's quest for knowledge is more of a social activity than what is found in other literary genres.

Many of these essayists have also held government posts. Fernández Retamar is the editor of *Casa de las Américas*, the official journal of the institution of the same name; Octavio Paz was Mexico's ambassador to India; and Alfonso Reyes was ambassador to Brazil. Through the essay the question of cultural identity, that is to say, the formulation of a concept of culture to support the idea of a Latin American literature, joins current politics and social and political thought in general.

But just because the essay has had, in the context of the problematic of identity, more contact with the overt formulation of a concept of culture, of an ideology of cultural homogeneity, it does not follow that the mythology of writing does not appear to disturb the calm of the classroom, the quietude of the lecture hall, or the polite exchange of the seminar. Even when the essay has appeared under the institutional tutelage of pedagogy, it has had to provide for its own performance a framework that soon betrayed disquieting figural choices. The essay, unlike a play or a sonnet, has no given form—it is not literature simply by being itself. Like the novel, the essay must pass for something else while acknowledging, contradictorily, that it is not what it pretends to be. The essay can pretend to be a letter, a confession, a lecture, a seminar, an oration, a scientific article, or a diary. In the essay the self of the author, bearing his or her public name, puts on a performance in which the possibility of persuasion depends on the role he or she assumes and on the fictional enclosure within which the performance takes place. Because the essay so often stakes out claims to truth and knowledge, we tend to overlook the rhetorical devices through which it stages its performance. Too much time and energy have been wasted in discussing the stylistic felicitousness of essays while ignoring their fictional self-constitution. Who has ever bothered to pursue the implications of the stance taken by Ortega y Gasset in *El espectador*? Has anyone ever analyzed the presumed genres of Unamuno's essays? Why not take into account the narrative element of the essay, its fictional construct, its rhetorical and poetic scaffolding? Why are

Borges's stories like essays, and vice versa?

If there is any one characteristic that pertains to the essay it is that the writer explores an issue while making his or her own presence and process of reasoning visible. The two main elements of the essay are, then, the self who explores and the process of exploration itself. But as the essay is not a scientific tract, and as there is no prescribed rhetorical norm according to which the process of exploration can or should be written out, a suitable fiction must be found. The elaboration of a relationship between the stated intentions of the self in pursuit of presence and truth and of the fiction created to carry out that pursuit is the main figural activity that allows the performance to take place.

The tropes socially produced by that activity are historically determined, just as the novelistic figure of the dictator, embodying a figuration of the author, is socially and historically determined. In the Latin American essayistic tradition that figure has been the pedagogical authority figure of the *maestro* because, until recently, education, as part of the liberal ideology on which modern Latin American nations are founded, was thought to be the solution to the continent's questions about its own mode of being and its future.[3] Sarmiento's dichotomy between civilization and barbarism as the main forces at work in Latin America is still alive in the pedagogical project of a revolution as radical as the Cuban, in which the most urgent project, once Batista was overthrown, was a literacy campaign. Dictatorial power exists, it is thought, because there is a lack of education among the masses. Reading and writing will banish violence. A novel like Gallegos's *Doña Bárbara* contains this contrary relationship between arbitrary power and writing. There is, of course, a contradiction in that novel, which also appears in my essay in chapter 2: autochthonous, telluric presence is illiterate, oral in its outward manifestation, whereas ideal knowledge resides in reading and writing. This opposition is at the center of the polemic between Sarmiento and Rodó, though not visible on the surface of the texts. What is important to note, however, is that the pursuit of "presence" and "knowledge," terms whose synthesis would yield cultural identity, is played out within a pedagogical fiction, a classroom drama in which reading and writing will supposedly be a liberation, but at the expense of the very culture that literature is attempting to define. Broadly speaking, the modern Latin American essay is generated within the seminal heat emanating from the friction inevitably produced by what is, from the outset, an insoluble dilemma at the very core of modern thought in the Western world since at least the eighteenth century.

Anyone familiar with the history of the Latin American essay will have anticipated, in reading the foregoing discussion, that I am leading up to an analysis of José Enrique Rodó's *Ariel*, the founding essay of the modern Latin American essayistic tradition. In terms of its influence on Latin

American thought and literature—indeed, on Latin American history—one could scarcely think of a more important text.⁴ My interest in *Ariel* is no doubt due somewhat to that fact, but also, as we shall soon see, to the way in which in this essay the figures (characters as well as tropes) dominating the Latin American tradition appear in full force, that is, in their own contradictory relationships. Though vilified as well as revered, Rodó's text has never been analyzed in a way that would lay bare its latent force as a text. I propose to do so both in a historical and in a textual way and to see how one of its key tropes reappears, though inverted, in a text by a very contemporary and even radical author, Severo Sarduy. What I intend to do here—as with Sarmiento in the essay on the dictator-novel—is to show how Rodó's text contains a founding fable whose influence (even while being vilified) extends to our days. The concept of Latin American culture that Rodó ostensibly proposes and its attendant idea of literature are obsolete, yet in formulating them the Uruguayan set in motion a submerged, subtextual psychodrama that endures.

2

ni del dorado techo
se admira, fabricado
del sabio moro, en jaspes sustentado.
—Fray Luis de León

No sooner was *Ariel* published in 1900 than its influence swept the Spanish-speaking world. Rodó's essay was reprinted, glossed, and commented on throughout Latin America and Spain. Societies were formed to discuss the doctrines it put forth, and commentaries appeared in scholarly as well as journalistic publications. The historical situation was propitious. Spain had just lost Cuba, Puerto Rico, and the Philippines to the United States in a war that demonstrated that the old metropolis was out of pace with the modern world. To what world did Latin America belong? Did its Hispanic roots still tie it to the Mediterranean, or was its future bound up with the new republic in the north, which was gobbling up its territory and touting a new way of life? Was Latin America Latin or American? Sarmiento had toured the United States and decided that Argentina at least was going to be "American" in the sense given the word by the United States. Martí first, and later Rodó, disagreed strongly, though from different points of view. Martí's revolutionary solution took long to be heeded. Rodó's call to be different from the United States by reaching back to the European tradition nearly became a cult. His was the first wide-ranging proposal for a Latin American identity. The opposition between Rodó and Sarmiento, like that between Plato and Aristotle or Vico and Descartes, in the European tradition, remains at the core of Latin American thought.

*Rodó
vs.
Sarmiento*

Even today not only essays like Fernández Retamar's *Calibán*, but also novels like Carpentier's *Reasons of State,* pay homage to this debate by reenacting it in the elaboration of the main character, the setting of the action in various moments in places that allude to Sarmiento's *Facundo* (Nueva Córdoba), and, above all, by giving the dictator's children Shakespearean names. The dictator's children, in the parodic world of Carpentier's novel, are like Rodó's many spiritual children throughout Latin America.

Ariel is subdivided into six brief chapters, preceded by an equally brief introduction in which the stage is set. Within the last chapter, but not set off, save perhaps by spacing, there is a finale in which the staging set up in the introduction reappears. The staging of this influential essay is, appropriately enough, a classroom. An old teacher, called Prospero by his students, holds the last meeting of a course in the teacher's book-lined study, a room dominated by a bronze statue of Ariel. The teacher has habitually sat next to the statue, hence the name given him by the students. Invoking Ariel as "my numen"—that is, the spirit within him—the teacher delivers an oration (the six chapters) to the students, telling them how to put their knowledge to use, how to behave in life, and what pitfalls to avoid.

The ideological background of this oration has been more than adequately studied by several commentators and need not be the object of much more discussion. Prospero's philosophy is, on the surface, a call in favor of spiritualism in the face of American pragmatism and utilitarianism. Rodó's sources are varied, but Gordon Brotherston's superb edition settles once and for all the predominance of certain French thinkers like Renan and Fouillée. In essence, Rodó exalts a supposedly Latin tradition of spiritualism, of disinterested humanistic contemplation, as a way of leading the mind to the moral pleasure of self-fulfillment. His pedagogical fiction—the essay is dedicated to "the youth of America"—has three main theses: the imitation of the good and the beautiful; the constitution of a self centered on an ideal of beauty and good; the creation of an elite of educated men, able to lead others not so fortunate in their capacity for inner growth, a sort of Darwinian spiritualism. At the end of the speech, the enlightened students leave the teacher's library in an ecstasy that is marred only by the presence of crowds in the streets through which they walk.

In a continent where the crowds are often made up of people whose racial origin could not easily be traced back to Latium, where elites had proved to be rapacious rather than enlightened, Rodó's message eventually became very polemical, though at first the "youth of America" readily embraced its ideas. In a sense, *Ariel* proposed a liberation from the encroaching ideology of capitalism and the possibility of founding an American self that, if not revolutionary, would at least stake out its own domain by refusing to collaborate with the aggressive American and European imperialism of the period. Rodó had recognized that the forces unleashed by the industrial revolution were now loose on the continent, eating away at the old Spanish empire in the name of new political and economic powers. The students who heard Rodó's message throughout Latin America understood this part of it, and many acted accordingly.

As time went by, however, Rodó's elitism became odious. The last episode of rejection is Roberto Fernández Retamar's *Calibán*, an essay that, from the perspective of the Cuban Revolution, denounced *Ariel*'s ideology and in which Shakespeare's monster is upheld as a more appropriate symbol of Latin America's people. Sixty-eight years after its publication, *Ariel* could hardly be expected to preserve its ideological currency. What it did retain, however, was the seductive power of its tropological structure.

Ideology and political relevancy are not the only elements of Rodó's essay that have aged. Perhaps its most obsolete aspect is its style. *Ariel*'s rhetorical flourishes, its allusiveness and self-serving, mellifluent, oratorical tone are barely tolerable today. Whereas Martí and Sarmiento, by their very passion, wrote in a prose that can still be enjoyed, Rodó's sounds hackneyed, edulcorated, and hollow. The paternalistic stance that Rodó takes through the figure of Prospero vis-à-vis the "youth of America" makes of *Ariel* even more of an outdated text. The figures that the essay brought to the fore still haunt the Latin American literary imagination, but Rodó's prose is hardly a model for today's writers. If this is so, however, how can we account for the presence of *Ariel* in today's Latin American literature? Straw men do not endure very long. I would venture to suggest that *Ariel*'s relevancy is due not only to the resiliency of the figures explicitly put on stage, but also to the way in which these figures engage in a polemical interplay beneath the surface of the essay, beneath the gloss of Rodó's elaborate nineteenth-century rhetoric. It is this compelling drama that engages the attention of modern writers, even those openly hostile to Rodó.

The basic elements in the drama that unfolds in *Ariel* set themselves off from one another as a result of the contradiction that emerges between the scene of *Ariel* and the overt theme of the essay, between the genre that it outwardly assumes and its actual performance, between the sense of what Prospero proposes and the image of his inner self that he projects and offers as example. On this level violence disrupts the tranquil surface of *Ariel*, prefiguring in the book's own self-dismantling the most radical critiques to which Rodó has been subjected by more recent Latin American literature.

Although Prospero refers to earlier meetings in the study that bears "the noble presence of books" as "our colloquia among friends" and, echoing a *fin de siècle* topic, alludes to Greece as having received from the gods at its birth "the secret of inextinguishable youth," I know of no critic who has called attention to the obvious fact that *Ariel*'s generic identification is with the classical dialogue. Once one notices the setting, it is impossible to deny the dialogic appearance of the essay: the master (Socrates, no doubt, as deduced from the slightly paternalistic tone), surrounded by his disciples-friends in a casual, yet organized, session. The same sort of prefatory session opens some of Plato's dialogues, which also have a concluding narrative like the one in Rodó's text. The example that most readily comes to mind is, of course, *The Symposium*, which also has the air of a final exchange on an important topic, a sort of send-off. There are in Rodó's text vestiges of dialogue, as when Prospero seems to be answering questions or doubts expressed by the students, but, of course, no dialogue takes place.

This appeal to the dialogic tradition in the deployment of the essay is significant in a number of ways. On the one hand, it is striking that Rodó, by means of this strategy, is returning to the very beginnings of the essayistic tradition. As Ciriaco Morón Arroyo has persuasively argued, the essay is a branching off from the classical dialogue in the sixteenth century.[5] As one of the interlocutors in the dialogue, the essayist could "speak" from an avowedly personal point of view, in a casual manner, to a specific audience. If in the dialogue the truth would presumably emerge from the dialectic established between the various points of view, in the essay it would issue from the meeting of minds of writer and reader. Though projecting an oral, intimate appearance, the essay is therefore thoroughly a product of a culture permeated by printing, that is to say, by writing.

I take this return to the origins of the essay as no innocent strategy on Rodó's part. Through the centuries the use of this dialogic origin had been lost. The essay persuaded through various rhetorical devices, and, no doubt, also through the very authority of the writer, whose signature is affixed to the text to identify him or her as belonging to a given social group. In *Ariel* Rodó abandons this boldy authoritative stance in favor of a strategy whereby the dialogic effect of the essay is restored. Part of the strategy, of course, is that, within the fiction of *Ariel*, the master's voice has been masked. It is not Rodó who speaks directly to the reader, but Prospero, who in turn supposedly engages in dialogue, and who furthermore purports to express someone else: Ariel. The polemics unleashed by *Ariel* throughout the eighty years since its publication make it difficult to reach, through the din of blatant political disputes, the mechanisms with which the text presents itself to the audience. It would be difficult to argue, however, that these mediations are insignificant. Once they have alerted our attention, they become embarrassingly obvious. The founding fiction of *Ariel* is that it is a dialogue, not a speech; a seminar, not a lecture.

There are clearly historical reasons for this appeal to the classical tradition, which are no doubt related to the *modernista* atmosphere of the essay. But beneath the décor—and décor, as we shall see, is all important—the essay's appeal to the origins of the genre is a way of exercising power over the reader. There is no dialogic exchange in the essay. The only speakers in the text are Prospero, a third-person narrator, who sets the stage, and

Enjolras, the student, who closes the essay with an allusion to the stars. There is a dialogic effect in *Ariel*, but the only voice is that of the teacher, who, through the ruse of the dialoguelike setting, is accorded a masterly and magisterial position. The reader in *Ariel*, given the situation, is always *in statu pupilari* and, though situationally in dialogue, is necessarily mute. The appeal to the form of the dialogue is a way of situating the audience, of placing it in a subservient position in relation to the speaker. Though ostensibly the dialogic form would appear to promote a dialectic, what it really allows is an enthronement of the voice of the master, a monophonic performance, an oration, in short, that strategically fosters the impression of polyphony: *magister dixit, magistri dicta.*

Recourse to the dialogic tradition in *Ariel* is also significant in a way that cuts deeper into the problematic core of the essay. In choosing Ariel as the symbol of the ideals he wished to impress upon the "youth of America," Rodó was appealing not only to the loftiness implicit in the figure, but also to its identification with air, with spirit, with voice. Air is the medium of voice, and the dialogue implies the use of voice to arrive at truth through both dialectic and the expression of the spirit. In the setting of the stage, Ariel is described as a "genius of the Air, [which] represents, in the symbolism of Shakespeare['s play], the noble part—the spirit with wings" (p. 4). Prospero, in the opening lines of his speech, invokes Ariel when asking the power of persuasion for his voice: "So I invoke Ariel as my divinity [numen], and I could wish to-day for my lecture [words] the most gentle and persuasive force [*unción*] that ever it has had" (p. 6). The association between voice, spirit, and air, as opposed to that between body, stone, and utilitarianism, is clear. The vaporous spirit will be exchanged through voice. In the voice of the master the truth will be communicated to the students. Though it is clearly to Derrida's credit to have driven a wedge between voice and truth as inseparable elements in the Western tradition, one hardly need to invoke the author of *La voix et le phénomène* to become aware of the presence of this uncritical ideological pairing in *Ariel*. The very figure Shakespeare's genie, whose name is of course derived from the word *air*, is enough to establish this association, which, together with the text's return to dialogue, makes even stronger the suggestion that truth, spirit, hope, and everything that is good dwell in the modulations of the teacher's voice.

But there is a further associative cluster that the essay contrives around the figure of voice. The very inner being of the master whence the air of voice issues is also made up of an ethereal substance. In the deepest recesses of his being, the architecture of which we shall have to examine in detail, "not an echo of that external gaiety, not a note of all that nature-concert, not a word from the lips of men e'er ventured past the thickness of those porphyrine sills to move an air [*una onda de aire*] within that forbidden hold. A religious silence brooded on the chastity of its sleeping air" (p. 36).

In this inner dwelling, "the perfume that prevailed was that of nenuphar, pure essence suggestive but of serenity and thought floated like an undissolvable wave the chaste perfume of nenuphar, the scent that suggests thoughtful serenity and the contemplation of one's own being" (p. 37). Within this abode the king "dreamed, there he freed himself of the actual; . . . there he turned his vision inward, smoothed and refined his thought in mediation like the pebbles all polished by the wave; there he bound to the noble forehead the youthful wings of Psyche" (p. 37). This interior is the place where air, voice, truth dwell. The slumbering air, the wave of air, is the transparent, unpolluted, chaste region of spirit.

"*Onda de aire*" is a curious expression. In Spanish it suggests sound, *onda sonora*, "sound wave," which exists in its vibrations, but here "*onda de aire*" denotes the absence of sound. It is only air, yet the phrase suggests sound. The contemplation of the self, the constitution of self, occurs within this undifferentiated, transparent, almost nonexistent substance in which reflection cannot be true. Here being can be itself, identity is found in chaste indivisibility, in inviolable self-presence. There is an obvious identification of the winged figure of Psyche with Ariel, whose statue is described in the opening lines: "The little statue, a real work of art, reproduced the Spirit of the Air at the moment [when], freed by the magic of Prospero, he is about to soar into the sky [skies], there to vanish in a lightning flash" (p. 4). Out of the master springs truth in the form of the airy figure of Ariel to strike the students' inner core and set it in motion with its vibrations. As the disciples leave, "of his sweet words there lingered in each the persisting vibrations through which the cry of the wounded glass is prolonged in still air" (p. 148). There is no doubt about the transcendental nature of this vibration, of the emanation of these oxymoronic waves of air. At the very end, the only "speaker" other than Prospero, the disciple Enjolras, whose name is drawn from Victor Hugo's *Les misérables*, refers to the stars and how they shed light on the masses of the unenlightened, with the same term used to refer to the dissemination of the teacher's words: "See . . . while the crowd goes by, it never looks up to the heavens: yet they look down upon the multitude . . . something descends upon the indifferent mass . . . the vibration of the stars reminds me of the waving arms of a sower, sowing seed. . . . While the crowd goes by, I notice that, although it never looks up to the heavens, the heavens look down upon the multitude. Something descends upon the obscure and indifferent mass of people, which is like the earth broken up in furrows ready for sowing. The *vibration* of the stars reminds me of the hands of a sower, sowing seed" (p. 150, emphasis added). The voice of the teacher vibrates with a truth that has its source in God; sound has turned into divine light.

The shift from the metaphor of sound to that of light is but a mild transformation in what really turns out to be the emergence of a series of contradictory figures that undermine the authority of the teacher, running parallel to the promotion of his voice as the carrier of truth. The teacher's innermost core, his heart, resounds, vibrates: "To it [the king's house] came he who needed bread and he who wanted balsam for a wounded heart. His own [heart] reflected, like a sensitive chord [*como una placa sonora*], the rhythm of others" (p. 34, emphasis added). Though it may seem aberrant to think of *placa sonora* as a sort of irreducible oxymoron, it is difficult not to see it as such within the tropological structure of the essay. From the *placa sonora* issue the vibrations that eventually become those of the stars, vibrations that in turn irradiate over the masses to enlighten them. The heart of the teacher is not a gaseous center where spirit is generated and released to travel as waves of modulated, unbroken air, but a hard, metallic kernel in which the vibrations of others are bounced and returned transformed. Though metallic, however, the king's heart is sensitive, *sensible*, which carries the meaning not only of being reactive to outside stimuli, but also of softness. The king's heart is at once hard and soft, mute like metal, yet vibrating with sound. If it can heal wounded hearts with its sound and softness, it could just as well bruise them with its hard, metallic edges.

This metallic center is to be found in the deepest recesses of the king's soul, where the air is still and chaste. From the metallic center issue waves of sound, suggesting an unbroken, harmonious response to others, yet the soul's very core is rent, divided, and at odds with the air that surrounds it in the farthest abode of the king's inner being. The architecture of this remarkable enclosure is the most suggestive part of Rodó's essay and the most pertinent for my reading of the text. As a house for the self, or perhaps as the very representation of the self, this building, half palace and half bunker, is as startling an inner landscape as there is in Rodó's writing and in Latin American literature in general.

The parable of the "hospitable king" is told, ostensibly, to illustrate and give force to Rodó's idea that, even when enslaved by utilitarian concerns, the soul can preserve its "inner freedom," that is, the freedom of reason and of feeling. No one, to my knowledge, has found the source of this story, if there is indeed a source. Within the fiction of the essay Prospero says that he draws the symbol of what our souls should be "out of a dusty corner of [his] mind." The closest I can come to a source would be Saint Teresa's *siete castillos del alma*, an elaborate inner architecture that the Spanish mystic possibly drew, according to Luce López Baralt in a 1981 lecture at Yale, from Arabic sources. If this were indeed the source, then a more real Orient than the one invoked by Rodó slips in through the back door in the form of a textual link.

In any case, the story of this "patriarchal" king is set "in the indeterminate and naïve Orient, where the joyous flock of stories likes to roost" (p. 34). It is clearly in an ambience of the *Thousand and One Nights* that the story is set, a sort of Victorian Orient. One should not dismiss that, in this fiction of the self, the protagonist is a king, no matter how magnanimous and hospitable. As with the more forceful figure of the dictator, power is the main ingredient in the constitution of being. But what is most remarkable is not the king himself but his palace, the most recent (per)version of which is the dictator's palace in García Márquez's *The Autumn of the Patriarch*, which also harks back to the *Thousand and One Nights*.

The outside of the castle bustles with the activity of people and of nature, as travelers from all parts of the world meet to exchange goods or engage in various forms of merriment under the paternal gaze of the old king. The outside of this palace, however, is not the most remarkable feature of this elaborate hypostasis of being. Inside the king has a chamber reserved for himself, which represents the deepest regions of the self.

But within—far within, isolated from the noisy castle (*alcázar*) by covered passageways, hidden from the vulgar eye like the lost chapel of Uhland in the most secret part of the forest, at the end of unknown paths, there was a mysterious hall where it was illegal for anyone to set foot, save for the king himself, whose hospitality turned to ascetic selfishness upon crossing its threshold. Thick walls surrounded the hall. Not an echo of the external gaiety, not a note from nature's concert outside, nor a word from the lips of men managed to get past the thickness of those porphyrine sills to move a wave of air (*onda de aire*) within the forbidden hold. A religious silence brooded on the chastity of the sleeping air. Light itself, filtered by stained-glass windows reached the inside languorously, with an even tone, and diluted itself like a snowflake that has chanced to land in a warm nest, in the midst of a celestial calm. There was no peace like this neither in ocean waves nor in the loneliness of the forest. Sometimes, when the night was clear and still, the decorated roof opened itself like two valves made of mother of pearl, allowing magnificently serene darkness to occupy its place. The perfume that prevailed was that of nenuphar, pure essence suggestive but of serenity, thoughtfulness, and contemplation of one's own self. Only grave caryatids guarded the marble doors, gesturing for silence. On the façade there were statues that express idealism, introspection, and rest. And the old king would assure that, though no one could accompany him there, his hospitality prevailed in that mysterious retreat just as generous and great, only that his guests there bidden were invisible, impalpable. There this legendary king freed himself from the actual, there he turned his vision inward, smoothed and refined in meditation like the pebbles all polished by the wave; there he bound to the noble forehead the youthful wings of Psyche. (pp. 36-37)

It would be difficult to imagine a more elaborately housed and armored inner self, a more bizarre enclosure or representation of being than this monstrous castle, which is reminiscent of the interiors portrayed in the engravings of the Hetzel edition of Verne's *Twenty Thousand Leagues under the Sea*. Even the least fanciful of visualizations of the building would have to take into account the clashing mixture of styles. The porticos remind one of classical Greek forms—the caryatids, above all—not necessarily Oriental ones, and the word *alcázar*, used instead of *castillo* to refer to the castle, is, of course, Arabic in origin, which immediately evokes lacelike patterns, numerous thin columns, pointed arches, and a mazelike interior plan. Within this already strange construction one has then to imagine a second, massive enclosure, walled off by marble, with heavy doors framed by caryatids, roofed by two mother of pearl, intricately inlaid valves that open up to the sky like a gigantic shell.

Like the *placa sonora*, this ornate building, containing the still air whence, nevertheless, the voice of the master issues in unbroken vibrations, is a contrary figure; rather than the lightness of spirit or the softness of voice, the building evokes the weight and substantiality of stone; instead of a free, generous exchange, it represents a defensive posture, an exclusion. No dialogic exchange here, but rather an enclosure in which the building, like a shell, hardens into shape around a vacuum. Only the most ornate interiors devised by Jules Verne to house his mad protagonists can compare to the castle of the hospitable king: the inside of the spaceship that will travel to the moon, the interior of Captain Nemo's submarine in *Twenty Thousand Leagues under the Sea*. The self, this monstrous self in which authority is invested, is shielded from nature, isolated from the world, by the most luxuriant artifice.

In a sense, what this elaborate building betrays is the strategic nature of the appeal to voice. Voice is but a ruse, for Prospero's is not merely persuasive but magisterial, even kingly. It is a voice that attempts to be inscribed, sealed, chiseled, wounded onto the listeners. It is no mere texture, but an *arch-texture* whose hypostasis is the imaginary *architecture* conjured up to envelop it. At the beginning, in the opening paragraphs, which describe the setting, the narrator refers to Prospero's voice as "a firm voice—the voice of the Master [*voz magistral*], which, to pass its ideas and [en]grave them deeply in the minds of the disciples, can employ either the clear penetration of a ray of light or the sharp blow of a chisel on the marble, the stroke of the painter's brush on canvas [*el toque impregnante del pincel en el lienzo*] or the touch of the wave upon the sands, [whose mark is] to be read in fossils by future generations" (pp. 5-6). At the end of the speech, as we have seen, the students carry within them this voice: "Of his sweetest words there lingered in each of the disciples the persisting vibrations through which the cry of the wounded glass is prolonged in the still air" (p. 148). The *"suave palabra"* is transformed here into the *"lamento del cristal herido"*; the "wounded glass" is the metallic plaque, giving off vibrations after being struck, only striking in this case is rendered as a form of incision or cut: the architecture of being out of which the magisterial voice emerges, the voice itself, has sharp edges instead of soft, vaporous contours. All of these figures used to represent voice, quite contrary to the intention to portray it as a gentle carrier of truth, culminate in the last example employed by Prospero in his speech. This illustration and the parable of the hospitable king are the rhetorical centers of the essay, the magnetic poles to which the various forces at work in the text are drawn and clash.

The example is part of Prospero's peroration, which begins with the extraordinary statement that he wishes his students to remember not so much his words as the statue of Ariel standing next to him, not the sound of his voice, but the visual image cast in heavy bronze. Once he has displaced the remembrance of his voice to the statue, Prospero asks that "the image, light and graceful, of this bronze, *impress itself* upon your inmost spirit" (p. 146; emphasis added). This request is followed by a new tale:

I remember that once, when looking at a coin case in a museum, my attention was struck by the device in an old coin that, though half erased on the decrepit paleness of gold, read *Hope*. Considering the effaced inscription, I meditated on the possible reality of its influence. Who knows what active and noble role it would be fair to attribute in the formation of character or in the life of several generations of human beings, to this simple motto acting upon their spirits as a persistent suggestion? Who knows how much timid happiness survived, how many generous impulses were carried to fruition, how many evil endeavors dissolved when eyes clashed with the encouraging word, impressed like a *graphic shout*, on the *metallic disc* that circulated from hand to hand? (pp. 146-141; emphasis added)

In the context of the figures we have been examining, Prospero's example could hardly be more suggestive. There is an obvious correspondence between the *metallic plaque* and this *metallic disc*, between the *wounded glass* and the souls of the students upon which the hard statue of Ariel is going to be impressed. The inescapable association of speech with coins is quite a contradictory figure; rather than the flow of speech, here we have the heavy, repeatable, yet divisible, materiality of coins. The coin, unlike undifferentiated air, is chiseled, written upon, set. It is a unit of repeated, yet distinct forms. Like the metallic plaque, the coin's inscription is an oxymoronic *graphic shout* that brings out the strident drama implicit in Rodó's essay, a drama based on the conflict between truth as a sharing of spirit and as ideological imposition. Like the castle of the hospitable king, the inscription on the coin houses truth, but truth congealed, in the molded shapes of the exceedingly ornate architecture or of the letters engraved in the gold like the vibrations emanating from the "wounded glass," the product of incision, chiseling. Instead of a free exchange of unmeasured spirit, we find a carved and minted piece of gold, the very measure not of timeless value but of contingent monetary exchange. Turned into a bronze statue, later into the inscription on the coin, the voice of the master begins to take on an ever more menacing shape; it is heavy, wounding, inscribed.

The very next sentence after the story about the coin signals a return to the statue of Ariel, which now becomes the heated metal mold ready to print or mint, to wound, so to speak, onto the metal, a text: "So may the figure of this bronze, *graven in your hearts*, fulfill in your lives this [the same] invisible yet determining part" (p. 147; emphasis added). The violence implicit in this sentence is so forceful that *graven*, despite its rather strong connotations, remains a weak version of the Spanish *troquelar*. *Troquel* is the actual mold used to mint coins, to engrave metal. Thus *troquelar*, as used in Rodó's text, has a meaning akin to branding, as in the branding of cattle, an image of writing that often appears in Latin American writing, particularly in Rómulo Gallegos's *Doña Bárbara*. I do not believe that I would be skewing the translation too much in favor of my reading if the sentence were rendered, "May the shape of this statue, once its figure has been branded onto your hearts, play a role as subtle as that of the inscription on the coin, but just as determining and durable." This sentence, dealing with the way in which Prospero's voice is going to be written upon his students, brings to a close a series of associations that mar the deluding calm of Rodó's text and points to a startling cohesiveness within a cluster of opposite meanings.

The magisterial rhetoric of *Ariel* conceals the violence by which it wishes to inscribe its doctrine and the self-criticism implicit in the cutting, the spacing, of the textual material. Perhaps the statue of Shakespeare's fairy is, indeed, the best representation of Prospero's message: a solid, heavy, metal figure of air. The cutting edges of this image are the ones that slit the source of the vibrations from the inner core, from the vibrations themselves, the ones that establish a space between the chaste air inside the king's secret abode and the space outside. These spaces mark the place of discontinuity and give way to repetition: no waves of sound or air, but vibrations made up of distinct, yet repeated, instances. Instead of the exchange promised by the dialogic setting, these edges are to brand the space of difference onto the other presences in the seminar. The soft voice that cures also wounds.

Rodó's elaboration of this magisterial rhetoric in *Ariel* reveals quite dramatically that the constitution of an American self through writing cannot be achieved without undergoing a complex process that halfway conceals the gaps inherent in the process itself and the willful nature of the impulse behind such an enterprise. The rhetorical power to sustain the magisterial voice consists in doing violence to an implied other onto whom one's words are to be cut. This reading at the center of Rodó's influential essay continues to be at the core of the Latin American tradition that follows it, and the emergence of Rodó's effort is connected to the first sustained efforts at the elaboration of an idea of a Latin American literature.

It is no accident that *Ariel* is a near contemporary of two major events in the history of Latin American literature: the publication by Marcelino

Menéndez y Pelayo of his monumental *Antología de poetas hispano-americanos* (1893), and of Rubén Darío's *Historia de mis libros* (1909) and *Autobiografía* (1912). The first is an institutional event of major significance. No matter what Menéndez y Pelayo's reactionary and Eurocentric biases were, his *Antología* conceived for the first time a literary space within which Latin American poetry could exist on its own. The publication of Darío's books is but a reflection of his own life as institution; that is to say, Darío lived and traveled all over the Hispanic world as a Latin American poet. The contradictory self that roams Prospero's study in Rodó's fiction is akin to Darío's own self as poet wandering the continent. But the fissure at the center of *Ariel*, the critical gap within which we can read the emergence of his wounded American self, leaves an imprint on the history of the Latin American essay that is just as important as the kinship of the essay with the works of Menéndez y Pelayo and Darío. The most visible repetition of the contradictory gesture of the essay is to be found in two books that put into practice many of Rodó's ideals, by two writers who would gladly have declared themselves to be disciples of the Uruguayan: Pedro Henríquez Ureña and Alfonso Reyes.

The essays by these towering figures that have often become standard texts in high schools and universities are *La cultura en la América hispánica*, by Henríquez Ureña, and *Ultima Tule* and "Visión de Anáhuac," by Alfonso Reyes.[6] All of these texts reach back to pre-Hispanic America in search of an origin of Latin American culture and find it in the rich civilizations that inhabited above all central Mexico and Peru. But although giving these cultures a foundational place, both Henríquez Ureña and Reyes usurp their capacity for verbal expression and thought. The metaphors to which they appeal hark back to Rodó's compelling tropological drama.

Reyes is interested, above all, in the founding American theme of Utopia, and his book on the subject, *Ultima Tule*, is an inevitable reference work on the subject. He sees universal history as being constituted by a series of violent rifts, which make people always yearn for a lost unity, which can be found either in the past or in the future. In pre-Hispanic America there had been such upheavals just before the Conquest, which was itself a catastrophe that broke apart the world known then to the natives of the New World. Reyes's conception of the march of universal history is mainly Hegelian, but the violence implicit in his conception of the crises of history reveals the same double sense of rending and mending, wounding and curing, seen in *Ariel*. Reyes writes in *Ultima Tule*,

In the various stages of history that we have gone over, we have witnessed a cosmic game in which a puzzle was being put together [*rompecabezas* (literally headbreaker)]. The scissor cuts [*golpes de tijeras* (blows of the scissors)] made by some whimsical demiurge have been slicing into fragments the original unity, and one of the fragments into parts, and one of the parts into pieces, and one of the pieces into bits. And the imagination, whose counsel we have agreed to follow, is whispering in our ear: "even if that original unity never existed, man has always dreamed." (XI, p. 77)

America would then be the restitution of that unity broken up by the slashes of the capricious demiurge, the elaboration of a fiction to smooth over the slits. But that movement toward a lost unity in the past is found, revealingly, in the stones of pre-Hispanic America, which are anything but a closing of the wound in themselves, unless some patch-up work is applied.

In "Visión de Anáhuac," one of the most remarkable and understandably famous essays in the Latin American tradition, Reyes posits that each culture is what it sees. Thus pre-Hispanic cultures have left a deep impression on the American soul with their pyramids, ruins, stone idols, and, above all, their hieroglyphs. Searching for the origin of modern Mexico, looking for that lost unity in the past, which can become a reflection of a unity restored in the future, Reyes sifts through the texts describing the Conquest until he finally reaches down to the hieroglyphs. These cuts in the stone are the irreducible origin, the original poetry of America. Yet these chiseled lines mean nothing to us and would be mute, the tracks of some monstrous pen doodling aimlessly and enigmatically on the rock. Open cuts without sound stand at the origin. But Reyes hears a sound: "Some crackling noises are heard [as the Indians of today speak]. The vowels flow and the consonants tend to turn liquid. The prattle is a delicious singsong. These *x*'s, those *tl*'s, those *ch*'s that are alarming to us [because they appear not to contain air, sound] in written form, trickle out of the lips of the Indians, sweeter than water and honey" (II, p. 102). Out on the stone, the *x*'s, which for us are signs of absence (the enigmatic cross at the center of the word *México*), the *tl*'s and *ch*'s, which appear not to contain sound, are fearful; when spoken, the stone turns to water and honey, caressing instead of wounding. Yet it is the vision of the stones that impresses itself on the soul. As in Rodó—as in Neruda and Paz—the stones speak through voice and writing.

Henríquez Ureña's gesture is even more revealing and in consonance with Rodó: he claims that the pre-Hispanic cultures were beheaded by the Conquest, leaving them with only their plastic arts as a contribution to the formation of Latin American culture.[7] Such a void is to be filled, of course, by the magisterial contribution of these two *maestros* and many others, who, like the Venezuelan Mariano Picón Salas in his *De la conquista a la independencia*, write in the tradition of Rodó. The magisterial rhetoric will then be the process of affirmation of the culture and the self, placed on the cut of the hieroglyph on the stone, the cut where the head was lopped off, supplying the necessary voice of wisdom and knowledge. Two other essayists in the tradition, the brilliant Mariátegui in his *7 ensayos de interpretación de la realidad peruana* (1928) and Lezama Lima in his *La expresión americana* (1958), put forth the idea that myths ought to be created to formulate the American identity, instead of passing off their ideas as truths derived from history or from the reality of the continent. Mariátegui, after a painstaking and scrupulous analysis of Peruvian history, which debunks many blatant ideological distortions in official history, sees the need to erect the Incaic empire as a sort of myth of natural communism to inspire the masses to a return to the past, which will in turn propel them into the future. A Marxist who begins his captivating book with a quotation from Nietzsche, Mariátegui points at the gap at the center of the project of formulating an American identity, an American self that can be at home in a well-defined American collectivity, and decides to cover it with a necessary fiction that is obviously contrary to the basic tenets of Marx's thought.

Lezama, on the other hand, posits the existence of a *sujeto metafórico*, a self with the poetic power to create an image of America, an image that will be composed through a poetic method of association. America will be an "imaginary era" for Lezama, an epoch with a distinctive quality that can be discovered by this metaphoric self capable of closing the gaps in language, a supplemental language conscious of its own supplementarity. Lezama's *La expresión americana* is the last and no doubt one of the most distinguished texts to have issued from the branding of the disciple's souls at Prospero's seminar.

The most recent vibration to reach us from the metallic plaque in Rodó's essay is *Barroco*, Severo Sarduy's 1974 book.[8] It may seem startling to bring Sarduy's book into this discussion, but, as I hope to show by way of conclusion, his version of Rodó's magisterial rhetoric is quite useful as a tool for analyzing the whole issue of the constitution of an American self and the reflection of this process in writing.

Sarduy's book follows Lezama Lima's idea that the baroque was the first autochthonous artistic movement in Latin America and that therefore it contains the kernel of the uniqueness of the Latin American self and its literature. *Barroco* does not follow Lezama beyond this general conception, but that is enough to reveal that Sarduy's book, following the heritage of Lezama and *Ariel*, is bent on discovering an American self and the culture of Latin American literature that sustains it and allows it to generate art. One need not follow here Sarduy's lines of argumentation about the baroque, which are only marginally pertinent to our discussion. Two aspects, however, have to be discussed, because they clearly echo Rodó's text in a fruitful way: the conception of the self, and the opening of the book through which the self is hypostasized.

Sarduy makes his entire conception of the baroque hinge on the figure of the ellipse, a figure of suppression and elision, through which the center—erased—is supplanted by another. The baroque is the excess, then, that covers the suppressed element, hence, the excess of ornamentation in baroque art. The functioning of this mechanism is akin to that of the subconscious according to Lacan, explained thus by Sarduy:

The baroque metaphor would be identified with a radically different mode of *suppression*, which consists in a change of structure: *repression (Verdrangung/-refoulement)*. It is on the level of the subconscious system where this operation is fully developed by means of which the representations of representations are kept at a distance by certain desires [*pulsiones*]. In the measure in which this is identified with an organization of the lack—and above all with an "originary" lack—repression sets in motion a metonymic mechanism that implies the indefinite flight of the object of desire; but in the measure in which through the symptom it allows one to see a possible return of what is repressed—the symptom is a signifier within an economy of neurosis—the symptom becomes indistinguishable from metaphor. (p. 74)

Symptom and metaphor are one because they are the end product of a cause whose effect is, so to speak, suppressed. The subconscious, then, is made up of these symptoms/signifiers that keep at bay the object of desire. The object of desire forms an absent core around which the symptoms gather, constituting the subconscious.

Given that the baroque is presented as the quintessential American art school, and that it is a representation of the American self, I do not think that it would be too rash to say that what Sarduy is providing here is a model for the constitution of the Latin American self. We can now see how the inner castle of Rodó's hospitable king, with its elaborate system of defenses or symptoms, is a sort of representation of a baroque American self in the manner Sarduy suggests. This system of defenses deploys itself around a lack, the void at the center of the castle, and a wound, the wounded, vibrating core.

This correspondence is made more plausible if we turn to the beginning of Sarduy's book. The book is organized following what is called a "scientific outline," meaning the various chapters and subheadings are numbered following a staggered system divided by periods: 1, 1.1, 2, 2.1, and so on. The first division, however, is in two parts, numbered *Uno* and *Dos*. The beginning of both parts is marked by the zero, which in turn becomes a graphic representation of the self that is repeated at the beginning of each half. *Uno* opens not with 1, to be followed by 1.1 or by 2, but with O., a chapter aptly entitled "*Cámara de eco*" (echo chamber). The first part of two, *Dos*, is named "*Cero*," though it is numbered 1. The chamber of echoes, appropriately repeated, is the entrance into the book, the portico of the self of the author, in what would normally be a foreword. But this self is composed of symptoms or echoes; therefore the self of the author appears here as this void encircled by the O. The echo chamber, as opposed to the core of the king's abode, is a vacuum in which all sound is always already an echo whose source has been suppressed. The graphic representation is itself significant in that it underscores the mark, the branding of the self by means of spacing. The book that follows that beginning before the beginning, which will expound on the American self through the circuitous way of a discussion of the baroque, is the symptom, the signifier of American culture, a signifier erected on the void of the suppressed object of desire, on the wound which is writing's violent inscription.

2. *Doña Bárbara* Writes the Plain

In this way the boundaries of the fields were fixed and maintained. This division, too generally set forth by Hermogenianus the jurisconsult, has been imagined as taking place by deliberate agreement of men, and carried out with justice and respect in good faith, at a time when there was as yet no armed public force and consequently no civil authority of law. But it cannot be understood save as taking place among men of extreme wildness, observing a frightful religion which had fixed and circumscribed them within certain lands, and whose bloody ceremonies had consecrated their first values.
—Thomas Goddard Bergin and Max Harold Fisch, *The New Science of Giambattista Vico.* Abridged Translation of the Third Edition (1744)

1

It is safe to say, without fear of sounding overly strident, that criticism of Latin American literature is in the midst of a crisis, a crisis that will be fruitful, to be sure, as is so often the case in the humanities. Signs of this crisis are everywhere. The most apparent is the absence of any school, ideology, or critical tendency enjoying even a modicum of shared acceptance among writers, critics, and intellectuals. Though it may seem to some that a critical consensus never did exist in Latin America, in point of fact there have been several periods of general accord, if only in broad and even diffuse terms, as to what Latin American literature is and how it should be approached.[1] I do not mean to suggest that these critical doctrines originated in Latin America, nor that their concept of Latin American literature was always propitious.[2] The fact remains, however, that there once existed dominant groups with general ideas about Latin American literature and a clear notion of what "our" literature was. When figures such as Alfonso Reyes, Pedro Henríquez Ureña, or Mariano Picón Salas made pronouncements about a specific writer or a broader literary theme, they did so with the sure hand of critics who work with acceptable and accepted doctrines.

Nowadays there are no figures that, like Henríquez Ureña or Alfonso Reyes, represent dominant literary doctrines, but rather a series of disparate groups, each unable to command the high ground of criticism. One finds, for example, critics whose orientation is Marxist, but there is not much agreement among them, nor has there arisen a critic of the stature that Mariátegui, the Walter Benjamin of Latin American letters, might have achieved, had he lived longer. And Juan Marinello, whose recent death was an irreparable blow to literary criticism in Spanish, was more of an artist than a critic. Incapable of theorizing successfully, the Marxist school in Latin America suffers from the same defects common to nearly all Latin American critical tendencies: a lack of patience for research; a disinclination toward close reading; the tendency to make quick, half-pondered judgments based on contingent political situations. Even though the work carried out by such journals as *Arte/Sociedad/Ideología, Casa de las Américas,* and *Revista de Crítica Literaria Hispanoamericana* is not without merit, the truth is that no Marxist school of criticism has developed in Latin America.[3]

One also finds critical groups loosely derived from French structuralism and poststructuralism, organized around journals such as *Texto Crítico.* But, despite the fact that Latin America has for the first time played an important role in originating a critical school, these groups have yet to produce a major critic.[4] Borges, for example, is rightly considered one of the founders, unwitting to be sure, of structuralist and poststructuralist thought, and both Severo Sarduy and Octavio Paz have been linked, each in his own way, to the movement, but Latin American structuralist and poststructuralist criticism has preferred to imitate its French models—doubtless because of the latter's more systematic nature.[5] Latin American structuralism has not produced the kind of major figure or major critical work that would achieve an original synthesis of structuralist tendencies. Journals such as *Texto Crítico* and *Escritura* have been unable to form a critical school, and their intellectual level is uneven at best; such is also the case with *Dispositio,* a journal published in the United States, which valiantly endeavors to promote a criticism of semiotic orientation. Even Noé Jitrik, the most tenacious Latin American disciple of French criticism in recent years, has failed to produce a work that would be for structuralism what Amado Alonso's book on Neruda was for *estilística.*[6] The closest we have come to a figure of sufficient caliber to impress a Latin American mark on French criticism is Severo Sarduy. He has, no doubt, had an impact on figures like Barthes and Sollers; however, like Borges and Paz, Sarduy is above all a writer whose best critical efforts, although often brilliant, follow certain French models (Derrida, Lacan) very closely, without quite crystallizing into a critical system of his own. I have no doubt that his eclecticism is his contribution to the *nouvelle critique*, particularly as it is practiced in his fiction, but it is hardly possible for such a position to create a school.

Latin America continues to have great critics among the poets, not only Octavio Paz, but also Guillermo Sucre, who is perhaps the most advanced critic of poetry in Spanish. But like Paz, Sucre is first and foremost a poet, not a creator of critical methods. Paz himself has noted this absence of critical schools in Latin America: "We have literary criticism; what we don't have is our own critical thought."[7] But the question remains as to whether, in the midst of this general crisis in Latin American criticism, it is not the very lack of a system and the presence of criticism in the work of creative writers that constitute Latin America's theoretical contribution to present-day critical thought, whether, in short, literature itself is not Latin America's critical thought.

In the essay quoted earlier, Octavio Paz attributes the absence of critical thought in Latin America to the intellectual weakness of our eighteenth century: "Since we didn't have an Enlightenment, nor a bourgeois revolution, neither did we have the great passional and spiritual reaction against criticism and its constructs: romanticism. Our romantics rebelled against something that they had not suffered: the dictatorship of reason."[8] I would not be quite so severe with our romantic age as Paz is, but I agree that the possibility of there being a Latin American critical thought like the European was eroded by the absence of the kinds of socioeconomic conditions that led to the romantic movement.

But to say this begs the question of why Latin America must have a critical thought like the European. Why must the master plot of Western European history, as devised by Western European historiography, be the one against which Latin American history is measured? To think in this fashion is to view history as do some simple-minded Marxists, who await the "bourgeois revolution" in Latin America before the "proletarian revolution" can take place. It may be true that the Enlightenment in Latin America was unlike Europe's, and one could say that there were no romantics in Latin America of the stature of their German or English counterparts. And yet Russia, a nation that never enjoyed an Enlightenment, was nonetheless able to produce both an original romanticism and, at the beginning of the twentieth century, a criticism that was in the very vanguard of literary studies. Another of Paz's observations from the same essay strikes me as more useful: "It would be very difficult to find one work in the literatures of Spanish America and Brazil in which there isn't, in one way or another, criticism. In this sense, our literatures are modern."[9]

If by "criticism" we mean the radical and systematic questioning of both values and the codes that transmit them, of both social and political practices, and of language and literature themselves, then we cannot help but agree with Paz. It is possible that, in this sense, there is no literature more critical than Latin American literature, and it is probable that it is for this very reason that Latin American literature is today the only one of truly international circulation. Thus we can conclude that, if Latin American literature has been critical, Latin American criticism itself has not. To what can these two phenomena be attributed? And what can critics do to aspire to the level of literature? In short, how can we best take advantage of the crisis?

2

The study of Latin American literature is in a state of crisis because the concept that has served as its base is for the first time being submitted to a radical and systematic questioning. This concept, an offshoot of nineteenth-century philology and of romanticism in general, holds that Latin American culture is so distinctive, so profoundly unique, that it has generated a literature that is fundamentally different from that of the rest of the West. This concept not only has influenced Latin American literary criticism, but also has been the visible ideology of Latin American literature itself, of the idea of literature in Latin America. Actually, the individual character of national literatures is a notion derived from romantic thought, one that has enjoyed a long life in the history of Latin American thought because the birth of Latin America as a discrete political entity coincided with the crest of romanticism.[10] It is no accident that the first great modern figure of Latin American letters was the poet-philologist Andrés Bello. The idea of Latin American literature rests on that concept, which postulates the existence of a synchronization, a perfect meshing of language, culture, and literature: this is the myth that gives it legitimacy and authority.

But today the concept of culture and the idea of literature are being studied from a historical perspective that reveals the ideological character of both. For this reason, the preeminence of the concept of culture, its place as the starting point for any study of Latin American literature, has become the object of analysis and debate, and not of implicit agreement. The Marxist perspective argues that cultural identity, as it appears in a certain kind of literature and in studies of literature, is a class concept, created to blur sharp social differences with an all-embracing category in which all individuals fit.[11] From a rigorous existentialist perspective, this option of identity as a by-product of culture is inadmissible, since ontological problems cannot be resolved collectively.[12] For the modern anthropologist, cultural identity enters into a vast and complicated system, one that integrates individual differences within a global coalescence.[13] And from the perspective of the most recent tendencies in literary criticism and theory, literature is the result of a radical split between language, culture, and individual consciousness.[14]

Even though the crisis brought on by these doubts has been apparent in literature for some time (it was also part of its constitution), it is only now that this crisis appears in an explicit form in literary studies and forces us to reformulate the problem.

Even the most cursory glance at recent Latin American critical speculation reveals that this restatement has begun in earnest. The most recent work of essayists as diverse as Roberto Fernández Retamar and Octavio Paz—who are continuing the tradition of Mariátegui, Reyes, and Henríquez Ureña—questions the notion that Latin America possesses a unique culture, and therefore an autonomous literature. Paz, in *Children of the Mire*, rather than insisting on the autonomy of Latin American literature, studies the particular way in which this literature forms a part of modernity.[15] Rather than examining how literature depends, in some vague way, on a collective spirit, Paz exploits the unique and contradictory way in which it partakes of Western literature. He maintains that modernity includes those differences that identify Latin American literature. Fernández Retamar, with a more political approach, questions the existence of a separate Latin American culture, demonstrating the historical role that "nuestra América," as he, following Martí, calls it, has played in Western literature.[16] In recent works, Fernández Retamar revises, with a Marxist approach that has begun to be coherent, the opinions expressed in his well-known essay *Calibán* and, in effect, opens the possibility for a critical rereading of both this essay and the tradition from which it arises.[17]

Fernández Retamar's work follows in the footsteps of the influential essay written in 1961 by Alejo Carpentier, "Literatura y conciencia política en América Latina."[18] In this essay Carpentier chastised his own generation for falling into the trap of a nebulous and sentimental *mundonovismo*, which blinded it to the political and social realities of the time.[19] This essay, along with some of Borges's critical formulations, the latest writings by Fernández Retamar, many of Paz's more acute and radical observations, and those of younger writers like Severo Sarduy, suggests that there is now in progress a critique of the work realized in the twenties, thirties, and forties by the generation to which Carpentier alludes.

Some of the older writers had already begun a critique. The key text by Borges in this regard is "El escritor argentino y la tradición," in which he says, "I would like to put forth and justify some skeptical formulations concerning the problem of the Argentine writer and tradition. My skepticism does not address the difficulty or impossibility of solving it, but the very existence of the problem. I think that we are faced here with a rhetorical problem, good for pathetic expositions. More than a real mental problem, I think it is a mirage, a simulacrum, a pseudo-problem."[20] Borges's affirmation is unquestionable, except that one must add that, since literature often hinges on rhetoric, simulacra, and pseudo-problems, the rhetorical theme he is discussing has undeniable reality, which is evident in his own work—not only in early books like *Fervor de Buenos Aires*, but in all of his work.

The most programmatic of Paz's essays in this regard is "Spanish-American Literature," where he writes,

The diversity of Spanish-American works cannot be reduced to a few characteristic traits. Isn't the same true of other literatures? Who could define French, English or Italian literature? Racine and Chateaubriand, Pope and Wordsworth, Petrarch and Leopardi, though they wrote in the same language, all inhabited different worlds. Why struggle to define the character of Spanish-American literature? Literatures have no character. Or rather, contradiction, ambiguity, exception and hesitancy are traits which appear in all literatures. At the heart of every literature there is a continuous dialogue of oppositions, separations, bifurcations. Literature is an interweaving of affirmations and negations, doubts and interrogations. Spanish-American literature is not simply a body of works, but the relationship among these works. Each of them is a reply, spoken or silent, to another work written by a predecessor, a contemporary or an imaginary descendant. Our criticism should explore these contradictory relationships and show us how these mutually exclusive affirmations and negations are also in some sense complementary.[21]

I owe a great deal to this essay, as shall be seen in what follows, but I nevertheless would make certain modifications. The problem is not only to seek to define the character of Latin American literature, but also *to inquire as to why Latin American writers (Paz among them) have so often sought such a definition.* I have no doubt that at the heart of all literature (which?) one can find the oppositions, contradictions, and negations of which Paz speaks, but one of the principal negations is that of literature itself; therefore, a dialogue is established not only among literary texts, but among *all* the texts of a given culture. To remain within the dialogue of a literary tradition is to reintroduce, through a so-called intertextuality, an essentialist notion of literature, which such an intertextual approach does not accept. Paz jumps from the Renaissance to the nineteenth century as if the definition of literature were not historical, including, above all, the definition that he tacitly employs.

The statements by Carpentier, Borges, and Paz find an echo in younger critics and writers. Even though, as shall be seen, the radical criticism that this new posture facilitated was already implicit in literature, more recent literature has made it explicit. Writers like Sarduy have parodied received ideas about cultural identity in works like *De donde son los cantantes, Cobra,* and *Maitreya,* whereas other writers in the language, like the Spaniard Juan Goytisolo, have done the same in an even more transparent way, in *Señas de identidad, Juan sin tierra,* and *Reivindicación del Conde Don Julián.* There are others, such as Carlos Fuentes, who, caught in the

Fuentes-
Derrida
y Américo Castro

middle of the crisis, seek a way out through the dubious, yet productive, integration of the latest critical systems with the ideological remnants of the concept of cultural identity—I refer to Fuentes's bizarre marriage of Derrida and Américo Castro in *Cervantes o la crítica de la lectura* and *Terra Nostra*, one of the most revealing and compelling episodes in recent Latin American intellectual history.[22]

Equally revealing is the orientation of some younger critics who have been affected by both recent Latin American literature and the theoretical turmoil of recent years. Guillermo Sucre, for example, asserts the following in a 1978 essay entitled "Poesía hispanoamericana y conciencia del lenguaje":

What we are actually surrounded by is the universe and language, and what we call culture is nothing else than the relation between these two terms. The history of any man, of any people, in any space, passes through and cannot but pass through the relation between language and the universe; even if this relation does not cease being dialectical, it would not be wrong to think of it as governed by language.

And he adds the following observation, which does not fail to be pertinent:

[N]ationality, with all its connotations, is the least important element in the poetic act. Like all literature, poetry is an open space in which there are only words—texts, forms, styles—that establish a dialogue among themselves, that attract or reject each other, above and beyond frontiers, races, epochs, and even languages. And, we should add, above and beyond and despite the author's intentions.[23]

Carlos Rincón, although with a very different critical formation than Sucre's, also insists on removing from the idea of literature that essentialist character that is inevitably conferred by the concept of culture promoted by previous generations of critics. In "El cambio actual de la noción de literatura en Hispanoamérica," Rincón says,

The pressure that social evolution on the continent has brought to bear on the ideological level has not only made all forms of reference explode, but has questioned the very mirage of there being a substantialist essence in literature. . . . When faced with the tests to which it has been submitted [of late], the literary text reveals itself not to be exclusively an object constituted by language, nor a generator of fictions, but the creator of specific effects.[24]

For her part, Irlemar Chiampi, after providing an interesting panorama of the Latin American essay dealing with the image of America, writes the following:

To discuss the degree of accuracy of the images of America [contained in the essays] would be interesting for a study of the signifying process of this discourse, of its semantic universe, which is not a primary system of objects and facts, but a second-degree system. To apportion value for being "true" or "false" to these images would carry us into metaphysical questions concerning the substance of the contents, making us lose sight of the semiotic, conventional nature of the language of these images. Thus we can say that the discourse interpreting America preserves a cognitive function about reality, but the information that it releases is no longer a direct given.[25]

Likewise, the Martinican Alfred Melon expressed the following in a lecture given in Havana a few years ago:

It should be understood that when one talks about the discourse concerning national identity one refers predominantly to intellectuals and above all to writers. In any case, the problematic of national identity, like the one about national consciousness, worries almost exclusively intellectuals and political leaders, without the Indians and the blacks taking part in this reflection, which is why they don't feel directly involved.

And Melon adds,

Until now the hegemony of Creoles, half-breeds, and mulattoes has been occasionally possible, but never that of Indians and blacks. In such circumstances, the discourse on national identity has for a long time played and continues to play an ideological function, which is to sustain the illusion of an already accomplished unity, concealing in that way inequities and the marginalization of the disfavored classes.[26]

Despite the obvious differences among these critics, they display a skeptical attitude toward the uniqueness of Latin American literature and an examination from without of the ideology that made this notion of uniqueness the standard point of departure for all studies of that literature. However, the purpose of such an examination should not be to do away with the concept of culture and the idea of literature, but rather to interpret the sense and the inner workings of the relationship between the two. Of course, it is not a matter of judging as true or false the concept or concepts on which the idea of Latin American literature has been based, nor of supposing that these concepts ever offered some kind of direct information, as Chiampi sees clearly. Nor is it a question of simply denying the ability of these previous formulations and venturing to establish a new one that would not take them into consideration. We must accept that we are dealing with ideological realities, whose function in engendering Latin American literature must be made manifest, not swept away. It is not that a mystification must be denounced, but rather that its mechanisms must be dismantled, since such a dismantling will reveal not information but the critical substratum of Latin American literature of which Paz speaks. In this substratum, in which apparent doctrine becomes polemical confrontation, the different components of the text bristle and pulsate instead of bending before the soothing breeze of doctrine.

Bello & the nature metaphor

3

It is not by chance that Henríquez Ureña, at the beginning of his influential book *Literary Currents in Hispanic America*, invokes the *Silvas americanas* by Andrés Bello. He returns to Bello in chapter 4, "The Declaration of Intellectual Independence." Henríquez Ureña appropriately recognizes that it is in Bello's work that a coherent idea of the modernity of America, and of the uniqueness of its literature, is first formed: "The desire for intellectual independence is first made explicit by Andrés Bello (1781–1865) in his *Allocution to Poetry*, the first of his two Silvas Americanas."[27] But it is not just for this historical reason that Henríquez Ureña refers to Bello's *Silvas*; to a great extent it is Bello's work that first weaves the metaphoric network on which the concept of Latin American culture and the idea of its literature are based. This network is, of course, that which nature provides; Henríquez Ureña's currents have their source in Bello's *Silvas*. The vigor of the nature metaphor has been so great in Latin American literature and criticism that it is difficult to find an important work that does not invoke it, from the beginnings of romanticism to *Piedra de sol*—nature and, more specifically, the metaphoric system that makes up the concept, have been the surface on which Latin American literature has inscribed the myth of its legitimacy. The relationship between culture and literature has been given coherence by nature, a sort of supreme text that, like an enormous vine, envelops and supports both.

It is on this myth of nature and its organic coherence that Latin American literature and criticism are founded, not on the idea of Utopia held by the Europeans who came to America in the colonial period. The validity of the colonial period as the origin of Latin American literature is that which modern Latin American literature itself has conferred on it. The nature myth arises toward the beginning of the nineteenth century in the works of the romantics, but first becomes coherent in the writings of the many European travelers who criss-crossed America in the nineteenth century and described it in rich detail: von Humboldt, Schomburgk, Koch-Grünberg, Robertson, Bonplant, Chevalier, and so many others (among them none other than Charles Darwin). The Renaissance idea of Utopia had lost all preponderance in the nineteenth century, and colonial texts had already begun to be described and edited; not so with those of European scientists of the nineteenth century, whose echoes were also heard throughout European literature itself.

Bello describes American flora with the passion of the naturalist, as do many other Latin American poets and novelists of the nineteenth century. In Cuba the elegant Plácido devotes delicate poems to coffee, cinnamon, and pineapple blossoms, and the *costumbristas* set out to describe not only the burgeoning cities but also, and above all, the countryside. The great romantic novelist Anselmo Suárez y Romero, author of an excellent Cuban abolitionist novel, delights in the description of Cuban landscapes.

European travelers

Plácido
Juárez y
Romero

Suárez y Romero's patriotism, or that of a Cirilo Villaverde, is intimately linked to this so-called *sentimiento de la naturaleza,* which was more than the critical commonplace may suggest. The sense of nature was, for these incipient Latin Americans, a sense of otherness, which was legitimized by the feeling of concrete ties between the variegated and wildly fecund nature of the continent and their own national and artistic consciousness. This is the great lesson that Sarmiento learns from his own writing of *Facundo*: there is no way around the nature that engenders Quiroga and Rosas; it expresses itself through Sarmiento himself. There is a fated link between the written text and the imposing jungles, the broad rivers, the strange plants, worthy of the attention of the naturalist and the color plates of the science book, the delicate and singular flowers that metamorphose into the rare and beautiful pineapple, sugarcane, and other fruits of the American cornucopia.

This exaltation of nature, and the concomitant definition of Latin American culture as proceeding from it, culminate in a powerful essay by Martí, "Nuestra América," which even today serves as a doctrinal base for many, despite the fact that it was written in 1891, in the midst of *decadentismo* and *positivismo*, for a Mexican newspaper during the Porfiriato. With phrases whose beauty will intoxicate even the most skeptical reader, Martí says, "Graft the world onto our republics. But the trunk of the tree must be that of our republics."[28] And he continues with a monstrous description that faithfully echoes nineteenth-century pathology: "We were a spectre, with the chest of an athlete, the hands of a fop and the forehead of a child."[29] Without overlooking the political impact of his influential essay, I must emphasize that Martí's concept of an *hombre natural* representing Latin American culture, and of the literature that such a figure would demand, forms part of a romantic ideology whose appeal in America was due to the factors already mentioned. As Antonio Cândido has said,

The idea of *patria*, of "fatherland," was clearly linked to that of *nature* and in part took its justification from this. Both led to a literature which compensated for material backwardness and the weakness of institutions by the supervaluing of "regional" aspects, making eroticism a cause for social optimism. . . . One of the ostensible or latent assumptions of Latin American literature was this connection, greatly exalted, between the land and the *patria*—taking for granted that the greatness of the second would be a kind of natural unfolding of the might attributed to the first.[30]

It was not just a question of legitimizing a new culture, or of laying the foundation of a new state, but also of an idea of literature inherited from romantic thought—the idea of organic form. This idea, whose origins can be found in Plato and Aristotle, had enjoyed a new currency among the romantics, many of whom, like Goethe himself, were amateur naturalists. Nearly all of the nineteenth-century European travelers who came to Latin America were naturalists. Their vision of America contributed in no small measure to the notion of the continent as an organic unit on all levels, including artistic form. Briefly, "organic form" refers to the congruity between the various parts of a work of art, a congruity that, for Goethe, led to the ideal of beauty; Kant also spoke of an organic congruity between parts, but for him this congruity led nowhere.[31] In Goethe, as in Coleridge, aesthetic feeling (in Coleridge, *imagination*) arises from the perception of regularities in nature. The perception of nature anticipates knowledge through our affinity with its repetitions and rhythms. The cohesion between this literary ideology and the concept of culture is the determining factor in the myth that legitimizes both culture and literature, or, also on a very visible plane, that denies this legitimacy. As a source of metaphors for the description of the origin and development of Latin American literature, the analogy with nature has not always been a positive one, as José J. Arrom demonstrated twenty years ago in his essay, "Tres metáforas sobre España e Hispanoamérica."[32]

Cândido has proposed, in the article already quoted, that metaphors relating to an exalted nature are prevalent until approximately 1930, when the focus changes to the concept of underdevelopment. I maintain that, although the cohesion that nature provides is simultaneously denied *from the first*, its vitality on the level of doctrine is much more enduring than Cândido proposes. The aforementioned book by Henríquez Ureña bears a "fluvial" title, and even today one finds a proliferation of the "roots of tradition" in literary studies. In addition, toward the middle of the 1920s, and thanks to the disseminating function of the *Revista de Occidente*, such German thinkers as Oswald Spengler and Leo Frobenius became popular throughout Latin America, along with their terminology, which was replete with metaphors taken from the natural sciences: Spengler spoke of "natural cycles" to describe the history of cultures; Frobenius referred to "geology." Even existentialist thinkers like Heidegger ultimately resorted to metaphors based on concepts taken from nature, such as "ground," although they often invested these concepts with quite a different kind of meaning. The predominance of nature in the constitution of Latin American literary discourse does not begin to crumble until Carpentier's *The Lost Steps* (1953), the first work to reveal the critical substratum that had always denied the sense and coherence supposedly provided by the nature metaphor. This break leads us to the most recent Latin American poetry and prose fiction, in which, as I have already pointed out, criticism of this myth of legitimacy becomes a very visible element.

Critical visibility has increased so because the legitimacy that this myth proposed is that of the propriety or pertinence of language. Modern literature—from romanticism onward—puts forth the idea that the language in which it is expressed is in correspondence with nature. This correspondence assures the close relationship between signs and things, between writing and the world. But *at the same time* modern literature is founded on a radical doubt as to whether such a correspondence exists, whether there really is a congruity between the world and the signs that presumably express it. This perverse misalignment opens a gap through which criticism enters. Writing, even as an exercise appropriate to a certain social class, is repudiated; its intelligibility as a doctrine or ideology is ruined, retracted.

As I have suggested, elaborating and skewing an idea of Paz's, all great works of Latin American literature possess this critical substratum, which consists precisely of a questioning of the central myths on which it rests; it is in the questioning that the modernity of Latin American literature resides. Criticism of Latin American literature has only recently begun to consider this corrosive element, rather than complacently echoing apparent myths or declared doctrines. Inspired by recent Latin American literature's reading of its own modern tradition, Latin American criticism can look to the critical substratum of literature as it endeavors to lay the foundations of a new critical structure worthy of our rich literary works.

As an example of what I am proposing, I would like to proceed with a reading of a work that, for many overzealous devotees of the recent Latin American novel, has been regarded as a quintessential example of the backwardness of our literature: Rómulo Gallegos's *Doña Bárbara* (1929). My reading does not so much pretend to be a new interpretation of Gallegos's novel as an effort to bring out a problematic that is, if not altogether a new method of reading, at least a new critical posture before the works of our tradition. This posture may allow us both to resist and to be seduced by the tropes that constitute Latin American writing.

4

I should perhaps begin with the following quotation from Lukács, which largely synthesizes what I intend to demonstrate in *Doña Bárbara*:

This ruthlessness towards their own subjective world-picture is the hall-mark of all great realists, in sharp contrast to the second-rates, who nearly always succeed in bringing their own *Weltanschauung* into "harmony" with reality, that is forcing a falsified or distorted picture of reality into the shape of their own world views.[33]

Doña Bárbara is the best known of what is called in Latin American literary history the *novela de la tierra*, a tag that can most productively be translated as both novels about the earth and novels of the earth, in the sense of belonging to the land or issuing from it. One of the better specialists on the works of Gallegos, D. L. Shaw, writes,

The three of them [*novelas de la tierra*], *Don Segundo Sombra* by Ricardo Güiraldes (Argentina), *La vorágine* by José Eustasio Rivera (Colombia) and *Doña Bárbara* itself, are the classic examples of the Latin American *novela de la tierra*. Their successful incorporation into fiction of the striking natural background, the *pampa*, the *selva* and the *llano* of the subcontinent, represented an important break with the imitation of European models and a great stride forward towards authenticity in Latin American literature.[34]

Shaw expresses succinctly how the ground, the *tierra*, is to be taken in these novels: as an outside referent whose own difference will make Latin American literature distinct and original. The ground is both origin and difference. This is the most basic idea governing the *novela de la tierra*: the ground itself, a metaphor of culture, is the source of authority. It informs the text, giving it referential validity and endowing it with the power to articulate the truth.

The *novela de la tierra* seems like an anachronism from the outset. First published in the 1920s, when narrative was passing through a stage of radical transformation in works like Joyce's, it was read by its critics and even promoted by its authors as the realistic novel that Latin America had lacked, as well as a politically committed literature. If we take into consideration that the *novela de la tierra* arose in a period of great economic, social, and political crisis, one that saw the rise of bloody tyrants and in which diverse ideologies became solidified, we have to admit that it was inevitable that works like *Doña Bárbara* would be seen in relation to the sociopolitical struggles of the time. We cannot deny, despite the double anachronism (that of the works themselves, and especially the critical anachronism), that the *novela de la tierra* fulfilled significant social and historical functions in its day, functions that were, of course, very different from those realized by the European realistic novel, which arose under distinct cultural and social conditions. The political activities of some of the authors within the genre demonstrate the degree to which the so-called *preocupación social* of the *novela de la tierra* corresponded to genuine impulses and peremptory necessities. But this far from exhausts the present-day relevance of these novels, whose critical substratum was disguised by their insertion within the specific and at the same time superficial dialogue of the moment at which they appeared.

The widespread circulation of the *novela de la tierra* beyond the borders of the respective countries of the authors within the genre is proof of its literary impact; it is the *novela de la tierra* that first begins to sketch out a truly pan-American landscape and gallery of characters.[35] The Cuban or Mexican reader of Gallegos comes to recognize the Venezuelan plain as part of his or her own literary landscape and discovers characters in Güiraldes who will come to compose a truly American typology. Today we know, despite what much of the criticism of the time claimed and despite what the authors themselves suggested, that those characters and that landscape were forged in relation to various local literary traditions in association with Western literary tradition. Despite its desire to present a compendious vision, the *novela de la tierra* gave a very limited view of the reality of its time, largely because of a clear ideological distortion. Cities, for example, which figured into certain works, such as those by Roberto Arlt in Argentina or Miguel de Carrión in Cuba, hardly appear in the *novela de la tierra*, despite the fact that Latin America already possessed relatively large and complex urban centers by the 1930s. The *novela de la tierra* elaborates a new Latin American literary reality, and it is precisely for this reason that it is so important today. It is the ground, the foundation, on which the present-day Latin American novel is erected.

This relationship with present narrative traditions is largely due to the anachronistic quality of these novels not being inherent; "the realism" of the *novela de la tierra* was a result of the inevitable partiality of critics and of the authors themselves—it was an effect, above all, of reading. Today, with the perspective of forty years, we can see that many of these novels, far from being realistic, were in fact allegorical, and as such presented a critical view of their own constitution that removed them from the realistic concepts of representation that criticism had elaborated. The best *novelas de la tierra* contained, in fact, mechanisms that were unusually modern, and that stand in contrast to the exterior appearance of the works and to the extreme archaism of their authors with respect to their literary ideology.[36] The modernity of the *novela de la tierra* is evident, despite the express will of its authors and despite what readers of the last two or three decades have wished to see in it. Only today, by examining how recent works read the *genre*, can we begin to recover this modernity.

By reading this venerable, but still vigorous, work from the perspective offered by two texts that figure among its wayward and motley offspring, "Big Mama's Funeral" (1967) by Gabriel García Márquez and *Cobra* (1972) by Severo Sarduy, I plan to expose here some of the mechanisms that make *Doña Bárbara* a modern novel. Although for rhetorical reasons I am going to respect the chronological order in which the three novels appeared, the truth is that the direction of my reading will be just the reverse: I read *Doña Bárbara* from the perspective of "Big Mama's Funeral" and *Cobra*.

In *Doña Bárbara* a certain mythology of writing begins to coalesce, one that links Gallegos's work with the modern novel. This mythology is the critical subtext, which subverts the primary plane of allegorical reading. The subtext alludes to the constitution and legitimacy of writing, without exhausting or closing off the theme, by elaborating a story that takes the form of what Freud called a "family romance," that is, the symbolic relationship established between individual characters who structurally compose a unit of kinship. I use the term here to designate a level of mystification with regard to its own origins that modern Latin American literature contains, a level involving precisely genealogy. I call this a "mystification" because we are not dealing with a level on which literature necessarily reveals a deeper truth, because, although the work in question alludes to its own constitution, it always does so through a projection to another level and, because, instead of cohering logically or formally, it remains fraught with contradictions. The plane is, if you will, an ideological one, but this ideology refuses to present itself in an explicit way, preferring instead to withdraw into the *enigma* of a narration.

What allows the inauguration of this mythology is precisely the allegorical character of the work. The allegory of *Doña Bárbara*, at the most visible and at the same time most abstract level, consists of the opposition of two forces that together make up Latin American reality: the presumed clash between civilization and barbarity, put forth by Sarmiento in *Facundo*. This conception is evident in the text, which contains enough material put into the words of the narrator to legitimize such an "interpretation." I put interpretation in quotation marks to emphasize that we are not dealing with a possible meaning extracted by the reader, but with a meaning inscribed in the text itself. The allegory on this level—which is not so much an ideological one as one of social and political doctrine—carries with it its own implicit reading.

But far from freezing meaning on this level, the allegory sets other mechanisms of signification into motion by showing the radical separation between signified and signifier (allegory is, etymologically, the discourse of the other). If the sign is not a fixed entity, but implies movement and duration, then it is possible to outline a series of permutations.[37] One of these has to do with the very nature of allegory: allegory consists of saying or interpreting more than what has actually been said; it is a supplement of meaning that escapes the intentions and rules imposed by the text itself. This essentially ironic situation implies a gesture in all allegory toward its origins, toward its signifier. That is, the signified pretends to acquire legitimacy by pointing backward, toward the form that set it in motion, in order to emphasize the *propriety* of the relationship that unites the two. The typical movement of all postromantic literature toward the origin—of history, culture, language, being—takes this form in allegory. There are certain manifestations of popular art in which the coupling achieved by this retrospective gesture is so unexpectedly perfect that it evokes laughter or derision. In allegory there is always a tendency toward excessive coincidence, which results in gigantism, the disproportion of form, and, in the hands of great humorists, a very special kind of grotesqueness. Popular literature, pop art, the *auto sacramental*, certain forms of revolutionary art, advertising, all exploit this kind of allegory, from which *Doña Bárbara*, when read on the primary plane of interpretation that I have mentioned, does not greatly differ.

But what interests me most is the plane of the retrospective gesture of allegory and the form in which that gesture manifests itself. In *Doña Bárbara* this gesture is related to writing and its origin, and the narrative in which it unfolds is that which refers to the sexual activities of the protagonists, in the genealogical as well as in the erotic sense. This is the "story" read by "Big Mama's Funeral" and *Cobra*; it is the inheritance, so to speak, that these texts collect from Gallegos's novel.

I do not think it would be difficult to convince even the most skeptical reader that one of the main problems in *Doña Bárbara* is that of writing; after all, the initial litigation between Santos Luzardo and Míster Danger, and between Santos and Doña Bárbara, has to do with the interpretation of the property titles that delimit Altamira.[38] There are two well-known scenes in which the characters dispute the interpretation of these texts, comparing them with other versions of what they supposedly explain and holding them up against the Law of the Plain. In the first of these scenes Míster Danger is able to invalidate Santos's accusations against him by brandishing property titles that have been adulterated by Doña Bárbara; in the second scene Santos is able to outwit Míster Danger and Doña Bárbara by appealing to fine points of the Law of the Plain, which are unknown to them and to Ño Pernalete. To this we can add, with respect to both land and animals, that the conflict hinges on the problems of *brands, marks,* and *boundaries.* The animals are branded with marks of the different haciendas; the boundaries marked off by barbed wire fences redeem the plain from nature's incoherence, from the total absence of signs. *Doña Bábara* constantly returns to the theme of writing, whether in the form of a pole stuck into the ground to mark off a boundary, or the red-hot iron used to sear the owner's mark into the hide of an animal, or the lines of writing in legal documents, writing that, like a black thread, interweaves the destinities of the protagonists.

Thus it is not only as a reflection of certain characteristics of Venezuelan society of the period that Santos appears as a lawyer. As a lawyer, he specializes in the encoding and in the interpretation of language in its relation to reality. In a very significant way he is a writer and a reader. Doña Bárbara is also a reader, since her supernatural powers enable her to read the future, not in documents but in the signs she discovers in the reality around her. She is a writer as well: she reiterates a number of times in the novel that she has rewritten the Law of the Plain and that the property titles, not to mention boundaries and cattle brands, have been rewritten according to her whims and to her desire to monopolize everything. Yet, there are fundamental differences between Santos's writing and Doña Bárbara's, and it is to these differences that we owe the previously mentioned mythology.

As a lawyer, Santos seeks a univocal interpretation of writing: his profession consists of comparing a given text with a specific situation or with another text and demonstrating the correspondence between texts, or between text and reality. The research he does before entering into litigation with Doña Bárbara and Míster Danger (analogous to that which a historical novelist would carry out), is a way of legitimizing writing by establishing its correct genealogy. But of course, tracing back this genealogy eventually leads him to the original patriarch, Evaristo Luzardo, his own forebear, who was the first to fence off the plain and who founded Altamira. But here we discover a contradiction that *Doña Bárbara* never resolves logically and that is therefore significant for our reading, because the legitimacy of this writing and the propriety that it concedes to Santos are based on an act of initial violence and arbitrariness on the part of Evaristo Luzardo el Cunavichero, an act that is illegitimate: "The man of prey [Evaristo] despoiled the aboriginal settlers of their just domain [*aquella propiedad de derecho natural*], and when they tried to defend it, exterminated them with fire and sword" (p. 108). Natural law is replaced by the law imposed by Evaristo. The dominion of written law that Santos attempts to establish clashes with this contradiction: the origin of that presumably harmonious dominion, of the sovereignty of correctly interpreted writing, has its origin outside of itself, in an act that is not proper to it but that remains its *principle*, both in the sense of beginning and of law. Violence and rewriting replace the mirage of a clear beginning, a legitimate principle.

Doña Bárbara, on the other hand, bases her readings on arbitrary rules, which are legitimized with the help of witchcraft, that is, on a savage and arbitrary relationship between reality and code. Her writing is based on an unbridled desire for power; the Law of the Plain is not founded on any genealogy, but, like Doña Bárbara herself, on the most primitive of desires. Doña Bárbara, substituting an immediate dissemination of signs for genealogical depth, uses her sexual allure to erase and rewrite. But there is an even stronger contradiction in Doña Bárbara than in Santos. Her desire to mark is motivated by the contradictory wish to eradicate all marks and thus induce a chaos of marks and boundaries, which will ultimately serve to abolish all marks and boundaries: to possess everything is the equivalent of eradicating all differences. It is a contradictory desire for self-annihilation, which in part outlines the tragic nature of the protagonist. If Santos is moved by a wish to fix meaning in writing. Doña Bárbara is motivated by a desire for permanent dissemination.

Luzardo's gesture in search of an origin, of the beginning of a genealogy and of the word, is a figuration in the text itself of the movement in allegory toward a coupling of meaning and form. The result is homologous in both. Contrary to the way it may appear on the primary doctrinal plane of allegorical reading in which civilization and barbarity confront each other, the radically allegorical reading that I am outlining here defies the possibility of such a propriety in the text's signifying task. In the case of Santos's inquiry, we learn that the origin of writing is impure, that Evaristo's initial violence has left his mark on the land, has made it his and his descendants' property. There can be no coupling between this initial violence and Santos's enterprise. However, this does not prevent him from pursuing his claim to its legitimacy. The violent origin is suppressed (even in its closest repetition, the struggle between Santos and his father), and writing is a simulacrum of legitimacy. The law is not natural, but imposed by force; its referential validity is a contingent, willful imposition, not a given.

The problematic that unfolds on the allegorical level is equally manifest in emblematic form in the novel's most obvious metaphor: the plain. With regard to the writings that parcel it up, to the laws that organize it and make it intelligible, the plain is an "original" text. The last bastion of writing is that which will be inscribed on the earth itself, where the nexus that makes signs and their referents coherent must necessarily be stronger. If nature has a pre-text, it must be the earth, the ground itself. But the plain in *Doña Bárbara* is as elusive as a Borgesian desert; the two poles that should organize it—its perimeter and its center—constantly undermine, so to speak, its steadiness, its power as source of authority:

Endless land of vigour and daring! The mirages circling the prairie [*el anillo de espejismos que circunda la sabana* (the ring of mirages encircling the plain)] danced before his eyes in a vertiginous whirl [the ring, *se ha puesto a girar sobre el eje del vértigo*], the wind whistled in his ear, the breaks parted and closed immediately behind him, the rushes tore and cut his flesh, but his body felt no hurt. At times the horses' feet rested on nothing but air. . . . One might ride on for days; there would always be more prairie ahead. (p. 100)

The plain—"prairie" does not carry the negational connations of the Spanish *llano*, which, like the English "plain," has a corollary meaning denoting absence—not only is endless, but disappears under the horses' hoofs. Yet, although endless, the plain does have a limit, only this limit is made up of false appearances that recede infinitely into the distance. The *anillo de espejismos* is the unfixed and elusive perimeter of the plain, always simultaneously announcing and postponing a limit. The Spanish *anillo de espejismos* conveys this contrary double thrust, for a ring is not merely a circle, but supposedly a hard one, denoting even the presence of a certain special covenant, and *espejismo* is not merely a mirage, but a sort of specular play of appearances. Standing on a kind of void at the always-present center of the plain, one is encircled by a display of appearances that denote a false, deceiving limit.

This *anillo de espejismos* is not a casual description of the plain, for it reappears near the end of the novel, when Doña Bárbara rides across the plain: "The parched chaparral crackled, the prairie glowed within the circle of mirages [*anillo de espejismos*] which gave the illusion of blue lakes, waters which drive to desperation the thirsty who go towards them, remaining always at the same distance away on the round horizon [*el ruedo del horizonte*]" (p. 433). Now naming the horizon a *ruedo*, in addition to *anillo*, is significant: *ruedo* means "arena," an enclosed surface where play occurs. The play in which Doña Bárbara performs takes place within this problematic perimeter, which at once proclaims a limit and declares it illusory. This infinitely regressing limit or mark is the counterpart of the barbed wire that Santos wants to use to set off proprietary rights; his would be the univocal text of the law, subverted by the white page of the plain, "a single land with a thousand different paths" (p. 56). The interplay between the vastness of the plain and the efforts to delimit it, later used by João Guimarães Rosa to great advantage beginning with his very title, *Grande Sertão, Veredas*, produces a shifting effect in the reader that effaces constantly the authority not only of the text but of the doctrinaire reading that the allegory, on a primary level of signification, promotes.

The source of the principal legal conflict in *Doña Bárbara* can be found precisely in the conjunction and disjunction between writing and the center/perimeter of the plain. The passages describing this relationship are most revealing in terms of the reading I am attempting here. After the death of Altamira's last proprietor, Don José de los Santos, the distribution of the land among his children leads to a dispute between José Luzardo and Panchita, who has married Sebastián Barquero. This first parceling out is contested by both parties:

[B]ecause of an ambiguous phrase in the will which described the boundary line as [reaching up to] "the palm grove of La Chusmita," discord arose between the brothers-in-law [*entre los hermanos* could mean "between brother and sister," though it probably alludes to all of them], for each declared that the phrase should be interpreted to *his* advantage [*agregándosele el inclusive que omitiera el redactor* (adding the *including* that was omitted by the person who drafted the document)], and thus they commenced one of those endless litigations which make the fortune of several generations of lawyers. It would have ended ruining them, had not the same intransigence which was making them waste a fortune over an unproductive bit of land also made them determine, when a settlement was proposed, to have "all or nothing." And since both could not have all, they both agreed that both should have nothing, and engaged to build a fence around the grove, which thus became enclosed and not a part of the property.

But the matter did not end there. In the centre of the grove was the bed of a channel which had dried up [*una madrevieja de un caño seco*]. In the winter this became a quagmire, a mudhole which was death to any man or beast attempting to cross it, and one day, when he spied in it a drowned steer belonging to the Barquero herd, José Luzardo protested to Sebastián Barquero, declaring that this was a violation of the neutral ground [*el recinto vedado*]. The dispute became heated; Barquero swung his whip at the face of his brother-in-law, and the latter, whipping out his revolver, toppled Barquero from his horse with a bullet through the head. Then the reprisals commenced, and with the partisans killing each other off, the population, composed as it was of practically nothing but the various branches of the two families, was in the end nearly wiped out. (pp. 19-20)

As we have seen, the initial act of appropriation of the plain by Evaristo el Cunavichero was violent; he wrested the territory from the Indians, who owned the land through "natural right." But there is no natural right; every act of appropriation turns out to be arbitrary, violent, and rending, as the passage just quoted shows. Though this is the first known division of the land, it is not the original one; it is the first since the family has "owned" the land. What follows is a story of the relationship between the parceling out of the land and the origination of writing.

José de los Santos's will, his intention, is going to turn into text, and this text, in turn, is going to be read. But we soon see that the text that issues from his intention is equivocal because it lacks something that must be added in the reading. That addition, uncannily enough, is addition itself; what has been left out is the *inclusive* that both readers of the text dispute and that the English translator, uncannily, also left out. The dispute turns out to be not so much over the text itself, but over the supplement. The text does not exist as such, except in the reading, and then what counts most is not the original intention so much as the addition that each reading supplies. It is not that this text is ambiguous, but that the very process through which textuality turns into appropriation is equivocal, not because the original intention was lacking, but because the very act of reading turns the origin into a lack that must be supplied. That act of supplying turns out, of course, to be violent, unnatural, and based on the political contingency of the moment. Authority is not gained so much from the origin as from the origin-become-supplement in the present. The dispute, significantly, is not now between blood brothers, but between brothers-in-law; blood, nature-turned-law, governs the process by which the plain becomes text.

The very disposition of the land reflects this process. What is disputed, the palm grove La Chusmita, is fenced off. Because it is the line of the break, the space between the two halves into which Altamira is presumably going to be divided, the grove is at Altamira's center. It is a center that is a void: its land is unproductive; it cannot be used by anyone. That which is at the center belongs to no one and to both; it is an addition to each of the two properties that, paradoxically, belongs to the other. This supplementary center is the object of the dispute. It is a hypostasis of the *inclusive* left out of José de los Santos's will. As center/origin of the dispute, the palm grove La Chusmita is made up of contradictions, and, on a certain symbolic level, is a sort of locus of nonsynthetic opposites. Although a center, the grove is always outside, like a supplement; it is the origin of the plain, yet it is not solid earth but, rather, a quagmire. It is nothing, yet it is fenced in; it is forbidden, yet a steer manages to get itself drowned in it to set in motion the feud. But more than anything, the palm grove of La Chusmita is an androgynous figure, a divided origin. On the one hand, there is the source of the quagmire itself, described as a *madrevieja*. A riverbed can be said to be a *madre* in Spanish, and when a river overflows its banks one can say that "*se salió de madre,*" it came out of its matrix or womb, so to speak. The quagmire is, paradoxically, a womb, a beginning of life, and the possibility of death to "any man or beast attempting to cross it." There can be little doubt that there is an opposition here between the primeval mire as a symbol of femininity and the vertical palms as symbols of masculinity: "The place was under a curse, surrounded by an unforgettable silence; there were numerous palm trees blackened by lightning, and in the center was a quagmire in which any living thing that had to cross perished in the quicksand" (p. 108). The palm grove is not a simple origin, a principle giving beginning out of which authority can be spun, but a divided origin: life/death, male/female, inside/outside, beginning/end. But this is not all, for the Chusmita palm grove is inhabited.

Marisela, Doña Bárbara's daughter by Lorenzo Barquero, and Lorenzo himself have been confined to La Chusmita, where they live in a semisavage state, near destitution. They are not a harmonious pair, but, again, a contrary one. Marisela, with whom Santos falls in love, is a sort of nymph. For her La Chusmita is an Eden-like garden, untouched by the evil of her mother and the hatred generated by the land division. Living in the beginning/end, in the lack/supplement of the grove, she is a clean start, hated for that very reason by Doña Bárbara, who sees her as a threat. For Lorenzo, on the other hand, La Chusmita is most certainly an end, not a paradise, but hell. Lorenzo is like a ruined deity, prostrate in the center of his own labyrinth. He is not just a drunkard, a victim of Doña Bárbara's unbridled lust, but the most intelligent of the Luzardo family (to which he also belongs, of course, though a Barquero), the most gifted, significantly enough, in terms of verbal capacity. Whereas Marisela lives in a sort of prelinguistic world—her favorite grunt is "Gua!"—Lorenzo possesses stunning eloquence. Having attempted to become a lawyer, his ability with language is what brings him into the problematic that we have been examining here.

While studying in Caracas, Lorenzo became an advocate of civilization, railing against the "centaur" (barbarism) that, according to him, all plainsmen carry within them. He was, moreover, what we would call today

Santos's role model when Santos was a boy. When Santos returns to Altamira, he goes to La Chusmita to see Lorenzo, put an end to the feud, and save him from the morass in which he literally lives. In this interview, Lorenzo reveals to Santos the true cause of his despair and abandonment: he has lost faith in the ability of words to signify to such a degree that he cannot even believe his own sincerity. His inner self appears to him as lies in which he can no longer believe. Lorenzo's revelation comes to him at the university:

That Lorenzo Barquero you spoke of was a lie. The truth is what you're looking at now. This land never relents. You've already heard the call of the ogress, you too, and I'll soon see you fall into her arms. When she opens them, you'll be the wreck of a man. Look at her. Mirages everywhere, one here, one there. The Plain is full of mirages. What fault of mine is it that you've been under the illusion that a Luzardo— a Luzardo, because I am one, though it hurts me to say it—that a Luzardo could be any man's ideal? But we are not alone, Santos. That's our only comfort. I've known many men, and you're one, certainly, who showed great promise at thirty. Double the age—[great promise in their twenties, but when they go around the thirty mark,] they're done for, ruined. The mirage of the tropics. But let me tell you this: I never made any mistake about myself. I knew that everything that others admired in me was a lie. I found that out right after one of my greatest triumphs of my student years, an examination for which I wasn't well prepared. I had to develop a theme I was totally ignorant of, but I began to talk and the words, pure words, did it all. Not only was I well treated, I was all but applauded by the very teachers that were examining me. The scoundrels! From that time on I began to observe that my intelligence, what everybody called my great talent, operated only when I was talking. Whenever I shut up the mirage was destroyed and I understood nothing about anything. I recognized the lies—my intelligence, my sincerity. You understand, realized the falseness of my own sincerity, the worst thing that can happen to a man. I felt the old hidden sore of that hereditary cancer in the bottom of my soul, just as it must feel in the deepest part of an apparently healthy body. I began to loathe the University, and city life, the friends who admired me, my sweetheart, everything that was the cause or effect of that self-deception. (pp. 119-121)

Living in the no-man's-land of La Chusmita, Lorenzo represents the defeat of language as well as its triumph: the defeat because it leads to no self-revelation, except to a negative understanding; the triumph because meaning, even if it is a series of lies, can only dwell in language itself. Lorenzo embodies this contradiction. If Marisela lives in a prelinguistic universe, Lorenzo inhabits a postlinguistic one. Lorenzo's insight makes him, paradoxically, given his constant state of inebriation, the most lucid character in the novel. He is in possession of the most dangerous kind of knowledge, that which undermines the illusions of all the others: the center/origin in which he lives is a sort of perpetual fission, a threshold that leads nowhere, a rending that never heals. Beyond the mirages that encircle him and everyone else in the novel, there is nothing; so he drinks to keep them there. But his most devastating insight is that the mirages repeat themselves. He does not in the end deny his being Santos's role model; on the contrary, he foresees in the young man a repetition of his own life. "Santos Luzardo, look at me! [*Mírate en mí!* (Look at yourself in me!)] This land never relents!" (p. 104).

Lorenzo's final transformation, into a mirror in which Santos can look at himself, is suggestive in another way. He can be a mirror that reflects reality—the reflections of other mirages, the *espejismos*—because he is a kind of figuration of the author. This is so, it seems to me, not only because of his ability with language, but above all because of his undeluded view of language itself and the position that he occupies in the fictional space of the novel. Lorenzo, because of his insight into the nature of language, is the final authority in the novel, the one who can deconstruct the fictions around him. But he knows that his own knowledge, rooted in language, is no authority at all. He can only think, he can only be, in language; there is no knowledge outside of it, yet he must think, outside of it to know also that language is made up of lies. Beyond that he must will the lies to defend himself from the void of the world and of his own inner self. His situation is analogous to the place in which he dwells, La Chusmita palm grove: a set of potential, mutually canceling forces that neither coalesce nor manage to obliterate each other. His condition as a physical and moral ruin is perhaps an image of the will from which the lies of language issue, the self of the romantics, which expresses the desires of man presumably into and through the text of literature. As a figure of the author, Lorenzo prefigures the dictators in the most recent Latin American novels, authority figures devoid of any authority other than the authority to deny their own presence.

The blood relationship of the inhabitants of La Chusmita is also full of implications. There is no suggestion in the novel of any incestuous relationship between Lorenzo and Marisela, but their being grouped like a couple in the quagmire is enough to call attention to the pervasive presence of incest in the novel. On one level, of course, the presence of the pair is in consonance with the androgynous nature of La Chusmita, but we cannot discount Lorenzo and Santos's near sharing of Doña Bárbara, their being uncle and nephew, and Marisela's becoming the nephew's beloved. The repetition suggested by the *espejismos* and by Lorenzo's metamorphosis into a mirror reflects, so to speak, this penchant for incest. Desire for an other who is the same as oneself is a desire to abolish difference, but the wages of this desire are violence and the spilling of blood.

Marisela's presence in La Chusmita can also be seen as a kind of substitution, projection, or even reflection of Doña Bárbara herself.

Marisela not only is her daughter, but resembles the young, innocent Doña Bárbara before she lost her first love, Asdrúbal, and was raped by his assassins. Doña Bárbara is there, however, in another sense. If La Chusmita is the symbolic center of the plain, with all that implies, the ogress cannot but be in that center, for she is at the center of the plain wherever she moves: "But I'm not so grasping as I'm painted. I'm satisfied with only a bit of land, enough so that I can be in the middle of my property, no matter where it may be [*donde quiera que me encuentre* (wherever I happen to be)]." She is the source of the disseminatory, capacious force that moves the novel, a force made up of contradictory desires and given to repetition rather than to distinction and difference. Like Lorenzo, she suffers for this power, as we shall see.

By carrying the above contradictions to the emblematic level, *Doña Bárbara* manifests a complex relationship with ideology that makes nature and, by extension, the land, the *nec plus ultra*. It is precisely in opposition to this ideology's central metaphors that the criticism emerging from contradiction orients itself. Read in this way, without evading any of its complexities, the question of writing becomes clear, but not simplified or reduced. If we consider the "logic" promoted by the text itself, we can see that Doña Bárbara is the incarnation of a concept of writing that is closer to that which governs the novel. The allegorical design is now more apparent: Doña Bárbara, illegitimate, possessing supernatural powers, endowed with a disseminating and contradictory erotic power, an androgynous being (the half-masculine devil within her [*el demonio andrógino*], p. 209) who is sacrificed in the novel, is an archetypal figuration of the *pharmakos* in whom the powers of writing are invested.[39] She is essentially split, divided; she is splitting and dividing herself. She and Lorenzo are victimized, but she carries Lorenzo within her, thus the tragic aspect of the protagonist. Doña Bárbara, like Nietzsche's Dionysius, is in more direct contact with the tragic essence of representation; she is able, in moments of hallucinatory lucidity, to read her own destiny. "She had a moment of uneasiness when she saw Luzardo, a flash of intuition telling her that the final drama of her life was about to be played" (p. 172). It is she who incarnates power and suffers it in the no-man's-land of her mixed and inconclusive genealogy. The allegory is resolved, not in the precise coupling of a meaning with a given form, but in this tragic fable about the contradictory nature of writing that, as has already been pointed out, invalidates the message contained on the doctrinal level and offers a critical view of literature itself. It is this aspect that makes this work by Gallegos modern. It is above all this problematic, and not merely characters and landscape, that *Doña Bárbara* bequeathes to more recent Latin American narratives.

5

In "Big Mama's Funeral" García Márquez returns to the figure of the powerful woman who commands a large area of Latin American land as an absolute ruler, but only by being aware of the critical level that we have uncovered in Gallegos's novel can we recognize the degree to which she is a "descendant" of Doña Bárbara's. In a way, "Big Mama's Funeral" is, within the fictive time of the Latin American narrative, a sort of sequel to or meta-end of *Doña Bárbara*, for it "takes place" after the death of the tyrant. By placing his fiction at the end or beyond, García Márquez casts a retrospective glance at the constitution of the fiction, a glance that allows him to lay bare through a series of technical mechanisms some of the elements of the critical level of Gallegos's novel.

Doña Bárbara, as we have seen, lived in the supplement, the *inclusive* presumably left out of the will written by José de los Santos. She is, herself, a sort of supplement, belonging to no clear genealogy. The supplement, however, being neither inside nor outside, is still the authority that parcels out the land, covering it with the marks of its proprietorship. In García Márquez's story the supplement has been hypostasized by the huge body of the tyrant: her breasts are "matriarchal," big enough to "suckle her whole family all by herself," and her buttocks "monumental."[40] (One imagines Big Mama to be very much like one of the figures in Fernando Botero's paintings.) Not only Big Mama, but all symbols of authority in the story are obese: it takes ten strong men to transport the aging Father Anthony-Isabel to the deathbed of the dying ruler; the president of the republic is "bald and chubby" (p. 168); Nicanor, Big Mama's nephew, is "gigantic and savage" (p. 154). But it is, of course, Big Mama who is outsized in every respect. She is all excess, from her absolute power to her buttocks. By making her fat, García Márquez is blowing up, as it were, the beginning/end character of the supplement, its being something added, presumably nonessential. ("Fat" in English has, of course, such a meaning—it is opposed to the meat of things; it is that which, being superabundant, one wishes were not there.) Her power, the control she exerts over the people of Macondo, and especially her funeral are all exaggerated, and the story is narrated in a hyperbolic style that seems to allow for anything to happen or grow: not only is national life paralyzed by Big Mama's death, but the pope travels in a gondola to Macondo to attend her funeral. Even the picture of her that the newspapers publish is a blowup: "That afternoon the inhabitants of the distant and somber capital saw the picture of a twenty-year-old woman on the first page of the extra editions and thought that it was a new beauty queen. Big Mama lived again the momentary youth of her photograph, enlarged to four columns and with needed retouching, her abundant hair caught atop her skull with an ivory comb and a diadem on her lace collar" (p. 162).

García Márquez's hypostasis of supplement as a fat woman harks back to my discussion of allegory. Instead of pointing to the break between the intended meaning of allegory and its conventional sign, García Márquez makes the coincidence so perfect that it elicits laughter. This technique, found incidentally in much of the popular art in Latin America, draws attention to the sign itself, which, because of its exaggerated proportions, is thereby devoid of meaning: Big Mama is like a huge and hollow plaster mold. If Doña Bárbara could presumably contain barbarism as a concept, including her own name, Big Mama must be big to embody, so to speak, her enormous power.

Like that of Doña Bárbara, Big Mama's power is contradictory. On the one hand, she rules with such absolute power that she raises all marks and boundaries; on the other hand, her capacity to distinguish, to set off, to cut, is such that the wounds she inflicts never heal. The central scene in the story, a scene that appears with significant frequency in Latin American dictator-novels, is the one in which Big Mama is dictating her will to the notary public. Her will, like José de los Santos's in Gallegos' novel, is the text in which power is apportioned:

Nicanor [her nephew] had prepared, on twenty-four folios written in a very clear hand, a scrupulous account of her possessions. Breathing calmly, with the doctor and Father Anthony-Isabel as witnesses, Big Mama dictated to the notary the list of her property, the supreme and unique source of her grandeur and authority. Reduced to its true proportions, the real estate was limited to three districts, awarded by Royal Decree at the founding of the Colony; with the passage of time, by dint of intricate marriages of convenience, they had accumulated under the control of Big Mama. In that unworked territory, without definite borders, which comprised five townships and in which not one single grain had ever been sown at the expense of the proprietors, three hundred and fifty-two families had lived as tenant farmers. . . . [H]istorical circumstances had brought it about that within those boundaries the six towns of Macondo district should grow and prosper, even the county seat, so that no person who lived in a house had any property rights other than those which pertained to the house itself, since the land belonged to Big Mama, and the rent was paid to her, just as the government had to pay her for the use the citizens made of the streets. (pp. 159-160)

These proprietary rights are marked, branded, as it were, in a maze of legal documents and preserved by a "sacramental fence [*alambrada sacramental*, a sacramental barbed-wire fence], within which uncles married the daughters of their nieces, and cousins married their aunts, and brothers their sisters-in-law, until an intricate mesh of consanguinity was formed, which turned procreation into a vicious circle" (p. 154). Her emblem or brand, naming the property as hers, is inscribed all over the district: "On the outskirts of the settlements, a number of animals, never counted and less looked after, roamed, branded on the hindquarters with the shape of a padlock. This hereditary brand, which more out of disorder than out of quantity had become familiar in distant districts where the scattered cattle, dying of thirst, strayed in summer, was one of the most solid supports of the legend" (p. 160).

Her power over branding, spacing, fencing off, writing, is counterbalanced by her control of rhetoric. After reading the list of her properties from the document prepared by her nephew, Big Mama begins to recite a series of clichés that constitute the language of official power, the language of the state as expressed in speeches. Needless to say, she does not own the things alluded to by these formulae, but the formulae themselves. This "invisible estate" that she dictates to the notary in "a domineering and sincere voice" includes

the wealth of the subsoil, the territorial waters, the colors of the flag, national sovereignty, the traditional parties, the rights of man, civil rights, the nation's leadership, the right of appeal, congressional hearings, letters of recommendation, historical records, free elections, beauty queens, transcendental speeches, huge demonstrations, distinguished young ladies, proper gentlemen, punctilious military men, His Illustrious Eminence, the Supreme Court, goods whose importation is forbidden, liberal ladies, the meat problem, the purity of the language, setting a good example, the free but responsible press, the Athens of South America, public opinion, the lessons of democracy, Christian morality, the shortage of foreign exchange, the right of asylum, the Communist menace, the ship of state, the high cost of living, republican traditions, the underprivileged classes, statements of political support. (p. 161)

Whereas in *Doña Bárbara* the relationship between the ideology of the land-as-origin and the language of power is present only in the critical substratum shown earlier, in "Big Mama's Funeral" the correlation is much more direct. From the depths of her enormous body, an allegorical representation of the mother, of the motherland, Big Mama enumerates the elements of her power in the language of official power; she dictates it, until she dies. Her enumeration is cut off by a belch, a nonlinguistic sound that, put on the same level as the dictation itself, mockingly represents an emanation from her insides: "The laborious enumeration cut off her last breath, frowning in the pandemonium of abstract formulas which for two centuries had constituted the moral justification of the family's power, Big Mama emitted a loud belch and expired" (p. 161). But the belch is also a cut, a break in language. As her spirit dissolves in the vapors of the belch, language reveals a cut, a fissure that was always there, at the very origin, through a cacophonous sound that is perhaps the ultimate speech act—an onomatopoeic sound meaning itself. This split is contained in the wild consanguinity through which she rules Macondo and ensures the continuity of her rule.

The split is present in the contradiction at the core of Big Mama: she dies an unrelenting virgin, yet she is the very representation of motherhood as origin and authority. She is the beginning and end of her genealogy, a source that is closed off, a disseminating virgin:

During this century, Big Mama had been Macondo's center of gravity, as had her brothers, her parents, and the parents of her parents in the past, in a dominance which covered two centuries. The town was founded on her surname. No one knew the origin, or the limits or the real value of her estate, but everyone was used to believing that Big Mama was the owner of the waters, running and still, or rain and drought, and of the district's roads, telegraph poles, leap years, and heat waves, and that she had furthermore a hereditary right over life and property. (p. 155)

The meaning of Big Mama's virginity is to be found precisely in the chaotic enumeration of her possessions; she is a simulacrum of natural authority who rules through the indirection of nephews and nieces, children who are of her own blood, yet not quite her own. The continuity and the break are both present in such an avuncular relationship, which reveals the ultimate arbitrariness of her property rights, in the propriety of the language of power and authority that she owns through accumulation without syntactical links. Her wealth is heaped pell-mell, without the sequential legitimacy of genealogy or grammar. This heaping, like her own bulk, is supplementary, not of the inside, or the essential, and, like the repetitious proliferation of her kind, leads nowhere but to death, to extinction, once the mirage of power is cut off by the cacophony of a belch.

A great deal of the charm in "Big Mama's Funeral," as well as a significant element in its relation to *Doña Bárbara*, is due to the story's being narrated in the hyperbolic style of a certain kind of popular journalism, but also in a style that is consonant with the process by which the critical substratum in *Doña Bárbara* is mobilized. But by bringing to the fore the critical substratum, García Márquez's story endows it with an authority that it could not achieve in *Doña Bárbara*, where it remained locked in dialectical combat with the doctrinal, ideological thrust of the novel. At the end of "Big Mama's Funeral," once the tyrant has been properly buried, there is a sense of relief and the indication that now the spell of repetition will be broken:

Now the Supreme Pontiff could ascend to Heaven in body and soul, his mission on earth fulfilled, and the President of the Republic could sit down and govern according to his good judgment, and the queens of all things that have been or ever will be could marry and be happy and conceive and give birth to many sons, and the common people could set up their tents where they damn well pleased in the limitless domains of Big Mama, because the only one who could oppose them and had sufficient power to do so had begun to rot beneath a lead plinth. (p. 169)

With Big Mama's wake, the break in genealogy can be covered.

Not so in Sarduy's *Cobra*, a novel that takes one step further the reach of the critical element present in Gallegos's novel.[41] The intricacies of this work are many, but mostly they revolve around an inversion of both the ideology under which the critical substratum lay in novels like *Doña Bárbara* and the subversion of what the new novel did with this critical substratum. In other words, *Cobra* would propose that Big Mama's death is not the end of negativity, that to erect as authoritative the language of criticism is to revert inevitably to the same structural situation present in *Doña Bárbara; Cobra* dismantles the metalanguage, bringing it back to the language of literature by means of an inversion to the second power.

This reversal begins to take place by having a series of critical or theoretical statements about literature appear in the body of the text like stage directions, or, better yet, reading instructions: "Writing is the art of ellipsis: in vain would we point out that of all the agendas Cobra's was the most crowded" (p. 6). Cobra is not, like Doña Bárbara and Big Mama, the ruler of land, but the queen of the Lyrical Theater of Dolls, a sort of elaborate brothel in which sexuality is entirely artificial. Cobra herself/himself is a homosexual, and the ellipsis from which s(he) suffers is castration at the hands of Doctor Ktazob, whereas her/his counterpart (?), la Cadillac, is endowed with a phallus by the same physician. The supplement here is always erected on the wound, not pretending to cover it. Instead of a polarity, we find a set of binary oppositions between characters of different sexes who simulate the genealogy of writing, but it is not the genealogy of writing that simulates that of the characters. The violent and contradictory origin of writing is inscribed on a primary level; the branding of animals in *Doña Bárbara* and "Big Mama's Funeral" now becomes the operations to which Cobra and Cadillac subject themselves. The binary opposition between them is not natural but artificial; both are the product of a cut. After the cut metalanguage is reinserted into literature, like Cadillac's artificial phallus; authority is artificial, willful, political. An allegory of an allegory, *Cobra* returns to literature the language of criticism that we had to excise from *Doña Bárbara* in order to read it, thereby undermining the very authority of my own writing and the power to extract from a text an element in isolation. Writing is the art of ellipsis, including the language of criticism.

Cobra is the naked subconscious of Latin American literature. Of course, through these inversions of inversions, "Big Mama's Funeral" and *Cobra* do not seek to criticize Gallegos's work, in the sense of diminishing its value or importance. Quite to the contrary, what they do is demonstrate the enduring relevance of *Doña Bárbara* while making manifest the degree to which, and the complex and enriching way in which, they are its descendants.

6

If Latin American literature is critical, then criticism of Latin American literature should put this critical energy into action, and not let itself be seduced by evident doctrines or by ideologies imposed from outside literature. No writing is more critical than literature itself. Literature's lesson is a stern one, since it always questions its own fundamental premises, and, indeed, everything that seems necessary for its existence. In *Doña Bárbara* we have seen how the language of nature, endeavoring to confer legitimacy on writing, ends in crisis, and how the emblems that are ostensibly most solid become blurry, give way, turn back upon themselves, and reveal their other side.

Naturally, to release the critical energy of Latin American literature is no easy task, and we should not be complacent with the recognition that this critical character is present. To exult over the fact that Borges may very well be a forerunner of Derrida, or that Paz may surpass Barthes in this or that formulation, is not tantamount to having a literary criticism, because Borges and Paz are not systematic critics, and their insights are not automatically applicable to critical efforts in general.

It seems to me that a more promising approach is to attempt a confrontation of texts from different periods—as I have undertaken here—in order to observe how these texts read one another within the tradition. I believe that such an approach can lead to ways of displaying Latin American literature's self-criticism, not only in the sense of what it reveals about previous literature but also of what it reveals about present-day literature. If, on the one hand, it is necessary to unveil how Latin American literature holds its own foundation myths in check, it is, on the other, necessary to examine how it reads and incorporates premodern works of the colonial period, such as the chronicles of the Conquest. The mystifications regarding the supposedly novelistic character of the chronicles comprise one of the most interesting chapters of contemporary Latin American literature and criticism. Also interesting, although to a lesser degree, is the way in which contemporary literature endeavors to incorporate pre-Columbian literatures, or those of non-European cultures, such as the African cultures in the Caribbean basin. What is needed is an un-reading of all of these foundation gestures, which will permit us to mobilize our own literary mystifications, even at the risk of turning criticism into literature, or of simply revealing the literary nature that it has always had.

It is the nineteenth century, Latin American literature's founding century, that gives rise to the most characteristic political figure in Latin American history: the dictator. And in *Facundo*, the first modern Latin American work of great narrative ascendancy, this figure combines for the first time with another figure, also born in the nineteenth century, the Latin American author. It is hardly a coincidence that these two are found united in this work, since they incarnate two modern myths, which since then have been interwoven in our continent with all the vigor, the beauty—and also the horror—that history always furnished in the concept of culture and the idea of literature. Today, works by writers such as Carpentier, García Márquez, and Roa Bastos make evident the relationship that exists between the figure of the author and that of the dictator and unknit the design whose careful weaving took more than a century. This continual weaving and unweaving of literature, this vertiginous process of making and undoing, is the challenge that we as critics must also accept.

3. The Dictatorship of Rhetoric / The Rhetoric of Dictatorship

la escritura que produce un dios subalterno
—Borges

Logos *is thus a* recourse [el recurso]. *One must turn to it, and not merely when the solar source is present and risks burning the eyes if stared at; one has also to turn away toward* logos *when the sun seems to withdraw during its eclipse. Dead, extinguished, or hidden, that star is more dangerous than ever.*

We will let these yarns of suns and sons spin on for a while. Up to now we have only followed this line so as to move from logos *to the father, so as to tie speech to the* kurios, *the master, the lord, another name given in the* Republic *to the good-sun-capital-father (508a). Later, within the same tissue, within the same texts, we will draw on other filial filaments, pull the same strings once more, and witness the weaving or unraveling of other designs.*

—Derrida

Canasta was Batista's favorite pastime in the waning months of his regime, as if he preferred the abstract strategies of cards to the all-too-tangible demands of the deteriorating military and political situation outside the presidential palace.[1] Inside he could shuffle kings, queens, and jacks, listen to their discreet rustle, deploy them according to precise laws. In the din outside, an army in rags was routing his U.S.-equipped and trained troops. By the time he quit Cuba, Batista had become as abstract as the kings in the cards. When the United States withdrew its support his army went through the motions of fighting, but without a sense of where the power lay. The power had vanished. It had become a figure shuffling cards on a table, a paper general. Batista disappeared, but his kind remains, as a recent picture of the dour Pinochet, staring back through dark glasses from a page of the *New York Times*, grimly reminds us.[2] And in the seventies, after the Boom, the Latin American novel takes up again the figure of the dictator, particularly of the ageing dictator, prey to the boredom of a limitless power he is on the verge of losing.

But what precedes the *and* that opens the previous sentence? Why, other than the fact that he is simply there, in Chile, Uruguay, Cuba, Argentina, does the dictator return to center stage in Latin American fiction? Beyond that primary, specular relationship, what is the link between dictatorship and the dictator-novel in Latin America? This question has been raised explicitly and implicitly often enough by recent criticism (often by studying the same texts that I analyze here), but a good deal remains to be said about it.[3] The answer proposed in what follows is by far more theoretical than comprehensive.

The most clearly indigenous thematic tradition in Latin American literature, the dictator and the dictator-book, can be traced as far back as Bernal Díaz del Castillo's and Francisco López de Gómara's accounts of Cortés's conquest of Mexico (structurally, López de Gómara's book is the most akin to the recent dictator-novels).[4] The modern tradition, which has its origins in Sarmiento's *Facundo* (1845), has produced masterpieces such as Valle-Inclán's *Tirano Banderas* (1925), Asturias's *El señor presidente* (1946), Carpentier's *The Kingdom of this World* (1949), and Rulfo's *Pedro Páramo* (1955).[5] What could be called the postmodern tradition consists essentially of three novels that appeared in 1974: Carpentier's *Reasons of State* (Mexico City: Siglo XXI), García Márquez's *The Autumn of the Patriarch* (Buenos Aires: Sudamericana), and Roa Bastos's *Yo el Supremo* (Buenos Aires: Siglo XXI). The revival that the dictator-novel is enjoying in these works is an inquiry not only into the nature and ways of contemporary political power, but also into the power, the energy that constitutes a literary text, particularly a novel, and the function within it of the figure of the author. In this sense it is not only a revival but a reappraisal of the tradition and of the Latin American novel in general.

I am interested here chiefly in the literary manifestations of the figure of the dictator in Latin American literature, not in the emergence and evolution of the dictator in history, a phenomenon much studied today by historians and social scientists dealing with authoritarianism and the state.[6] It should be obvious that literature *reflects* this process, but reflection does not mean copy or reproduction, much less scientific analysis; in literature, more often than not, reflection means, precisely, distortion. Novels dealing with dictators do not establish clear-cut distinctions between the various types that appear in history but tend to deal more abstractly with authority figures and with the question of authority. Of course, authority figures coalesce the historical and psychoanalytic realms. The dictator, Primer Magistrado, Comandante en Jefe, Supremo, El Hombre, is a paternal figure who in turn embodies yet another fiugre, the *macho*. In this sense, then, the dictator becomes, in literature, a figure as complex and, if one wants, abstract as Don Juan, and perhaps just as original and philosophically rich. In the Hispanic tradition and guided by purely literary sources, it is easy to see that the figure goes back to the Arabic presence in medieval Spain. As Américo Castro has so persuasively shown, El Cid, "El Señor" in Spanish, was a mirror image of his Arabic counterparts in the peninsula, thus his Arabic name.[7] (In a forthcoming essay on Lope de Aguirre, Ricardo Diez claims with good reason that El Cid is the first dictator figure in Hispanic literature.)

In addition to the Arabic background, one should recall that Visigothic kingdoms in Spain had a tribal structure in which individual vengeance was favored over recourse to legal action in cases involving injury to one's honor; the rule of mighty males prevailed against the influence of Roman Law. Menéndez Pidal has shown in a beautiful book how these atavistic values persist in Spanish literature throughout the centuries.[8] Leaping to the fifteenth and sixteenth centuries one might recall the *comendadores* who appear so often in Golden Age plays, particularly Lope de Vega's. These *comendadores*, who felt that they had the power to rule despotically over the territories they had wrested from the Moors, were budding dictators. They were above the law, or better yet, they were the law. In Lope's plays they come into conflict with the centralizing effort of the Catholic kings. This centralization, on the other hand, culminates in Philip II, who created a vast bureaucracy to rule all of the *caudillos* who, imbued with the spirit of the *comendadores*, felt the urge to create their own empires in the New World. The best-known case, of course, is Lope de Aguirre. It could be argued that the clash between a central authority governing large states and small, feudal-type *caudillos* that beset nineteenth-century Latin America is prefigured in the struggle between Philip II and the seditious Aguirre.

But postindependence dictators are clearly the product of different historical forces. Although I am sure that political scientists have by now a much more refined analysis of the origins of the phenomenon, I am still persuaded by Mariátegui's descriptive analysis:

Military *caudillos* were the natural product of a revolutionary period that had not been able to create a new ruling class. In such a situation, power had to be exercised by the military men who had fought in the wars of independence. They enjoyed on the one hand military prestige because of their war deeds, and on the other were capable of maintaining themselves in power by the force of arms. Of course, the *caudillo* was not immune to class interests nor to clashing historical forces. He found support in the inconsistent and rhetorical liberalism of the urban population, or in the conservatism of the land-owning class. He was inspired by his clientele of legislators and lawyers belonging to the urban democracy, or by the literati and rhetoricians belonging to the land-owning class.[9]

The rhetoric, as it were, of these literati was also permeated by nineteenth-century philosophy, which, from Hegel to Nietzsche, was enthralled by the figure of the powerful, willful individual. I believe that the first modern consideration of the figure of the modern political leader appears in Hegel's *Philosophy of History*, written in the wake of Napoleon's exploits. Hegel writes, speaking of Caesar,

Such are all great historical men—whose own particular aims involve those large issues which are the will of the World-Spirit. They may be called Heroes, inasmuch as they have derived their purposes and their vocation, not from the calm, regular course of things, sanctioned by the existing order; but from a concealed fount—one which has not attained to phenomenal, present existence—from the inner Spirit, still hidden beneath the surface, which, impinging on the outer worlds on a shell, bursts it in pieces, because it is another kernel than that which belonged to the shell in question. They are men, therefore, who appear to draw the impulse of their life from themselves; and whose deeds have produced a condition of things and a complex of historical relations which appear to be only *their* interest, and *their* work.[10]

Marx's debunking of this concept of heroism in "The Eighteenth Brumaire of Louis Bonaparte" is well known. From our (literary) point of view, Stendhal's consideration of Napoleon's figure through the eyes of his sensitive, artistlike protagonist in *Le rouge et le noir* (1831) is the most suggestive, for Julien Sorel within the fiction sees the emperor through a biography that sparks in him the anxiety of being like the hero. As we shall see, the imaginary collapse of the dictator-figure with the boundless desire for power embodied in the nineteenth-century intellectual or artist, particularly of the novelist, is crucial in the development of the novel, particularly in Latin America.

Sarmiento's passionate analysis of the life of Facundo Quiroga was the first full-fledged treatment of the *caudillo* and the first work in which, in dealing with such a figure, the author asked him- or herself about his or her own relationship to such a creature. Sarmiento's book, of course, was his own way of coming to terms with Rosas's dictatorship. As a liberal with progressive ideas, Sarmiento had to explain to himself as well as to others how Rosas had come about. How could independence have bred such a monster? What had gone wrong? The drama in *Facundo* is Sarmiento's gradual realization that the *caudillo* could not simply be wished away with liberal ideology, that he was an inevitable product of historical and telluric forces. Facundo and Rosas form part of a historical foundation, and in Sarmiento's book they become both a foundation myth and a literary myth.[11] From here to declaring that the *caudillo* was a providential figure there was but one step, and Sarmiento did not hesitate to take it. Rosas's violent regime was only a necessary upheaval that would eventually usher in the forces of progress. He becomes an abstract historical entity, a cog in a large providential design.

Just as Sarmiento is absorbed by this historical dialectic, so is he drawn by an equally compelling literary dialectic. Quiroga may be a barbarian, but he is a powerful, attractive figure who dominates the book, as well as the agent of a beneficial process that he only understands darkly, if at all. There is a beguiling analogy here between the *caudillo* and the author, another bold step that Sarmiento is not hesitant to take, and he declares in Flaubertian fashion, "I am Facundo Quiroga." At this point the modern dictator-novel is born. Sarmiento realizes that the power of his own consciousness in the book, the energy allowing him to interpret history in order to write it, is analogous to the power of his own creature, Facundo Quiroga. Nowhere is this identification of writer and dictator more evident than in the following passage about Rosas:

Rosas finally has the government in his own hands. Facundo was killed a month before. The city has surrendered to his will. The people have confirmed in the most authentic way this surrender of all rights and institutions. The state is a tabula rasa upon which he is going to write a new, original thing. He is a poet, a Plato who is going to bring about his ideal republic according to his own conception of it. This is a work that he has thought about for twenty years, and to which he can now give birth, unencumbered by obsolete traditions, preoccupations of the times, plagiarism of Europe, individual rights, functional institutions. He is a genius, no less, who has been lamenting the errors of his century and preparing himself to destroy them with one blow. Everything is going to be new, the product of his own mind. Let us behold the miracle.[12]

Rosas is going to write an original work, free of plagiarism, which is going to issue out of his own imagination. In the book, the *caudillo* would be a hypostasis of the author. Properly read, Sarmiento's interpretation of the writer is as complex and rich a theoretical statement as those of Flaubert or any of the other European writers of the period.

When we evoke the great novelists of the nineteenth century—Dickens, Balzac, Galdós, Flaubert—we think of powerful individuals whose imagination "created" vast societies that paralleled and even rivaled the world of their times. The modern printing press gave these men enormous power, the power emanating from Rodin's head of Balzac, an imperiousness we associate with the novelist's demiurgic creativity. Lukács is wrong when he declares that the novel is an unheroic genre.[13] There may no longer be, as in the epic, heroic protagonists who are at the center of harmonious totalities, but there is the implicit, powerful author, who probes the inner workings of an entire society to lay them bare in his or her novels, and who, within the confines of the text, is a partially veiled god. The author has the vision afforded by a reflexive and self-reflective consciousness, less grandiose than Hegel's spirit, but, in the fiction, just as omniscient. At the end of the century, Unamuno saw clearly how the novel was the projection of a powerful self:

Yes, every novel, every work of fiction, every poem, when it is alive, is autobiographical. Every fictional being, every poetic character created by an author is part of the author himself. And if such an author puts in his poem a man of flesh and blood whom he has known, it is only after having made him his, a part of himself. Great historians were also autobiographical. The tyrants described by Tacitus are all himself, because of the love and admiration that he has bestowed upon them. One loves and admires even that which one abhors and struggles with. . . . Oh, how Sarmiento loved the tyrant Rosas; he has appropriated him, made him himself.[14]

This view of the writer, which Unamuno fostered with his own works, is of course an ideological distortion of where power lay in nineteenth-century society, a trope whereby the consciousness of the bourgeoisie attained imaginary power over the world. The ideology of modernity—from the eighteenth century on—enthroned the individual.[15] The individual is producer and consumer. Individuals make their own laws to govern their conduct. The world is there for them to possess and consume, particularly the colonial world opened up by Europe in Asia, Africa, and Latin America, as well as the more "backward" regions of the individual's own country. The rise of the bourgeoisie glorifies the entrepreneur, the engineer, the man of action, who believes that he alone has the necessary knowledge and energy to make the world consumable. This figure appears again and again in the nineteenth-century novel. Pepe Rey, in Galdós's *Doña Perfecta*, is a good example, if we wish to remain within a Hispanic context.

The image of the novelist that we saw before is the counterpart of this entrepreneur. The latter conquers whole continents through commercial colonialism, whereas the former invents new worlds and new stories. Traditional narrative *repeated* tales handed down by the collectivity, whereas the novelist "invents" new plots and characters. The man of action created new values through his far-flung commercial ventures and his domination of nature through technology; the man of letters created and occupied new regions for the imagination. This is why the novelist is seen to have such power in society and also why, within the text of the novel, it is the novelist, through the voice of omniscience, who has replaced God. The third person is the novelist's unholy, yet powerful, ghost.

As the power of the bourgeoisie recedes, as the colonialist ventures begin to fail, it is precisely the figure of the author that comes to be questioned in literature. The postmodern novel, let us say, from Proust and James on, tells the tales of woe of an author fragmented, sick, who is called to task, whose apparent power has vanished. Unamuno's *Niebla* furnishes the paradigmatic example. The author, who still holds the seat of power (the setting of the scene is significant) is confronted, challenged, and cursed by the protagonist. The author no longer controls undisturbed the omniscient device of the third person, the voice of rhetorical power. In *A la recherche du temps perdu* there is a similar, though considerably more complex, situation. A sickly, hypersensitive, marginal individual, Marcel, can exert power, if at all, only over himself. We imagine Balzac—the fictional, rhetorical Balzac—pacing up and down his study, dictating with a powerful voice his novels, playing out the parts of the various characters, modulating with precision the voice of the narrator. (Mark Twain actually gave "readings," performances of himself as novelist, for a fee.) We can no longer imagine such a scene when we think of Marcel. The precious language, the proliferation of details, approach the rhetoric of the intimate diary, written for oneself. James's speculations about narrative point of view and the *writerly* nature of his works falls within that problematic. When we reach Joyce, the dictating scene is totally out of the question. *Ulysses* and *Finnegan's Wake* do not have the air of dictated pieces. They have been written, to the point where a good deal of the "action" in *Finnegan's Wake* would be lost without recourse to the visual text itself.

The great figure of the author has been replaced by the uncertain figure of the writer. The former controlled whole continents and centuries, the latter, perhaps a city, twenty-four hours of the life of a nobody. But most of all what has been lost is the rhetoric of fiction. As that hypostasis of the modern individual, the powerful entrepreneur, is degraded, so is the grip of rhetoric eased. The novel was a long discourse by that third person in authority; it contained snippets or long tracts of dialogue by other characters, but was nevertheless a speech by one voice, which "told" the story. Now there is no such mediation, no filtering, no power. The nineteenth-century novel was a potent ideological instrument because through it each individual was convinced, by the boundlessness of that typically nineteenth-century faculty, the imagination, of his or her own power.

The beginning of the disintegration of the society within which the novel emerged makes for the change in the figure of the novelist from author to writer. This reduction is a demystification. The novel, being one of society's more persistent forms of self-analysis, was also one of its more fruitful mechanisms of self-delusion. The real author was no more powerful, even metaphorically, than the entrepreneur, who was a cog in a larger system that he could barely understand, and certainly did not control. The postmodern novel, even going as far back as Flaubert, holds a mirror, so to speak, up to that image of the author-dictator, of the author-rhetor, and reveals instead a weak and fragmented *scriptor*, who is the secretary of a voice no longer enthroned, no longer his or hers. The Latin American dictator-novel undergoes and reflects a similar process.

Sarmiento's *Facundo* evokes, in Latin American terms, the problematic outlined above. Sarmiento may want to be Quiroga, but in fact has become his, and Rosas's, Boswell. Who is the master and who the slave in this mythology of writing? For all his barbarism Quiroga incarnates the true will of history, whereas Sarmiento is a mere exegete, a commentator, the representative of an ideology. But at the same time, neither Facundo nor Rosas "know" that they are the sacrificial victims of a broader historical beginning. Facundo and Rosas need Sarmiento—as the master needs the slave in Hegel's dialectic—in order to record their predestined, ritualistic immolation: the author dies, the dictator is killed, the secretary remains to tell the "true" story. The mythology of writing conceals an Oedipal subplot: the king, the father, is killed for the story to be told. Sarmiento is not really Facundo. When he says, "I am Facundo," Sarmiento is really wishing for an illusory time when totalities were possible, when discourse encompassed the wholeness of being—the self and its object united in one moment of ecstatic self-delusion.

Many of the elements that we discover in *Facundo* reappear in the three recent dictator-novels mentioned earlier: *Reasons of State, The Autumn of the Patriarch,* and *Yo el Supremo.* The intermediate dictator-novels, from *Amalia* to *El señor presidente,* repeat the myth of authority, whereas the novels of Carpentier, García Márquez, and Roa Bastos deconstruct the myth, often by returning to that original mythology of writing already set out in *Facundo.*[16] There is, in fact, a progression in that deconstruction that goes from Carpentier, to García Márquez, and finally to Roa Bastos. It is, of course, not a chronological progression, since the novels appeared in the same year, but one in which that mythology of writing to which I alluded is unfolded in a kind of fictive time. I will, therefore, avail myself of this fictitious chronology and discuss these three books in that order.

The very title of Carpentier's book announces what is at stake in his novel.[17] *El recurso del méthodo,* the original title, is obviously a garbled version of Descartes's *Le discours de la méthode.* The ageing, capricious dictator, who surrounds himself with venal academics in *fin de siècle* Paris, where he spends most of his time, authorizes outlandish political atrocities, justifying them by allusion to some of Descartes's dicta (some drawn from the *Traité des passions de l'âme*). The parodic nature of the novel is clear on this level. And in a historical sense, the First Magistrate is the monstrous product of the application of European (i.e., French) liberal philosophy to Latin American sociopolitical problems. In the First Magistrate the *libertadores,* the *padres de la patria,* repeat themselves, but as farcical, despotic ideologues who have become the staunch defenders of class interests. He would be Sarmiento's European dream-become-nightmarish reality. Carpentier's Francophile First Magistrate has turned liberal ideology into mere oratory—his forte is his rhetorical skill, his ability to deliver bombastic speeches laden with topics "borrowed" from European writers. His passion is opera, and indeed the whole of *Reasons of State* takes place in what appear to be operatic settings: the half-constructed plaza where the First Magistrate delivers a speech that turns out to be a translation of Renan's *Prayer on the Acropolis*, the capitol housing an enormous statue representing the motherland, all display the monumental yet insubstantial quality of operatic stage props. Indeed, one of the revolts against the First Magistrate breaks out during a performance of *Aida* that he had staged in his capital to raise the cultural level of the country. His power resides in his command of voice, a voice that externalizes that (mock) Cartesian consciousness through a rhetoric that becomes operatic, that is, melodic, hollow, contrived, and ultimately ridiculous. *Reasons of State* is a kind of comic melodrama.

But if Descartes's presence is felt from the very title, Vico also appears from the beginning. *Reasons of State* alludes to Vico's *ricorsi*, the convolutions of history that repeat past events in not quite mimetic fashion—repetitions that are original acts.[18] Needless to say, Vico polemicized against Descartes, and in this sense Carpentier's novel opens up again a debate that is situated in the beginnings of modernity. These *ricorsi* are present throughout the novel in the spiral trajectory of history, the recurrence of revolutions that eventually bring about the downfall of the First Magistrate. Each repetition leaves a residue, the nonmimetic produces a comic effect that is at the base of parody, but that also opens up to the future and the next turn of the spiral. Carpentier manages in this fashion to fuse the comic spirit of the novel with a political statement. If the *caudillo*, as in *Facundo*, is a providential figure, the parodic corrosion of the ideology that spawns him marks his appearance and announces the coming of a revolution, a revolution that, even if carnival-like in outward appearance, will nevertheless be a significant new beginning.

Vico, however, is present in more than just this representation of history, for the Cartesian *cogito* that it undermines is also an important factor in the novel's own critique of authority. As the novel opens, the First Magistrate is awakening in his Paris apartment (the various moments of awakening are, incidentally, a parody of *A la recherche*):

But I've only just gone to bed. And the alarm has gone off already. Half past six. It's impossible. Quarter past seven, perhaps. More likely. Quarter past eight. This alarm clock would be a marvel of Swiss watch-making, but its hands are so slim that one can hardly see them. Quarter past nine. That's not right either. My spectacles, quarter past ten. That's it. Besides, daylight is already shining through the yellow curtains with morning brilliance. And it's always the same when I come back to this house: I open my eyes with the feeling of being *there*, because . . .[19]

The First Magistrate's mind is not filled with clear ideas, nor is he able to perceive surrounding reality sharply. The narrative focus of the novel shifts, accordingly, from his mind to an indirect, third person, or to Peralta, his obsequious assistant and secretary. We also find this lack of precision in the historical background. The First Magistrate is not a specific historical figure, but a composite of various Latin American dictators: Estrada Cabrera, Machado, Trujillo, Porfirio Díaz, Batista. More than a mere abstraction, however, he is a mythic figure, in the Viconian sense: the compendium of the people's recollections that constitute a foundation myth.[20] In this sense the novel is detached from Carpentier, though careful historical investigation would no doubt reveal that most of the historical background comes from the Machado years in Cuba, when the then-young novelist was involved in subversive activities directed against the dictator. (For Cuban readers, particularly, the novel is a sort of compendium of stories from the Machado years, told and retold since then.)

But there is a way in which the novel is not that detached from its author. One cannot but see in the music-loving, erudite First Magistrate, who divides his life between Latin America and Paris, a parody of Carpentier himself (Carpentier has also given us a self-portrait in the character of the rebellious student, whose general features, however, correspond with greater historical accuracy to Julio Antonio Mella and Rubén Martínez Villena). Carpentier's parodic self-portrait harks back to Sarmiento's solemn identification with Facundo Quiroga, and the self-parody is made even more obvious in the text of *Reasons of State* by the presence of oblique references to Carpentier's own earlier work. The recourse, the rebound, could not but strike at the author himself, and a great deal of the significance of this novel within the field of Latin American literature lies precisely in this factor.

Known for his methodical, architectural structures, Carpentier opts in *Reasons of State* for a monumental but insubstantial, cardboardlike construction that betrays its opera-stage quality. Singing at the center is the First Magistrate–Author, who can hear only the distortions of his own voice in the multiple echoes his goons provide of it, particularly Peralta, the parasitic secretary, who is the counterfigure of the dictator. Carpentier's novel demystifies the authority of the dictator-author by means of a parody of political rhetoric in which speech is the product of a muddled mind. At the same time Carpentier demystifies the notion of authority by identifying himself with the dictator. Though the parody withdraws from the figure of the dictator its solemnity, Carpentier preserves the providential structure suggested by *Facundo*, only he plays out more thoroughly this mythology of writing by insisting on the "passion" of the First Magistrate, whose demise is the very condition of history.[21]

García Márquez's anxiously awaited *The Autumn of the Patriarch*—his first long work since *One Hundred Years of Solitude*—has a great deal in common with *Reasons of State*. Like Carpentier's novel, *The Autumn of the Patriarch* takes place in a mythic Latin American republic, though located in the Caribbean basin, and the figure of the dictator is again a compendium of dictators. But whereas Carpentier has set his novel at the turn of the century—between the end of the *belle époque* and the beginning of the "roarin' twenties"—García Márquez encompasses a much broader temporal span. What could be termed the present time of the action (sometime in the early twentieth century) takes place in the waning moments of the dictator's life, but by means of his muddled memory and owing to his prodigious longevity, the novel encompasses the whole of Latin American history, from the arrival of Columbus to the heyday of U.S. imperialism (the dictator sells the Caribbean Sea to the Americans to settle his foreign debt, and the Americans cart it away in numbered pieces to reassemble in the Arizona desert). Carpentier's is a mock foundation myth whose origin is modernity; García Márquez's is a mock foundation myth whose ultimate model is Christianity itself. A great deal of fun at the expense of (particularly) Colombian popular piety is present in *The Autumn of the Patriarch*, and, as in *One Hundred Years of Solitude*, the Bible lurks just beneath the surface.[22] But more to the point, the dictator, with his "holy family," his providential advent to "save" the republic (from utterly obscure origins—he is fatherless, but for more worldly reasons than Christ), and his "resurrection" at the very beginning of the book make him a farcical *figura Christi*. This resurrection is made possible, of course, by the existence of a perfect double who is killed, allowing the dictator to catch red-handed those who revel at his wake and try to divide the spoils. There are many more instances in which New Testament scenes are evoked in this parodic fashion.

Even at this substructure of myth, García Márquez's penchant for hyperbole is at work. From Sarmiento on, as we have seen, the figure of the dictator is part of a foundation myth that attempts to account for the modern history of Latin America. But García Márquez has gone farther, to the very dawn of Western tradition, to show that the figure of the dictator is but a repetition of the figure of the *bouc émissaire*, a version of the repeatable story of Christ. The parodic repetition of such a basic story also involves, as we shall see, a profound reflection on the nature of the novel.

García Márquez's dictator is more primitive that Carpentier's, more like the early *caudillos* than the *déspota ilustrado* of *Reasons of State* (correspondingly, *The Autumn of the Patriarch* is much less erudite). Kept in power by English and American imperial interests, the dictator flounders about in the tedium of absolute power. He is mired in a chaotic atmosphere in which terror and magic coexist, babbles clichés about the fatherland, and gives outrageous orders. The history of Colombia parades in chronological disorder behind the incidents narrated, a history, as in Carpentier, rendered "mythopoetic" by individual and collective memory, without a structuring function in the sequence of events. History is simply a series of outrages perpetrated by foreign nations, by the dictator, or by both with the object of securing and maintaining absolute power. If in *One Hundred Years of Solitude* there was a rigorous order behind the apparent discord, *The Autumn of the Patriarch* is a chaotic universe that begins near the end and returns to the end at the closing of the book without there being a sense of cyclical recurrence. It is as if everything occurred simultaneously at the end, without order. If Colonel Aureliano Buendía's all-encompassing glimpse as he faces the firing squad has the hallucinatory rigor of dreams, the dictator's senile recollections in the waning moments of his life are a confused jumble of memories. The central, repeated image in the novel is *chapaletear*, to thrash around in the mud, to muddle through. *Chapaletear* accurately describes the text itself and the dictator's palace, where most of the "action" takes place. The palace is a possible emblem of the novel's fictive universe: teeming with beggars, concubines, cows and their leavings, chickens, made up of countless rooms, the palace at times recalls a biblical temple, at others a bazaar from the *Thousand and One Nights*. One is never sure of the palace's location, nor of its interior plan; rooms connect with others or have balconies facing the courtyard or the street according to whim or need. The dictator's abode is the ruined version of the king's secret chamber in *Ariel*; each is an emblem of the self of the author at different stages in the subterranean history of Latin American literature that I am attempting to uncover.

There are hardly any periods in *The Autumn of the Patriarch* and no paragraphs. The rambling syntax (technically made up of a few interminable anacolutha) moves from speaker to speaker without transition, and the topics change with equal arbitrariness. It is a syntax without a fixed subject, which shatters all the usual commonplaces about point of view in fiction by exposing the grammatical conventionality of what we call "perspective" (the uncritical association of grammatical person, narrative voice, and the mechanics of dialogue between people). This syntactical chaos is a model of the system of power that enthrones the dictator. His power lies in *being thought to be there*, at the center, giving orders, assuring a link with the origins of self and history, being the Self, the Super Self, the *überselbst* that grounds syntax and rhetoric, the Voice of the Subject. (There is an ironic mention of RCA Victor's famous commercial in which a dog recognizes the voice of his master on a phonograph record. In Spanish the commercial simply says, "La voz de su amo," which no doubt alludes to the question of the voice and the self, which can be reproduced to perform an authoritative function when the self is no longer there. The voice of the master can fool only a dog.) Here we are far from the notion that the collective voices create the dictator. The dictator is, for the most part, absent in mind and body from the center of power. Readers are made aware both of his absence and of the need for his presence as they read on without a sense of "whose" mind they are inhabiting.

Once into the novel the need diminishes and we too abandon ourselves to the flow of the manifold, multiperson prose, a radically predicative, headless writing. This effect is of the utmost importance. The illiterate dictator rules through voice, but after a while no one pays attention to his real existence, hence his voice and image are re-created by electronic devices. The *dictator*, the one who dictates, can be *reproduced*, and it is that reproduction that rules. The same occurs at the syntactical level. The rambling syntax may in the beginning evoke the apparent free-flow of conversation; we are at first taken aback, then reassured by what appears to be a direct transcription of a rambling monologue. But in fact, since grammatical persons do not rule this prose, it is the furthest possible thing from being a dictation—it is rather a textual web, a game of mirrors that both reconstruct and deconstruct the figure of the dictator, the missing subject. Needless to say, we as readers are also caught and deconstructed by that game in which all our most basic expectations are shown to be arbitrary conventions. Are we a second person being addressed by the text, a first person who enters the text to put it in order, or an impassive third person who just watches? Who (is, am, are) (you, I, we)? Without persons, or with multiple persons lacking clear ontological status—even in representational terms—or grammatical identity, there is no one to reconstruct a text that is simply there, as the most devastating critique of dictatorship beyond the more obvious political messages of the author. In his earlier "Big Mama's Funeral," by making the dictator female, García Márquez had already cleared the ground for this critique of dictatorship, as I have already explained.[23]

The return to Christ, the mocking of the Christ-myth through the figure of the general (of the universe, no less) becomes more significant now. Christ, like all great teachers in the Western tradition, did not write; his precious dicta were gathered and written by adoring disciples whose collaboration produced the New Testament, in the same way that Plato's work made available the Socratic dialogues.[24]

The dictator too is supposed to rule through voice, a "voice" much like that of an author—that is to say, the tics and quirks that make writing his or hers, the marks that identify him or her. This nodule of associations is clear in the novels of Carpentier and García Márquez. In both cases the problematic generated by this association is determined by a return to *Facundo*, and more precisely by a deconstruction of Sarmiento's relationship to the dictator. For in the end the dictator is shown not to be the bearer of power through voice, but a figure needed to show by his demise the controlling power of writing—it is not the voice, but writing, it is not the dictator-author, but the secretary-writer, who reigns, even if he is nothing but a Carnival king.

But the secretary, the agent of the text, can only be secretary, and the Figure of Authority is still needed: "We are Facundo—First Magistrate–General of the Universe in the texts," seem to say Carpentier and García Márquez, "but only because of a textual need born of a certain ideology that enthrones the subject. We are *figurae*, not present-unto-ourselves bearers of the truth about Latin American history. Our texts celebrate in advance, prefigure the real absence of dictator-authors, the coming of the TEXT. But we can't do this without posing as victims, without being beheaded by our texts, without the spectacle of our own demise, without our public sacrifice. We too must be victims of a textual assault." (In Severo Sarduy's *From Cuba with a Song—De donde son los cantantes*—the figures of the General and Mortal Pérez sketch this problematic in ways that there is no room here to discuss.) The novel was made possible, according to Auerbach, by the advent of Christianity's *sermo humilis*, which led to the realism of certain medieval texts and then on to Cervantes. And the presence of the Christ myth at the core of *The Autumn of the Patriarch* is also a way of underlining that writing takes place in the realm of the son, in the kingdom of this world, so to speak. But the humor, the chaos, the luxurious disorder and sensuousness of this world of writing underline too that this is not an authoritative world, except through representation, through the theatricality of the king's public sacrifice.

Roa Bastos's *Yo el Supremo* takes to their ultimate consequences many of the problems raised in *Reasons of State* and *The Autumn of the Patriarch*. In a sense, only after reading *Yo el Supremo* can we perform on the previous two novels the sort of reading that I have suggested, for in many ways Roa Bastos's text is the most theoretical of the three, that is to say, the most detailed in its consideration of the question of power, rhetoric, and the novel raised before.[25]

A significant difference between *Yo el Supremo* and the two other novels is that it deals manifestly with a historical figure exclusively, Paraguay's notorious Dr. Francia, and not with a composite of various dictators. The significance of this is to be found not in the relative truthfulness of this novel in contrast to the other two, but in the presentation of "facts," the author can attribute to history, not to himself, the very factuality of the book. This is important because Roa Bastos has exhausted the well-worn games of illusion about found manuscripts, long-lost documents recovered, and the like. *Yo el Supremo* is composed, for the most part, of real texts by Dr. Francia or about him. These texts range from personal memoirs by members of the opposition to translations of chapters from the books written by two British merchants, the Robertson brothers (*Four Years in Paraguay, Comprising an Account of that Republic under the Government of Doctor Francia*, 1838; *Letters on South America*, 1848), passages drawn from

Carlyle and the defense of Dr. Francia

Captain Richard Burton's *Letters from the Battlefield of Paraguay* (1870—a book, incidentally, dedicated to Sarmiento), works by the French botanist Bonplant and the Swiss doctors Rengger and Longchamp, and even a text by Thomas Carlyle (actually a defense of Dr. Francia, printed first in the *Foreign Quarterly Review* in 1847 and later included in his *Critical and Miscellaneous Essays*). All of these texts are arranged by an editor who has also furnished quite a few footnotes in which he sometimes corrects what is said in one text by comparing it with another, and offers other pertinent information. These notes also tell the story of how the book was put together, and they constitute in a very real sense the most important strand in the plot of the novel. This story ends with the editor's own explanation in an "Editor's Note," in which he declares his faithfulness to the texts and not to his own whims or creative impulse: "The reader will have already noticed that, unlike common texts, this one has been read first and written later. Instead of saying and writing a new thing, it has done nothing but faithfully copy what has already been said and written by others. There is, then, in this compilation not a single page, a single phrase, a single word, from the title to the final note, that has not been written in this manner" (p. 467).

We cannot, however, take this disclaimer literally, for the editor is the final authority in this collection of texts that compose *Yo el Supremo*, no matter how weak an authority he may appear to be in comparison to an omniscient narrative voice. The body of the novel is composed of a polemical collection of versions of Paraguayan history. A mere description will no doubt make clear what I mean by "polemical."

There are three main kinds of texts, in addition to the footnotes, the "Editor's Note," and an occasional unclassifiable document, such as a list of toys ordered by the dictator. The first kind of text is what the Supremo dictates to his secretary, Policarpo Patiño, about what is happening in the present. This record includes the constant abuse that the dictator heaps on his secretary ("*fiel de fechos,*" roughly, "inspector of facts," but the irony is more intense in Spanish because *fiel* literally means faithful) for his alleged lack of faithfulness in taking down what he says, and also for his presumed ambition to topple the Supremo in order to become King Policarpo I. The hapless Patiño, who takes dictation while soaking his enormous, sore feet in cold water, protests his innocence throughout the novel (the big, sore feet are an obvious identification of Patiño with Oedipus).[26] The story told here, as rambling and vulgar as Nixon's tapes but far more amusing, involves the dictator's attempt to discover the authors of a pasquinade in which it is announced that the Supremo is dead and instructions for his burial are given. The Supremo urges poor Patiño to discover the culprits, and the docile secretary pores over every single scrap of paper in the republic (Patiño knows by heart every official document in the archives), but to no avail. The author of the pasquinade is never found, though even the paper and its watermark are scrutinized, not to mention the calligraphy, which perfectly imitated the Supremo's own handwriting.

Finally there is what the Supremo writes himself in his "Private Notebook," which is mostly an account of his life, attempts to write fiction, diatribes against Patiño and his kind, philosophical musings and ramblings, and other sundry exercises. Most poignant in this section are Supremo's words about his stepfather, whom he allowed to die without forgiving him some trivial insult (like all the other dictators, Roa Bastos's lacks a precise genealogy: history begins with him). All of these texts have been edited, for one finds in them, besides the footnotes, indications in italics and within brackets such as "on the margin it is written," or "there is a hole in the paper here." So that, although they do not compose a homogeneous text, held together by the rhetorical power of a narrative voice, and in fact are anything but homogeneous, these texts, in these discreet marks and indications, bear the presence of the editor.

Dr. Francia's fear of the pasquinade, his abuse of Policarpo Patiño (to whom he dictates his own—Patiño's—death sentence), his constant worry about writing, all stem from the fact that he has found and used the power implicit in language itself. The Supremo defines power as being able to do through others what we are unable to do ourselves: language, being separate from what it designates, is the very embodiment of power, for things act and mean through it without ceasing to be themselves. Dr. Francia has also realized that he cannot control language, particularly written language, that it has a life of its own that threatens him. So, he takes it out on poor, obese Patiño, who represents the scriptors, who are even capable of corrupting the oral tradition:

Don't use improper words that do not go well with my feelings, that are not impregnated with my thoughts. I am bothered by this dependent, mendicant relationship. What is more, your style is abominable. A laybrinthine alley, paved with alliterations, anagrams, malapropisms, barbarisms, paranomasias of the kind paroli/parulis, dumb anastrophes to impress dumb queers who get erections under the influence of queer inversions of the sentence, like: to the ground from the tree I fell. Or this one, even more violent: Stuck in the Square, the pike winks at my head of the Revolution. Old rhetorical tricks that they use now as if they were new. What I now reproach you for is that you are incapable of expressing yourself with the originality of a parrot. You are nothing but a palavering biped. A hybrid engendered by different species. A donkey-mule pulling the wheel at the well of the Government's Office. As a parrot you would have been more useful to me than as an inspector of facts. You are neither one thing nor the other. Instead of transposing to the natural state what I dictate to you you fill the paper with pompous gibberish, wicked things written before you by others. You feed off the carrion of books. You have not yet ruined the oral tradition because that is the only language that cannot be sacked, stolen, plagiarized, copied. The spoken language lives sustained by the tone, the gestures, the countenance, the looks, the accent, the breath of the speaker. (p. 64)

Patiño is the quintessential writer, thus Supremo's diatribe against written language and his impassioned defense of oral communication. But toward the end of his life, in one of his dialogues with Sultán (another potential dictator?), his dog, Supremo expresses fear that he might lose his speech, his ability to remember in language. His recourse is to remember Patiño, who has become his memory, so that he too feels himself in the clutches of written language, as embodied by the apparently defenseless secretary.

In spite of the death penalty imposed on him, Policarpo Patiño outlives his master. He does not attain the power that Dr. Francia feared he might achieve and dies an obscure death. But did he not have the last laugh? Did he not attain some sort of posthumous power? In a long footnote that invades nearly four complete pages of the book, the editor tells the story of how he got hold of the pen Supremo used. This pen, a sort of writing Aleph, not only could write, but could project between the lines a series of pictures, "optical metaphors," which translated writing into a language of images. In addition, the editor supposes, the pen could also project the phonic temporality of language, thus combining simultaneously three texts. This pen is given to the editor by Raimundo "Loco-Solo," a fourth grandchild of Policarpo Patiño.

There is a link, a very significant link, between the Supremo's amanuensis and the editor of the book we read. The editor, who arranges the various texts and annotates them, who thereby exercises final authority over Dr. Francia's versions of himself, is the heir of Policarpo Patiño. The editor is a sort of Super Secretary, the Bureaucrat of Bureaucrats, the Collector of Writing, the Fervent Devotee of the Letter, a Scholar, in short. There is, in fact, a completely new twist in *Yo el Supremo* in relation to the earlier two novels: there the dictator appears as the victim who was sacrificed to history; here the sacrificial victim is Policarpo, who dies, so to speak, so that the story may be written, edited, through the ministrations of a distant heir. *Yo el Supremo* does not pretend to tell so much a founding myth as to constitute a founding text: its composition is more akin to that of sacred books, like the Bible, than to that of the versions of an oral myth that literature often seeks or pretends to emulate. Layers upon layers of text are compiled, gathered together, edited, arranged, to preserve texts at the expense of coherence or the elimination of contradiction. *Yo el Supremo* is the final victory of the text.[27]

Perhaps the brief analysis of a recent book whose structure is the very opposite of the dictator-novels studied here—their correlative opposite—will serve to clarify the discussion. I am referring to Guillermo Cabrera Infante's *View of Dawn in the Tropics*, published in the same year as *Reasons of State*, *The Autumn of the Patriarch*, and *Yo el Supremo*.[28] *View of Dawn in the Tropics* was the title of Cabrera Infante's brilliant novel *Three Trapped Tigers* when the book won the Biblioteca Breve Prize in 1964. As the author has explained, he decided to delete from that original version a series of vignettes dealing with the struggle against Batista. These vignettes served as a counterpoint to the sections dealing with the nightlife of Havana, which became the core of *Three Trapped Tigers*. It is very probable that the present book consists, for the most part, of those deleted sections, which are very much like the vignettes that Cabrera Infante had inserted in his first book, the short-story collection *Así en la paz como en la guerra* (1960). It is also clear, however, that some of what is included in *View of Dawn in the Tropics* must have been written after the publication of *Three Trapped Tigers*, because it is based on historical events that occurred afterward. In any case, though the question of the relationship between *Three Trapped Tigers* and *View of Dawn in the Tropics* cannot be analyzed with precision without having access to the manuscript that won the prize, the latter must be considered a 1974 book.

View of Dawn in the Tropics consists of a series of vignettes retelling salient events in Cuban history. The totalizing intention of the book is evident in that these vignettes are organized in chronological fashion and cover the period from the geological upheaval that lifted Cuba out of the sea to counterrevolutionary activity in the eighteen years preceding 1974. *View of Dawn in the Tropics* presents violence as the constant reenactment of a historical birth, a dawn that announces a day that never comes. At one point (p. 118) the book refers to itself as an inventory, and this is a fairly accurate description of the detached, monotonous cadence of the narrating voice; its repetitiousness and simple syntax level off the different moments in an effort, it would appear, to reduce them to a single, abstract instance, a conglomeration of the same.

The incidents related are those that supposedly have become fable: the execution of the Indian rebel Hatuey by the conquering Spaniards; José Martí's death in Dos Ríos on 19 May 1895; Fidel Castro's attack on the Moncada garrison on 26 July 1953; and so on. Many of these incidents are documented and are part of the official history of the island (Portuondo's standard textbook is quoted in the front matter), whereas others belong to what could be called historical lore in the sense used in our discussion of *Reasons of State*. In some cases, what is described is not the historical incident per se (if indeed such is possible), but its inscription in history, particularly when this inscription is of a visual nature. For instance, in the account of Hatuey's execution, mention is made of the label of the beer bearing his name; the description of the maroon being attacked by "Cuban hounds" is actually a description of the well-known painting by Landaluze (Víctor Patricio Landaluze, d. 1889). In other instances, the inscription is of a textual nature. For example, the assassination of Manolo Castro is retold by alluding to Hemingway's "The Shot," and the plot to kill Clemente Vázquez Bello and blow up Gerardo Machado and his cabinet at the funeral recalls Carpentier's "Manhunt."

But these *urtexts* are not grafted onto the text to establish what the current cliché would call a "textual dialogue," or to manifest an "intertextuality." In fact, the opposite occurs, for all these texts are subsumed in the monotonous, impersonal, and stylistically faceless narrating voice. That voice effaces their contours, blurring all differences and making them part of a given thematic. There is an inescapable moralistic and ideological sense to *View of Dawn in the Tropics* that is lodged precisely in that monotony. The soothing monotone tries to persuade the reader that there will always be an established order against which futile and heroic acts of violence will be committed (there is pathos verging on bathos in many of the vignettes— Manolo Castro is killed with thirty-five cents in his pocket).[29] The totalizing thrust of *View of Dawn in the Tropics* and the effacement of textual differences seek to promote a transcendental truth, a truth that lies before writing, in that impersonal voice that repeats it in every instance from behind the transparency of the text. Whereas in Carpentier, García Márquez, and Roa Bastos textual heterogeneity shatters the presumed transcendence of any foundation myth, Cabrera Infante's monophonic text purports to enthrone a voice that would be "imperishable and eternal," as the book grandiloquently declares Cuba to be in the last sentence.

Besides, the totality promoted by *View of Dawn in the Tropics* is in fact quite partial. It is significant that a book that attempts to offer such a global view of Cuban history should leave out all the violence visited upon Cuba by the United States. The Bay of Pigs invasion is a glaring absence, as are the many other CIA-sponsored attacks against Cuba. Such a selective presentation of history belies the totalizing character of *View of Dawn in the Tropics* and reveals its true intention, which is what could be called the promoting of contingent political argument, as authoritarian a move as that found in books issued under the aegis of the Cuban revolutionary apparatus. Though directed against a dictator—Fidel Castro—*View of Dawn in the Tropics* reflects the dictator's authoritarian hold on truth and power. The link between this book and the dictator-novel is to be found there, in that rhetoric of abstraction and power that is dismantled in texts such as *Reasons of State*, *The Autumn of the Patriarch,* and *Yo el Supremo*, not to mention Cabrera Infante's own *Three Trapped Tigers* and "Meta-Final."

The erosion of authority that has prevailed in postmodern Western literature has been played out, performed in Latin American literature in the form of the recent dictator-novel. This performance consists of the cancellation of a central authority, a conscience to whom, even within the fiction, a certain intention can be attributed, an intention whose discovery would in turn be the object of our own act of interpretation. The text is there to be read without a governing purpose or previously set meaning, a collage of other texts, gathered by a secretary who is not accountable (a "scholar" whose "objectivity" does not allow him more than the collation of texts).

But this does not mean that the dictator-novel does not reflect the nature of current dictatorships; it is, in fact, a truer reflection of modern dictatorships than the group of novels written in the twenties and thirties. We know that it is not Pinochet who rules Chile, but a complex web of interests whose emblem could very well be International Telephone and Telegraph—a transnational communications empire, a TEXT. Somoza, Videla, Franco in his final years, were/are also puppets of what are now called the multinationals. So perhaps the most characteristic "dictator" of the current age was Howard Hughes, the figurehead of a vast financial and communications empire that had no legitimate affiliation to any given country and whose power lay not in the drugged and senile tycoon who was carried around by zealous assistants, but in the hands of the multiple secretaries, technocrats who control today's electronic communications systems. The figure of the tottering, doped Howard Hughes, being secreted from country to country by his entourage, allows me to make some final commentaries about how the postmodern dictator-novel has reappraised and in a sense rewritten the tradition of the Latin American novel in general.

Brian J. Mallet is right when he says that the dictator-novels by García Márquez and Aguilera Malta undermine the myth of the dictator and create a game of mirrors that corrodes the relation that earlier novels had established between myth and history.[30] The dictator-novels that we have been studying here explode precisely the two pillars on which the "mythic" novel rested: the author, and culture, the latter understood as the homogeneous, unspoken code that gives meaning to social activity. The novel that appealed to the conjunction of these two claimed to present a transcendental truth about history by having access to the very origin and fountainhead of all signification, an origin that in the specific case of the Latin American novel took the form of the "primitive" cultures of the continent, be it Mayan in the case of Asturias or African in that of Carpentier. The author's spirit—through the medium of his or her voice—plumbed the depths of time, conquered history, and brought forth an original truth that was the guiding power of the work. The postmodern dictator-novel shatters this delusion by showing that it represents a dream of power and authority through which the Supreme Self of postromantic ideology still secures its throne. This new novel demonstrates in its very structure that in reality dictators are not powerful telluric forces, but ideological diversions, shadows cast by the true powers in today's world.

By relinquishing its claim to a transcendental truth, the new novel—"the textual novel"—does not renounce knowledge. On the contrary, recent Latin American fiction takes on what must appear to many to be a very "philosophical" mold. (The title of Carpentier's novel, as we saw, alludes to a philosophical work, and one could easily be reminded of *The Twilight of the Gods* by García Márquez; Roa Bastos's title also has a Nietzschean ring to it.) And indeed what the new novel has done is to include philosophy within its textual web, not to reject it for being bookish, as the earlier writing has done. The separation of literature and philosophy by the fiction of the twenties, thirties, and even the fifties and sixties was a way of privileging the former while suppressing the possible power of the latter. Today's writing privileges neither, and in this, as in so much else, it may be taking a cue from Borges, who, from the thirties on, has included philosophy in the elaboration of his fictions not as a superior code, but as one more among the many kinds of texts produced by society.[31] Today's Latin American writing—the dictator-novel being one of its more compelling manifestations—includes what, anachronistically, we could still call philosophy.

Roa Bastos's *Yo el Supremo* reveals one last twist, with which I shall close. Policarpo Patiño does have a sort of posthumous victory, but, precisely by being posthumous, it reveals its lack of finality. His dying puts him in a position analogous to that of the Supremo: both are absent from the end; neither is present to claim victory. Patiño too has been sacrificed, and this uncovers the sense of the mythology of writing that has been observed in all the books analyzed. If only the holder of knowledge and power were victimized in order to make communication possible, then we would be in the presence of a kind of prelapsarian myth, which would make of this story the vestige of an initial act of exchange, prior to ideological distortion and to the differentiating mechanisms of language. By dying, Patiño "shows" that once he has attained power over the other he must go, that the struggle for power in this mythology of writing is essentially a repetition that lacks a first, unrepeated act. In other words, his death demonstrates that the nontextual nature of the dictator, his claim to truth and authority, was also a sham, a necessary disguise for the ritualistic actualization of difference. The sacrifice, the Christian and Oedipal reminiscences, are thereby shown to be unavoidable, but nondetermining, tropes, reflections on repetition that are themselves repetitions, translations.

The novels of the Boom—*Hopscotch, One Hundred Years of Solitude, The Death of Artemio Cruz*—brought about a literature that no longer needed to be "typical" or representative of Latin America, but still was an exploration of what Latin America was. All of them (perhaps *The Death of Artemio Cruz* being the most clearly oriented toward such knowledge by its relation to Octavio Paz's *The Labyrinth of Solitude*) centered on the delusion that a certain total knowledge of Latin America must be sought through its literature. The post-Boom novel, as we have seen in our study of the dictator-novel, deconstructs the assumptions about the power of the self and its representation in fiction, which supported such a literary ideology. But in doing so, the novel has not replaced the myth of the self with that of a collective unconscious, or of a class consciousness, a proletarian ideology that would replace the fallen self of the bourgeois author. In a way, that correlative literary myth of the class or collective authorship is also deconstructed by the new textual novel.

All such pipe dreams are obsolete, for what the new literature is doing is dismantling Literature itself, not replacing a relation of power with another within an unchanging concept of literature. And this is present not only in Borges and his heirs (though Borges's literature had been announcing this crisis for a long time), it is present even in Sovietized Cuba in the work of authors such as Miguel Barnet and others in the tradition of the *novela testimonio*, the so-called documentary novel, the best known being *Autobiography of a Runaway Slave*. A valuable recent example of this trend is found in Reynaldo González's *La fiesta de los tiburones* (1979), which deals with the emergence of dictatorship in Cuba during the early republican period, but does so by combining "oral" testimony with a collage of newspaper clippings of the times, plus a critical apparatus consisting of footnotes, chronologies, and the like. Perhaps González's work is the most representative of the new literature, for it combines openly and without literary games textual production and criticism, thus effacing the conventional line that literature established between these two modes of writing. But this may be a delusion on my part, a prelapsarian dream such as assaults literary critics and scholars periodically; a dream, after all, of power, for we too are secretaries to great writers and works and often desire to supersede them by showing how, without us, they could not communicate their message to mere mortals.

When the Sandinista troops entered Somoza's bunker they found on a bed a crumpled, flaccid military uniform, like a discarded skin. The snake had fled.

4. *Terra Nostra*: Theory and Practice

In an essay that was widely read in the sixties, Alejo Carpentier maintained that the novel is above all a form of knowledge, not an object of aesthetic pleasure: "The Spanish picaresque, born unwittingly from the comical nucleus of *Lazarillo de Tormes* and continued until the premonitory autobiography of Torres Villarroel, fulfilled its true novelistic function, which is to violate constantly the naive principle of being a story destined to cause 'aesthetic pleasure to its readers,' to become instead an instrument of analysis, a way of knowing epochs and men; a way of knowing that goes beyond, in many cases, the author's intentions."[1] As on many other occasions, Carpentier is echoing here an idea of Unamuno's: the knowledge of humankind in general can be achieved through the artistic observation of the local culture.[2] Carpentier's essay, "Problemática de la actual novela latinoamericana," proposes a vast theory about the relationship between texts and contexts in the Latin American narrative, a theory that is a synthesis of ideas with a long history in Spanish-language intellectual circles.[3]

These ideas, linking the peculiarity of local culture and history to literary production, are the main preoccupation of essayists like Unamuno and Ortega in Spain, and Alfonso Reyes, Mariátegui, Henríquez Ureña, Lezama, Paz, and many others in Spanish America. The central concern of these writers was to distinguish what is specifically Spanish or Spanish American in their own literatures and to show how this specificity issues from a broader code, a culture that renders that difference intelligible. These ideas culminate in *Terra Nostra*, where they are subjected to a very severe test, and where they show, by "going beyond the author's intentions," the very complex fashion in which novelistic theory and practice are articulated using such presuppositions. If the very term "culture" is based on a metaphor of tilling the earth, *Terra Nostra*, from its title, announces its intention to provide the ground for a mutual understanding—a telluric communion, a common ground. *Terra Nostra* could perhaps be seen as the last gasp of the *novela de la tierra*, the latest rewriting of *Doña Bárbara*.

The relationship between *Terra Nostra* and these ideas is so strong that the novel comes with a sort of manual in which the theory about the "knowledge of men and epochs," and the instruments for its achievement, are revealed to the reader. I am referring, of course, to Fuentes's essay *Cervantes o la crítica de la lectura*, in which one reads, "In a certain way, the present essay is a branch of the novel that has occupied me for the past six years, *Terra Nostra*";[4] also, under the heading "Bibliografía conjunta" ("Joint Bibliography"), "In the measure in which the present essay and my novel *Terra Nostra* are born out of parallel impulses and obey common preoccupations, I indicate in what follows the twin bibliography of both works."[5]

It is not unusual, of course, for a novel to appear with one or several expository pieces by its author that "explain" its origin and execution. Among Latin American books, such is the relationship between Carpentier's *The Kingdom of this World* and *La música en Cuba*, and more recently between Severo Sarduy's *Cobra* and *Barroco*. In the case of Fuentes, there is a similar relationship between his essay *La nueva novela hispanoamericana* (1969) and several of his earlier novels. In a way, what I propose to do here, to pit the theory expounded in *Cervantes o la crítica de la lectura* against the practice of *Terra Nostra*, is analogous to my study of *The Kingdom of this World* and its relation to *La música en Cuba* and various other of Carpentier's essays. I intend therefore to pry apart that relationship to see how the impulse to intelligibility and knowledge present in the essay is thwarted in the fiction, how, against the explicit and implicit intentions of both the essay and the novel, the latter renders the link between cultural specificity and literature questionable. In the case of *Terra Nostra* this approach will also allow me to make some observations about the recent history of the Latin American novel.

And what do we find in that "joint bibliography" at the end of *Cervantes o la crítica de la lectura*? In addition to some recent theoreticians and critics such as Derrida, Foucault, and Cixous, and many others extremely familiar to the Hispanist such as Américo Castro, Valbuena Prat, and Stephen Gilman, one finds, of course, Cervantes, Fernando de Rojas, Juan Ruiz, and Quevedo, not to mention the Spanish editions of the *Summa contra gentiles* and the *Summa theologicae*. Needless to say, not all of these books and critics play the same rôle in both of Fuentes's books, and there are others, not included in the bibliography, that have a very prominent place in *Terra Nostra*, namely, several important novels by Latin American writers: *Explosion in a Cathedral, Hopscotch, Three Trapped Tigers, The Obscene Bird of Night, Manuel's Manual,* and *From Cuba with a Song*. It is evident, therefore, that *Terra Nostra* is an inquiry into the origins of the culture of Spain and Latin America, through an analysis of the literary myths created by them.

Such a study of culture through mythology has its most remote source in Plato, of course, though it was Vico who legitimized it in modern times. Fuentes's most recent source, however, is Spain's Generation of '98 and the *modernistas*. It is difficult to avoid the sensation, when reading *Terra Nostra* or *Cervantes o la crítica de la lectura,* that Fuentes is moved in these books by anxieties very similar to those found in *Vida de don Quijote y Sancho,* "El sepulcro de don Quijote," *Don Quijote, don Juan y la Celestina, Clásicos y modernos,* or *La corte de los milagros (Meditaciones del Quijote* also comes to mind, and Ortega's *Obras completas* appears in the joint bibliography). The figure who links these Spanish writers and Fuentes is Américo Castro, for whom there are three entries in the bibliography: *El pensamiento de Cervantes, España en su historia,* and *La realidad histórica de España.* Castro also serves to ground on a historical "reality" the Orientalist metaphoric penchant of the *modernistas,* who often cast Latin America and Spain in terms of the Orient. There is a clash in Fuentes's novel between the historical knowledge of the origins of culture pursued by the *noveintaiochistas* and the artificial image of Hispanic culture of the *modernistas.* This clash is, of course, within an ultimately homogeneous literary ideology that has enveloped modern literary production in Latin America since the middle of the nineteenth century, but that is beginning to give way now.[6]

It does not matter here that the books by Américo Castro exemplify three very different moments in the ideological evolution of the Spanish professor. Fuentes's link with Spanish intellectual history is determined first by the overall importance the relationship between Spain and Mexico has had in this century. The exile to Mexico of great Spanish intellectuals—many of whom had been disciples of Ortega and through him had delved into the thematics of the Generation of '98—is a most important chapter in the history of ideas in Mexico. One must add to this that Mexican intellectuals and artists have had a very tortured and anxious notion of the role Spain played in the origin of Mexican history. The "return" to Spain evident in both of Fuentes's books is clearly also a return to origins in search of identity, of a beginning that informs the present. The best-known interpretation of the paradoxical love-hate relationship with the mother country is Octavio Paz's *The Labyrinth of Solitude,* a book written under the influence and even the tutelage of the exiled Spanish intellectuals, and one that has had a lasting impact on Fuentes's work. In a sense *Terra Nostra* is still a reaction to Paz's 1950 book. If in *The Labyrinth of Solitude* Paz spoke of a schism at the core of the Mexican's soul, torn by scorn for a whorish mother (Malinche) and admiring hate for a violent father (Cortés), in *Terra Nostra* Fuentes attempts a reconciliation, a reconciliation that would include not only an acceptance of the liberal Spain whose tradition Paz already claimed, but also of the dark, violent, and retrograde Spain that most Latin Americans and Spaniards abhor.

The "joint bibliography" reveals, then, what every reader of *Terra Nostra* suspects: Fuentes's voluminous novel represents a considerable effort to achieve an absolute knowledge of Hispanic culture, a knowledge binding its two branches on both sides of the Atlantic. The novel, after all, centers on the moment that would be the beginning, in history, of its modern peculiarity: the sixteenth century, when America was conquered and Spain underwent telling historical upheavals. As one reads in *Cervantes o la crítica de la lectura*, "The three dates that make up the temporal references in the novel can also serve to establish the historical background of Cervantes and *Don Quijote*: 1492, 1521, 1598."[7] The dates correspond to historical events that are reenacted several times in the novel: discovery of America, defeat of the *comuneros*, death of Philip II. If the literary figures—Celestina, Don Quijote, Don Juan—serve as an access to knowledge of the culture in which they are engendered, the historical events and figures give the blueprint of the history out of which that culture unfolds. *Cervantes o la crítica de la lectura* builds the foundation for the construction of *Terra Nostra*, gives the bases of its intelligibility in the widest possible sense. Culture and history are a structure of knowledge, a key for the comprehension of everything that precedes the text and gives it meaning.

The ideological underpinning of Fuentes's construct on Hispanic culture and history is Américo Castro's theories on Spanish history. Fuentes's appropriation of Castro's views is somewhat more insouciant than Juan Goytisolo's.[8] Neither is it clear from *Cervantes o la crítica de la lectura* or from *Terra Nostra* whether Fuentes is aware that *El pensamiento de Cervantes* (written in the early twenties), which emphasizes Cervantes's debt to Italian humanism, and *España en su historia* (published in 1948 after Castro had proposed his theories on caste struggle) are hardly compatible. Nor are we sure whether he knows that there is a vast gulf between *España en su historia*, which stresses the Arabic component of Spanish culture, and its "rewriting," published in 1954 and retouched many times under the title *La realidad histórica de España*, which gives far more importance to the Jewish element. Be that as it may, Fuentes promotes the idea, derived from Castro, that Hispanic culture is fragmented, owing to the struggles between Jews, Moors, and Christians that resulted in the victory of the last group and the violent suppression of the first. Such fragmentation, which would have broken a previous harmonic fusion of Arabic eros, Jewish wisdom, and Catholic militant imperialism, is responsible for the contradictions, clashes, and contrasts that have characterized Spain and its American colonies since the sixteenth century. Although Américo Castro and his disciples have exhausted the possibilities of relating this fragmentation to the birth of modern Hispanic literature, usually appealing to an existentialist ideology,

Fuentes manages to supply a version in a new key.

The fragmentation is now rendered as the separation between words and things, which Foucault perceives as the transition from a medieval to a "classical" *epistemé* in *The Order of Things*. Given that Foucault begins his book by analyzing two Spanish works—*Don Quijote* and *Las meninas*—it is not difficult to see how Fuentes would be tempted to conclude that the fragmentation of codes in the modern world originates in Spain. But one can hardly agree with him, particularly because the ideological foundations of Castro and Foucault are so divergent, and because Foucault, though working with Hispanic works does not touch on any other peninsular examples to support his analyses.

We know, however, that Fuentes is really seeking a "literary" link to connect these theories. That link is none other than Lukács in the guise of Octavio Paz. At the beginning of section 2 of *Cervantes o la crítica de la lectura*, Fuentes alludes to Paz's *The Bow and the Lyre* to explain how the epic is the literature of a unified community, whose homogeneity is reflected in the lack of ambiguity of the epic text and of the epic hero, whereas the novel is the literature of a fragmented society, whose plurality and ambiguity are reflected in the novelistic text and hero. Anyone familiar with Lukács's *The Theory of the Novel* will recognize without much difficulty the source of these ideas. In *The Bow and the Lyre* Paz uses this view of the novel as a contrast to poetry, in which unification is sought through a plunging into the abyss of language and its promise of a return to a oneness of meaning.

In *Cervantes o la crítica de la lectura* Fuentes makes a similar use of Lukács, though now he has also brought in Américo Castro and Michel Foucault. A synthesis (or reduction) of the implicit argument of Fuentes's essay would run as follows: the caste struggle (Castro) resulted in a fracture, a separation between words and things (Foucault), which produced the modern novel (Cervantes), which is the product of fragmented societies (Lukács). But the plot does not end in such a catastrophe. If the novel reflects the fragmentation of Hispanic culture and history, Fuentes proposes a reconciliation analogous to the one he pursues between Latin America and Spain. The return to a basic set of figures and events is a demolition prior to a reconstruction that reader and writer will accomplish through a ritualistic exchange. Projecting onto Joyce a capability that he would wish for himself and that is similar to Cervantes's, Fuentes writes in his essay,

Joyce tells the reader: I offer you a *potlatch*, an excremental ownership of words, I melt down your bars of verbal gold, throw them in the sea and challenge you to make me a gift that is superior to mine, greater than the gift of loss, I challenge you to read mine/your/our words according to a new legality in the making, I challenge you to abandon your lazy, passive, linear reading to participate in the re-writing of all of your culture's codes, going all the way back to the lost code, to the reserve where savage words circulate, the words of the origin, the words of the beginning.[9]

Terra Nostra is, then, an effort to reach back to those original words found in a prediscursive logos that retains the keys to a homogeneous Hispanic culture, a reserve that is a common ground whence those keys have emanated throughout time and history. In spite of the "criticism of reading" that the essay appears to promote, *Terra Nostra* attempts to abolish all possible criticism through a return to the origins of language, a golden age where there is no mine or yours, a moment before dispersion that is an apotheosis of the legible. Such a plenitude of meaning would be the kind of knowledge that Carpentier and the Generation of '98 wished to attain, and also a reunification of *las dos Españas*, with Latin America included for good measure.

Reading is not an abstract issue in *Terra Nostra*, but a quite concrete problem that begins with the very size of the book and also includes a variety of modernist narrative techniques plus an avalanche of cultural allusions. There is no question of aesthetic pleasure, in the sense Carpentier spoke of, but of discipline; few works bite so much into the reader's real life. Of course, these problems of reading lead to more theoretical issues and hark back to the question of knowledge and culture, of intelligibility posed at the outset. In a brilliant article to which I am indebted, Lucille Kerr maintains that *Terra Nostra* is a book in which the quest for absolute knowledge is frustrated, in which the author, whose hypostasis is El Señor in the novel, succumbs before finding the key to the labyrinth that he himself has wrought, and with the solution of which he has been teasing the reader for the 783 pages of the text:

The thematic and structural paradoxes are still as dominant at the end as they were at other points in the novel. In and of themselves, these mysteries have a power over the reader; Fuentes' strategy is to increase their potential force by pretending to underscore their decipherability. The author manipulates us to make us believe in an ultimate truth that he, as author, pretends to possess. But in the end he refuses to reveal or invent it. In this way, Fuentes himself pretends not to desire or to be able to play that privileged role of the truthful voice, since the problems about which he writes in *Terra Nostra* are ultimately unanswerable in the extraliterary world as well.[10]

There is a great deal to be learned from Kerr's scrupulous analysis, and in the end I must agree with her that, in the text, power gives way before the impossibility of knowledge, and that, even when such power attempts to exert control by masquerading strategically as a weakness, many of the enigmas remain unsolved. I believe, however, that Kerr gives up too soon on the riddles of *Terra Nostra* and that the relentless cultural and historical allusions are more decipherable than she allows. A text is not the dialectical potential of paradox—a reservoir of mutually cancelling contradictions— but the rhetorical performance of contradiction. The moment of illegibility does arrive, in a manner not too dissimilar to Kerr's description, but first there is a very sustained display of knowledge and "readability." It is in that interval that the issue of culture and literature is played out, against the ideological background sketched in *Cervantes o la crítica de la lectura*. The metaphor of "mystery text" that Kerr applies to *Terra Nostra* is very appealing, but there is much more in the novel than the solution of a discrete enigma: *Terra Nostra* pursues a broad self-recognition and collective self-discovery that the many recognizable cultural and historical allusions make very clear.

No matter how great the apparent dispersion, *Terra Nostra* repeats, unifies, and reduces Spanish and Latin American history to a set of literary and historical figures, almost all of them from the 1492 to 1598 period. It is evident that the characteristics of El Señor come from various Spanish kings, but El Señor, even if in the future he is projected as Francisco Franco, is Philip II. The Chronicler is Cervantes, even if inescapably he may appear to be Carlos Fuentes in the future. The young woman with tatooed lips is Celestina, the multiplying, shipwrecked young man, the protagonist of Góngora's *Soledades*. Guzmán is Antonio Pérez, though perhaps also Guzmán de Alfarache. These figures, it is true, are multiplied, not by differentiation, but by repetition. The most spectacular case is the whole New World, which turns out to be the double of the Old: "Quetzalcoatl, Venus, Hesperia, Spain, identical stars, dawn and dusk, mysterious union, indecipherable enigma, but cipher for two bodies, two lands, cipher for a terrible encounter."[11]

On the level of these repetitions, the problem in *Terra Nostra* is not so much that of obscurity, but of a blinding clarity. From a thematic or ideological perspective the text displays concepts about Hispanic culture the sources of which we have already seen. Philip II incarnates authoritarianism and orthodoxy, which are but sublimations of a burning concupiscence. Don Quijote, Don Juan, Celestina, and the shipwrecked youth project various facets of the split matrix-figure of Philip; unshakeable faith that obliterates reality and covers it with a fiction, the uncontrollable desire that tricks and violates, the all-powerful sensuality that corrupts everything, the lack of identity that is supplemented with ornate language. At this level, time and space lose their differentiating power: to the West, the Escorial, a temple of death, becomes an Aztec pyramid, a temple of death; to the past, Philip becomes Tiberius Caesar; and to the future, Franco or Maximilian (and the Escorial, the Valle de los Caídos).

But are these figures truly the same? Has Fuentes hit upon founding myths, a reservoir, a "lost code," the "savage words," the "words of the beginning"? Has he not, rather, returned to what has always already been said? Is he not collating, instead, texts that scatter in his own the clutter of history? The clarity of the hieratic figures of the origin turns out to be instead the pollution of time and history, not original words, but the used words of the *modernistas*, the artificial words of the worldly. *Terra* stands not for virgin soil of the Garden, but for the earth of the trash heap of time: Fuentes's mystification in *Cervantes o la crítica de la lectura* about the possibility of going back to original words, to a prelapsarian common ground, is opposed by the novel's insistence on the proliferation of the particularizing details of history. History is like the bric-à-brac of *modernista* poetry, a decor without support, but veiling that absence. The text, like history, is a question of the unfolding of para*dox* into contra*diction*, and of the undissolvable residue of what is said, of the *dicta*. Against the mystification of myth the text offers the proliferation of history; against the clarity of repetition, the density of difference.

Terra Nostra suggests (inevitably) a way of domesticating, on the level of enunciation or performance, the issue of repetition and difference. Lucille Kerr has also noticed, with great insight, the importance of murder in all structures of power set up in the text. The assassination of the double is the violation that inaugurates temporality, history. As one annihilates the similar, repetition is broken, difference established, and temporal succession begun. The presence of death is really the ingredient needed to set in motion the potlatch, the give and take of time in the world. But of course, there is a paradigmatic story of Christ's sacrifice, and *Terra Nostra* not only includes it, but makes it a part of the most historically remote time-segment in the novel. It becomes another origin, set at the time of Tiberius Caesar, the first authority figure, the first dictator in *Terra Nostra*. Christ is like the Father, but submits himself to the unrepeatable individuality of time.

The irony that does not allow this act to become dogma in the novel is Tiberius's own murder, which is only the first of what will be many repetitions of the story of Christ. At the very moment when *Terra Nostra* is going to claim a clear beginning, the unrepeatable also glides into repetition, but a repetition that differentiates through deformation. Tiberius dies to reveal the thirst for knowledge and power implicit in Christ's sacrifice; knowledge is always a mask for power. It is not difficult to see here a clear correlation between the figure of Christ, the dictator, and the author himself. It is in this correlation above all that one detects, contrary to the generous exchange between writer and reader that Fuentes posits in *Cervantes o la crítica de la lectura*, contrary to his claim that a shared knowledge of culture will come from a shared rewriting, that his will is to exert authority and power over the reader.

It is therefore not in a feast that the Señor/Author circulates the codes containing knowledge, a shared knowledge that would become culture (Hispanic, Hispanic American), but in a polemic struggle with the reader, a struggle that is prefigured in the one between the dictator and his secretary, that renders the act of reading the book I have on my desk a mortal combat with Fuentes for its possession. Given that the master signs are unreachable and that knowledge prior to the use of language is not available, the Señor/Author uses the knowledge of history to control the reader. Culture thus becomes not the repository of pristine knowledge, but the conglomeration of the trivia of history. The Encyclopedic Señor, the Master of Bibliographies, the Master Scriptor encrypts in writing, preserving rather than sharing.

The very choice of dictators is revealing of this attitude. Philip II not only controlled the vast Spanish empire, but did so through writing. He was the King Bureaucrat, Secretary to Himself. Tiberius Caesar also ruled through writing, governing his Roman Empire, by correspondence. I have shown in "The Rhetoric of Dictatorship/The Dictatorship of Rhetoric" that in the modern dictator-novel in Latin America the figure of the dictator—the one who dictates, whose voice is an authority before writing—is demystified and replaced with that of the secretary, a subordinate who usurps power by being able to supplant truth and knowledge with simulacra. In *Terra Nostra* such power has not been relinquished; the subaltern god, the son, has not slain the father, but pretends to be both father and son to contain a knowledge of both history and the master codes from which it issues. The Dictator/Scriptor incarnates a duality that leaves out the reader. The book, this huge, baroque enclosure, is a retreat, an inner core, well-armored self, similar to the king's in *Ariel*. There is in this egotistical suppression of the other a *performed* insight into Hispanic culture that in some ways confirms the worst premonitions of Unamuno, Baroja, and Valle Inclán about the Spanish and, by extension, about the Spanish American man.[12] We see, then, in this real contact between reader and book an insight into people and epochs that validates indirectly Carpentier's assertion about the rôle of the novel as a form of knowledge.

The Latin title of *Terra Nostra* contains, in a curious way, an emblem of the sort of contradiction that I have examined here: a hoarding, a preservation of knowledge encrypted in a writing that is not to be shared, but that is used to exert power over the reader. It is obvious that by writing the title in Latin Fuentes is "naming" the origin-oriented thematics of his novel, that origin in which, presumably, writer and reader will share common words, unpolluted by time. But Latin is not a shared language; it is an abstract, unspoken code, the chiseled letters on monuments, not the language of exchange. Our common code—Spanish—has dissolved the cryptic atemporality of Latin by splitting its pristine vowels, by diphthongizing the accented long *e* and *o* into *ie* and *ue*. *Terra Nostra* would be *Tierra Nuestra*, extending the vowels, giving them time and differentiating them phonetically and graphically. Like the Dictator/Scriptor, who monstrously wishes to contain both the voice of authority and the inscribing, disseminating power of writing, *Terra Nostra's* title pretends to be a shared language in which there is no time, no difference, no exchange. The encyclopedic knowledge—because of its vastness and its hasty, pell-mell origin—of the figure of the author therein obtained is that of a resentful, narcissistic, and solemn possessor of truth. Once these mechanisms in the novel are unveiled, we become aware that *Terra Nostra* wishes to pass its ideological bulk as truth, that, though its mystifications are more insightful than its ideology, the latter is part and parcel of the very structure of the novel, of the very attitude that the text assumes before the reader.

There is another possible reading of *Terra Nostra* that undermines the one I have just performed, and through which the novel is linked, less obliquely, to the *modernista* version of Hispanic culture, rather than to the Generation of '98. Here the source of Fuentes's experiment is to be found in a Borges story, "The Garden of Forking Paths," even if that source is disguised as Giulio Camillo's "Theater of Memory."[13] The key both to Camillo's work and to the novel mentioned in Borges's story is the same: simultaneity, complementarity. Fuentes's novel attempts the same by giving various, mutually exclusive solutions to several episodes. In "The Garden of Forking Paths" Yu Tsun relates the discovery that the British sinologist Stephen Albert has made in reference to the novel written by his ancestor Ts'ui Pên: "In all fiction, when a man is faced with alternatives he chooses one at the expense of the others. In the almost unfathomable Ts'ui Pên, he chooses—simultaneously—all of them. He thus *creates* various futures, various times that start others that will in their turn branch out and bifurcate in other times. This is the cause of the contradictions in the novel."[14]

A series of violent deaths is related to the labyrinthine novel of Ts'ui Pên: he is killed by an unknown assassin; Stephen Albert is killed by Yu Tsun to transmit a message thereby; and Yu Tsun writes on the verge of execution for his crime. The seriousness of the matter, one might say, led Borges merely to sketch the plan for the novel and its impossible nature rather than actually to write such a book. Be that as it may, it is important to note that Borges has chosen as his novelist the representative of a millenary culture, one whose collective self-recognition we would expect to be easier. Yet every act of communication of knowledge is thwarted and leads to death. Yu Tsun "writes" by means of Albert's death and thereby condemns himself to death.

The close correlation between knowledge, writing, death, and the novel in Borges's story forecloses the kind of rewriting of the codes of culture that Fuentes proposes in *Cervantes o la crítica de la lectura* and attempts to carry out in *Terra Nostra*. Writing is the accumulated residue of all those codes gathered on the verge of death, both the total absence of knowledge and absolute knowledge. The presence of Orientals, but more so of the

Orientalist Stephen Albert, links the story to *modernismo* and its image of history and culture as museum.[15] In the museum, the Tinkerer, like the writer, rearranges objects that bespeak death, not the origin. Borges's story is the most powerful link in Latin American literary history between *modernismo* and postmodern fiction, not because of its eccentric theory of the novel, but because it offers this image of the writer.

Terra Nostra's end, which, chronologically, is also the beginning, contains such a caveat, rendering the intervening seven hundred pages a disclaimed foundation. At the end, which occurs in 1999, in Paris, there is a game of cards being played by a group of characters drawn from recent Latin American fiction: Oliveira (*Hopscotch*), Cuba Venegas (*Three Trapped Tigers*), Humberto Peñalosa *(The Obscene Bird of Night)*, and others, including Pierre Ménard. The cards being used are topics of Latin American history and literature: dictatorships, police goon-squads, prisons. " 'Full house! shouted Buendía. 'Masferrer's Tigres, Duvalier's Tonton Macoutes, and the Brazilian DOPs, plus an Odría and a Pinochet.' 'That's shit, you're wiped out, you and your momma and your papa.' Oliveira crowed triumphantly, spreading his four Prisons on the card table: the cisterns of the Fort of San Juan de Ulúa, Dawson's Island, the cold plain of Trelew, and the Sexto in Lima. . . . O.K., top that.' "[16]

This game is being played on the verge of Apocalypse and parodies the gathering of various tellers in Boccaccio's *Decameron*, who have, however, fled the city to save themselves from the plague. The nature of the "cards" and of the "players" themselves, plus the fact that the game is being played while the world is on the brink of extinction, is a comment on literature, its relation to history and to a knowledge of the artificiality of writing that is not too far from that of Borges's story. In mobilizing so many literary figures, from Celestina to Yu Tsun, from Doña Inés to Cuba Venegas, *Terra Nostra* demonstrates that the language that unites us, the *tierra nuestra*, is not the words submerged in a logos before language, but the already uttered words that are circulated in works like *Don Quijote, Vida de Don Quijote y Sancho*, and "Pierre Ménard, autor del *Quijote.*"

Terra Nostra ends where the most radical new Latin American fiction begins, calling attention to a curious phenomenon in the history of the Latin American novel: the established novelists who rose to fame during the Boom have become the epigones of a younger group whose most important figures are Severo Sarduy and Manuel Puig. Fuentes in *Terra Nostra*, Mario Vargas Llosa in *Captain Pantoja and the Special Service* and *Aunt Julia and the Scriptwriter*, Juan Goytisolo in *Count Julian*, have all abandoned the novel of cultural knowledge in favor of fictions in the vein of Sarduy and Puig in which indeterminancy in all realms and the "universalizing" force of popular culture demystify literature's claim to a deep insight into Hispanic culture through a fusion with myth, language before writing, or any sort of primitivistic ideal. *Betrayed by Rita Hayworth*, and particularly *From Cuba with a Song*, had already undermined to such a degree projects like *Terra Nostra*, or even recycling and renewing gestures like *Count Julian* or *Captain Pantoja* that there is a certain pathos in the end/beginning of Fuentes's book.

5. *Los reyes*: Cortázar's Mythology of Writing

Although I refer to *Los reyes* in my title, I do not intend to carry out an independent literary analysis of what no doubt is a callow work. My design, at once broad and reductive, is to deal with the somewhat dated and embarrassing problem of how to read an author, not a book.[1] Is "holistic" criticism viable? Is it possible, in other words, to read Cortázar instead of engaging in a series of isolated exegeses of his works? And if it is worth attempting such a reading, how does one avoid turning it into a thematic gloss, a formalistic reduction or a biographical narrative? How, other than as a rhetorical license, can we continue to use Cortázar's name in reference to what is already a vast and diverse body of writing, encompassing texts belonging not only to various genres but also to criticism and theory? And what can one make of a text as bizarre as *Los reyes*? In what way is it also Cortázar's?

These questions do not arise from an abstract, speculative whim, but from Cortázar's work itself. They are, as I hope to argue here, the fundamental questions posed by Cortázar's texts, and not only by such obviously autobiographical books as *La vuelta al día en ochenta mundos, Ultimo round,* and *Fantomas contra los vampiros multinacionales.* I intend to use *Los reyes* to sketch a primal scene, to delineate what might very broadly be called Cortázar's conception of writing—conception, that is, both in its etymological sense of insemination or generation, and in its more common meaning of notion or idea. By determining Cortázar's conception of writing in both these senses, I hope to legitimize a critical discourse that will atone for its reductiveness by providing a critical insight into the totality of a literary enterprise.

While discussing a problem similar to the one just sketched, Roland Barthes remarks,

There is no doubt that the "civilized" work cannot be dealt with as myth, in the ethnological sense of the term. But the difference [between the "civilized" work and that of the "primitive"] has less to do with the signature of the message than with its substance. Our works are written; that imposes upon them certain constraints of meaning that the oral myth could not know. It is a mythology of writing that awaits us, that shall have as its object not certain determined works, that is to say, works inscribed in a process of determination where a person (the author) would be the origin, but works *traversed* by the great mythic writing in which humanity tries out its significations, i.e., its desires.[2]

As often happens in discussions of myth, whether those myths be "civilized" or not, Barthes's own formulation has become part of the myth that it attempts to uncover. For, if there is a modern mythology of writing, it centers on the question of authorship versus general determination—a question, in other words, of the origin or generation of writing. That "great mythic writing" of which Barthes speaks has as its object the disappearance of the author, or, in more current critical idiom, the abolition of the subject; it is a search for meaning in a universe abandoned by both man and the gods.

Although current and certainly modern, the abolition of the author is not new. In *The Dehumanization of Art*, synthesizing a whole current of modern thinking, Ortega said that "the poet begins where man ends," and added, referring to Mallarmé, that the fate of the "poor face of the man who officiates as poet" is to "disappear, to vanish and become a pure nameless voice breathing into the air the words—those true protagonists of the lyrical pursuit. This pure and nameless voice, the mere acoustic carrier of the verse, is the voice of the poet who has learned to extricate himself from the surrounding man."[3]

The work of philologists and mythographers during the nineteenth century (the Grimm brothers, later Bédier and Menéndez Pidal) brought to the fore the question of authorship. As Foucault has shown, once representation as a synchronic, complete system mediating between the subject and the world is shattered, the various languages of literary expression, as well as the question of being, become historical—language and being become a matter of depth.[4] Philology seeks the origin of language, just as ontology seeks the origin of being in man's passions (Rousseau). The urgency of this question of origins, in its double thrust—language, being—determines that most salient characteristic of modern writing, self-referentiality. By alluding to itself and by probing into its own mode of being, modern writing is always in the process of offering an implicit statement about its own generation, a conception of its conception, as it were.

It would be a naïve and predictable undertaking to show that self-referentiality occurs in Cortázar, since *Hopscotch* has already become a classic of self-referential writing. But it is precisely in self-referentiality that the mythology that I intend to isolate manifests itself. As Jean Hyppolite has shown in his study of Hegel, self-reflexiveness is a regressive movement, a circular journey back to the source.[5] In literature self-referentiality is a return to origins in order to take away from conception its claim of originality, of constituting a single, fresh moment of beginning, an ordering principle and principium. Rather than the joyful game that it is often taken to be, self-referentiality is a deadly game in Cortázar, a violent ritual in which Cortázar is at stake. *Los reyes*, the first book signed with his own name (an earlier work had appeared under a pseudonym), presents, under the guise of the Theseus myth, this ritual. By reenacting this ritual, Cortázar's writing labors to define itself, to cope with the opposition of the individual/original versus the general/collective, in short, the issue of generation. Who writes?

The most superficial consideration of *Los reyes* immediately leads to the issue of individuality and origin. The very appeal to classical mythology, to the dawn of Western literary tradition, is suggestive of a concern about the beginning of writing. The recourse to classical mythology is in itself hardly original, but rather a characteristic of the modern tradition: Nietzsche, Freud, Joyce, Pound, Unamuno, all take recourse to classical figures. In Latin America there is a strain of classicism of this sort that runs from Lugones and Borges through Reyes, Carpentier, and Paz. It is not a neoclassical spirit that leads these modern writers to the classical tradition, since they do not imitate classical models, but instead (particularly in Nietzsche and Freud) a philological quest for a mythology of origins. A perfect example of this would be Carpentier's story "Like the Night," which begins and ends with an episode drawn from the *Iliad*, a double thrust away from and back to the origin of Western literary tradition. There is throughout Cortázar's work a recurrence of classical motifs and figures that answers to this general philological trend.

All myths, as we know, appear in many versions, but if one reads the most complete account of the Theseus myth, that of Plutarch, one is struck by the confusing number of contradictory accounts extant of this particular story. The charm, in fact, of Plutarch's rendition is his juggling of so many different versions in one and the same text, versions that cancel each other and blur or abolish altogether the possibility of a master version. To read Plutarch is to realize that the myth, although organized around a certain implied narrative core, is not a fixed text but a set of superimposed narratives. Thus we already have in the myth chosen by Cortázar the outlines of the question of conception: although set at the dawn of Western tradition, which classical mythology represents, the myth cannot claim originality in the sense of constituting a single source.

If the versions of the myth of Theseus offer, simultaneously, the promise of uniqueness and multiplicity, of singularity and plurality, so do the many readings of which the particular incident of the Minotaur has been the object. Theseus's slaying of the Minotaur and his escape from the labyrinth have often been interpreted as the victory of reason over ignorance, so much so that to some the myth is a parable of the Greeks' founding of Western thought after conquering superstition. According to this reading, the

Theseus myth would mark the birth of reason. Moralistic interpretations also abound in the form of allegories, particularly in the Middle Ages. A creature half bull and half man is the image of humanity driven by its lower instincts, imprisoned in the materiality of its senses, unable to exercise its spiritual and intellectual powers. Dante's inversion of the figure, making the lower half of the Minotaur the animal, points to such a moralistic interpretation.[6] Theseus's victory would in this case be a moral one, the triumph of the higher faculties of humanity over its lower instincts. The victory would thus mark the birth of morals. A political reading is also possible and common. Theseus's victory over Minos is the triumph of political principle over arbitrary rule, of Athens over Crete, the defeat of the old order and the coming of the new. The very abstractness of these readings underscores again the question of singularity, of individuation: Theseus's victory is that of reason, of higher instincts, of political principle. The specificity of the text vanishes as we glide into allegorical abstraction and accept the plurality of potential readings that the myth contains.

The same problematics appear when it becomes evident that Theseus's slaying of the Minotaur displays a series of elements that relates the episode to other myths. The confrontation of Theseus and Minos is the well-known struggle between the old king and the prince. Theseus's journey into the labyrinth, the regressive voyage in search of origins, the slaying of the Minotaur (who is, after all, also a young prince), the hero's struggle to assert his individuality—all of these elements link the myth to other myths of generation, such as the Oedipus myth. It might be remembered here that Theseus not only defeats Minos, but also, though inadvertently, like Oedipus, kills his own father, Aegeus, by forgetting to change the sails. Moreover, as in the cases of Oedipus and the Minotaur, Theseus's origins are clouded by mystery: it is not clear whether he is the son of Poseidon or the son of Aegeus. His journey to the center of the labyrinth, like his earlier journey to Athens, is a journey back to the source to establish (or reestablish) his own beginning. As soon as we insert the Theseus story into a general mythology, it begins to lose its specificity; its own origins begin to recede into infinity or to dissolve and multiply as if in a gallery of mirrors. The thematics of genealogy that pervade the readings of the myth—it represents the birth of reason, of morals, of political principle—perhaps reflect this dialectic that subtends its structure.

What we find in *Los reyes* is, then, necessarily not a version but a subversion of the myth of Theseus. To begin with, as Cortázar himself has emphasized on many occasions, his Ariadne gives Theseus the clue only in order to free the Minotaur, once the monster has killed the hero. As Alfred MacAdam perceptively notes, *Los reyes* contains a "double tragedy."[7] Instead of triumph, Cortázar's version offers a mutual defeat: Theseus's quest leads not to heroic distinction, but to indifferentiation. The Minotaur, which would represent such indifferentiation and thus be the victor, is dead. Theseus's pursuit of individuation is thwarted from the start: he constantly recognizes himself in others, not only in the Minotaur, but also in Minos. What is emphasized in Cortázar's version is the violence that Theseus commits against himself in defeating Minos and killing the Minotaur. Instead of the erection of individual presence, Theseus's regressive voyage creates a vacuum at the center; the Minotaur is dead; Theseus has fled.

The clash, the violence of conception suggested by the erotic act of *contra naturam* by which the Minotaur was conceived, is repeated at the end of Theseus's journey. The blood of Pasiphae has been spilled again. Whereas previously the "lord of games" (the Minotaur) inhabited the labyrinth,[8] it now stands as an empty gallery of winding walls. Theseus's victory has led to that other labyrinth suggested by Borges: the labyrinth of total indifferentiation, the desert, the white page. The I, the you, and the we float in a space without perspectives and dimensions, as interchangeable masks of primeval chaos and apocalypse.

This confrontation of the monster and the hero constitutes the primal scene in Cortázar's mythology of writing: a hegemonic struggle for the center, which resolves itself in a mutual cancellation and in the superimposition of beginnings and ends. The very image of man unborn, the Minotaur, is the possessor of the immediate but naïve knowledge of man before the Fall. His speech is the incoherent, symbolic language of a savage god. Theseus, on the other hand, not only is a dealer in death, but is the very image of death. His linear, cogent language is temporal, discursive—it is discourse. In his enclosure the Minotaur speaks a perishable language, which is not temporal but which is reinvented every day. The words he utters are, even if momentarily, attached to the things they represent:

Oh, his pained monologues, which the palace guards heard in wonder, without understanding them. His profound recitals of the recurring waves, his taste for celestial nomenclatures and the catalogues of herbs. He ate them pensively, and then gave them names with secret delight, as if the flavor of stems had revealed their names to him. . . . He raised the whole enumeration of celestial bodies, and seemed to forget it with the dawn of a new day, as if also in his memory dusk dimmed the stars. And the next night he took delight in inaugurating a new nomenclature, ordering sonorous space with ephemeral constellations.[9]

If in other versions of the myth the birth of reason, morals, or politics is at stake, what we have in *Los reyes* is the violent birth of writing. The catalogue of herbs that the Minotaur "tastes" is a series of disconnected words, without syntactical and therefore temporal, structure, linked to their individual origin through their "stems." By killing the Minotaur, Theseus attempts to replace the perishable sound of individual words with the linear, durable cogency of discourse, a cogency predicated not on the stems of words but on their declensions, on the particles that link them in a structure whose mode of representation would not be sonorous but spatial—writing. The irony, of course, is that once writing is instituted, Theseus does not gain control of the labyrinth but becomes superfluous and flees. Because writing cannot be dimmed, like the stars, with each dawn, because it is not a memory whose traces can be erased, Theseus is not needed to reinvent it, as the Minotaur reinvented his nomenclatures every day. Writing is the empty labyrinth from which both the Minotaur and Theseus have been banished, the same textual labyrinth left by both Supremo and Patiño in *Yo el Supremo*, the enclosure-crypt of both the king in *Ariel* and the author in *Terra Nostra*.

This primal scene appears with remarkable consistency in Cortázar's writing. I do not mean simply that there are monsters, labyrinths, and heroes, but rather, that the scene in which a monster and a hero kill each other, cancel each other's claim to the center of the labyrinth, occurs with great frequency, particularly in texts where the nature of writing seems to be more obviously in question. The most superficial consideration of Cortázar's first novel, *The Winners*, would no doubt reveal the existence of the primal scene, but I would like to examine two briefer texts, "All Fires the Fire" and "The Pursuer."

The title of "All Fires the Fire" is drawn from Heraclitus and suggests the indifferentiation obtained when all things return to their primal state, and ends and beginnings resolve into one.[10] The story is in fact two stories that reflect each other, that are told simultaneously. One is a lover's triangle in, presumably, contemporary Paris and told for the most part through a telephone conversation. The other also involves a lover's triangle of sorts: it is the story of a gladiator whom a Roman consul (jealous of his wife's interest in the gladiator) makes fight a gigantic black slave.

In the first story (I use "first" here for the sake of clarity, but there is no hierarchy of this kind in the text) Sonia calls Roland to plead with him and to announce that Irene is on her way to his apartment. Their conversation is made difficult by a bad connection. A mysterious voice in the background keeps reading a series of figures—is it a gambler? These figures, in their stark meaninglessness, are remindful of the Minotaur's "celestial nomenclatures." They oppose the flow of speech, the discursiveness that Roland wants to achieve. The dark depths from which the sounds in the telephone line seem to emerge also evoke the labyrinth and Ariadne's clew. Roland's cool and logical entreaties aimed at Sonia, who finally commits suicide, are Theseus-like in their reasoned discursiveness. There is, furthermore, (although very obliquely suggested) a potential "monstrosity" in Sonia, whose interest in Irene seems to be as strong as her interest in Roland.

In the other strand of the story the primal scene is present in much more obvious fashion. The hero-monster confrontation is clear, and there is, moreover, an echo of one of the versions of the Theseus myth offered by Plutarch in which the Minotaur, instead of being a monstrous creature, is a powerful and hateful man named Taurus, whom Theseus defeats in combat at the Cretan games.[11] Although, naturally, some of the details are different in Cortázar's story, the basic situation is essentially the same. The young gladiator has risen from the ranks because of his heroic deeds to become known as an individual, and by competing for the affections of the consul's wife he has also become a potential usurper.

There are other, more direct echoes of the primal scene in the text of the story. When the black giant enters the arena, he does so through the gallery the beasts use, and the description of the gate through which he passes evokes the act of birth: "They have raised the creaking gates of the dark passages where they have wild animals come out, and Marcus sees the gigantic figure of the Nubian retiarius appear, until then invisible against the background of mossy stone."[12] The labyrinth is evoked in the description of the arena, where it appears sketched on the sand as a trace, "the enormous bronze eyes where hoes and palm leaves have sketched their curved paths darkened by traces of preceding fights." It is, of course, at the center of that maze that Marcus and the Nubian retiarius stage their combat.

As in *Los reyes*, there is no victory at the end of "All Fires the Fire," but rather a mutual annihilation. The fight between the Nubian retiarius and the gladiator is resolved when both fall dead on each other in the sand. The mutual killing and the sand, which suggests the desert, prefigure the fire that kills everyone at the end, the fire that destroys the arena and also levels the apartment building where, centuries later, Roland and Irene have fallen asleep on each other, like the dead gladiators, after making love. The stories merge at the end, not only on the level of the action but also at a conceptual level: love and war, presumably opposites, mingle to evoke the topic of the *ars amandi, ars bellandi*. Like the gladiators and the lovers, the two stories have a common end, which abolishes their difference and returns the text to the indifferentiation of origins—all texts the text.

In "The Pursuer" the various elements of this mythology are even more directly related to writing. The story tells of the last months in the life of jazz saxophonist Johnny Carter, as reported by Bruno, a writer who had published a biography of the musician. It is rather easy to discern in the story the general outline of the primal scene. Bruno's visit to Johnny as the story opens is reminiscent of Theseus's journey into the labyrinth. The jazzman lives in a small, dark, walk-up apartment, a sort of lair, and he is described in animal terms: "But he's making gestures, laughing and coughing at the same time, shivering away under the blanket like a chimpanzee."[13] Johnny is also described as a huge fetus or newborn monster, naked and coiled onto himself and making inarticulate sounds: "And I saw Johnny had thrown off the blanket around him in one motion, and I saw him sitting in the easy chair completely nude, his legs pulled up and the knees underneath his chin, shivering but laughing to himself" (p. 184).

Whereas Johnny appears as a monstrous fetus, Bruno, the writer, stands for order and profit. Bruno wants to "regenerate" Johnny, to make him abandon his intuitive cavils about time, his drugs, and his visions. But Bruno's apparent good intentions conceal his desire to kill Johnny, to reduce him to that image that Bruno's book has created. Johnny's death at the end of the story appears to take place in order to round out the book:

All this [Johnny's death] happened at the same time that the second edition of my book was published, but luckily I had time to incorporate an obituary note edited under full steam and inserted, along with a newsphoto of the funeral in which many famous jazzmen were identifiable. In that format the biography remained, so to speak, intact and finished. Perhaps it's not right that I say this, but naturally I was speaking from a merely aesthetic point of view. They're already talking of a new translation, into Swedish or Norwegian, I think. My wife is delighted at the news. (p. 220)

The last two sentences, the conclusion of the story, indicate the measure to which Johnny's death also signals Bruno's defeat. The allusion to the translations, and particularly the vagueness of the allusion, shows to what extent the text has already been taken away from Bruno—how, in a sense, he is out of the picture. The laconic last sentence, in its homely triviality, reinforces this notion by showing how the pleasure generated by these new versions of the biography is deflected away from Bruno. Like the labyrinth, the text is empty at the end. The book has become a funeral monument, a tomb.

But in a sense it is the whole story that reveals Bruno's defeat. In spite of his naïve assertion that his book is "intact and finished," "The Pursuer" is a postscript or supplement to that earlier book, and, more than the story of Johnny, it is the story of Bruno's futile attempts to commit Johnny to writing. Bruno's writing of "The Pursuer," his return to the book that he had already written, is like Theseus's journey into the labyrinth, the very image of self-reflexiveness. The pursuer is Bruno, not Johnny, who, on the contrary, is the epitome of hieratic immobility. Johnny lives unreflexively, a sort of inarticulate monster who is more on the side of things than of words— his means of expression, the saxophone, is not verbal. The rivalry between Johnny and Bruno is apparent from the beginning in their playful banter, in which the musician mocks the writer's practical sense. Bruno himself is aware that his relation to Johnny is an exploitative one, that he and all the others who hover around him are "a bunch of egotists": "Under the pretext of watching out for Johnny what we're doing is protecting our idea of him, getting ourselves ready for the pleasure Johnny's going to give us, to reflect the brilliance from the statue we've erected among us all and defend it till the last gasp" (p. 182). Johnny's retaliation is to tell Bruno that his book has missed the point, that the real Johnny is absent from it: " 'Don't get upset, Bruno, it's not important that you forgot to put all that in. But Bruno,' and he lifts a finger that does not shake, 'what you forgot to put in is me' " (p. 212). Bruno winds up writing about himself, subjecting himself to the same operation to which he submits Johnny. The text of the story is in the end Bruno's pursuit of himself, a pursuit that turns into a flight—the vanishing of infinitely receding sequences. "The Pursuer" is a postscript to Bruno's biography of Johnny, but it is also a postscript to the story it tells, a postscript that can only be a prologue to a further story.

As in the previous texts I have analyzed, the hero's regressive quest leads not to individuation and difference, but to a notion of indifferentiation: empty labyrinth, desert, fire, the infinite, where ends and beginnings merge and dissolve. One of Bruno's reflections brings out, in a metonymical play, this dialectic of ends and beginnings:

It drags me to think that he's at the beginning of his sax-work, and I'm going along and have to stick it out to the end. He's the mouth and I'm the ear, so as not to say he's the mouth and I'm the . . . Every critic, yeah, is the sad-assed end of something that starts as taste, like the pleasure of biting into something and chewing on it. And the mouth of Johnny moves again, relishing it, Johnny's big tongue sucks back a little string of saliva from the lips. (p. 167)

We shall have to look at this passage in the original, not only because the translator, Paul Blackburn, got carried away and became too explicit, but because there is in it an anagrammatic clue that is important to note:

Pienso melancólicamente que él está al principio de su saxo mientras yo vivo obligado a conformarme con el final. El es la boca y yo la oreja, por no decir que él es la boca y yo . . . Todo crítico, ay, es el triste final de algo que empezó como sabor, como delicia de morder y mascar. Y la boca se mueve otra vez, golosamente la gran lengua de Johnny recoge un chorrito de saliva de los labios.[14]

There is a complex and compelling metonymical and anagrammatic network here that leads to the notion of the mutual cancellation of Johnny and Bruno. If Johnny is the mouth and Bruno the ear, or the anus, they both stand for absences, holes. What remains between them is the saxophone, a curved gallery of air, or, to continue the physiological metaphor, the labyrinthine digestive track (or the Eustachian tube).

This imagery of absence is the same as that in Octavio Paz's poem "La boca habla," incorporated by Severo Sarduy into *Cobra*:

La cobra
habla de la obra

en la boca del abra
recobra
el habla:
El Vocablo.[15]

It is an imagery of absence conveyed by the repetition of the *o*'s, a figure of the hole, as in "El es la boca y yo la oreja, por no decir que él es la boca y yo ..." It was not reticence that kept the obvious word out, since it is more conspicuous in its absence, but the desire both to create a gap at the end of the sentence and to stop on "*yo.*" That "*yo*" is already, by its very orthography, the hole, the void, the last letter of Bruno's name, but also the beginning of Johnny's—"Jo." In fact, by taking the beginning of Johnny's name and the end of Bruno's, by practicing with their names the operation that the sentence suggests, we have "*yo no.*" Ends and beginnings merge, and the result is a negation, a canceling out.

Cortázar plays this philological game more often than has been suspected to undermine the notion of individuality. A clear instance of this, but on another level, is Francine in *Manuel's Manual*. She so obviously stands for France and French values that she becomes an ironic abstraction. Not as obvious, though here the literary device is much more traditional, is Andrés, the protagonist of that same novel. His name means, of course, Everyman. One might further note in this connection that the *o* plays a key role in the names of many of Cortázar's characters: Nora, Wong, Oliveira, Toland, Romero, Roberto. That *o*, or zero, is the grapheme that designates an absence, a dissolution of individuality, a sphere demarcating nothingness. In chapter 148 of *Hopscotch* Cortázar quotes one of Aulus Gellius's etymologies in which it is suggested that the origin of the word *person* is related to that *o*, which occupies its center:

A wise and ingenious explanation, by my lights, that of Gabio Basso, in his treatise *On the Origin of Words*, of the word *person*, mask. He thinks that this word has its origin in the verb *personare*, to retain. This is how he explains his opinion: "Since the mask covers the face completely except for an opening where the mouth is, the voice, instead of scattering in all directions, narrows down to escape through one single opening and therefore acquires a stronger and more penetrating sound. Thus, since the mask makes the human voice more sonorous and firm, it has been given the name *person*, and as a consequence of the formation of this word, the letter *o* as it appears in it is long."[16]

The suggestion that the voice would then be the distinguishing mark is clear; but the voice is no mark at all. In the case of Johnny, where the voice is made firmer and more sonorous by his musical instrument, we would find the mark in the saxophone, not in him.

If "*yo no*" is the cryptic message of Cortázar's mythology of writing, what then of our initial question about how to read an author? And if conception denies the possibility of conception, if a cogent and distinguishing theory of literature appears to be foreclosed by the ultimately negative gesture of self-referentiality, how is Cortázar's literary production held together? What can we *retain* as the distinguishable mark of his work?

It is not by accident that Cortázar's mythology of writing, as I have represented it here, should bear a Nietzschean imprint, since it is a Nietzschean problematic that seems to generate it. "Who writes?" is an essentially Nietzschean question. The struggle between the Minotaur and Theseus is analogous to that between Dionysus and Apollo in *The Birth of Tragedy*. In "The Pursuer" this Nietzschean quality is particularly evident. Johnny, whose musical instrument is a direct descendant of the Dionysian *aulos*, exists as if in harmony with the vast forces of the universe—with truth and actuality—and suffers as well as experiences joy for it. Bruno, on the other hand, the Apollonian seeker of light, deals in illusions; his aim is to domesticate Johnny's savage wisdom. The birth of tragedy, according to Nietzsche, is generated by the confrontation of these two figures. The birth of tragedy signaled the victory of Dionysus over Apollo, for tragedy could emerge when the god of reason spoke the language of the god of music.

In Nietzsche there remains a vestigial theodicy that confers meaning to the death of the hero. It would be reassuring to be able to say the same about Cortázar. But the analogy between the birth of tragedy and Cortázar's version of the birth of writing can only be carried so far, and beyond that point is where Cortázar emerges. Nietzsche, still the philologist in this early work, traces a curve that represents the birth of tragedy and its gradual decline, a decline provoked by the counteroffensive of Apollonian powers. Not so in Cortázar, where, as we have seen, each confrontation leads to a mutual cancellation, each conception carries with it its concomitant death. Writing in Cortázar must be born anew in each text; the whole of writing must emerge with each word, only to disappear again—not an eternal return, but a convulsive repetition of construction and deconstruction. A formal reflection of this might be found not only in the heterogeneity of Cortázar's longer texts, but also in their reliance on dialogue.[17]

Cortázar emerges, then, at the point of the cancellation, of the negation. He must therefore be read whole, establishing no generic distinctions nor privileging either the fictional or the expository texts. Each text must be read as if it were the totality of his production, given that each begins and ends in a question so fundamental as not to be transferable from one to the other. Rather, each must be repeated in each text and in each reading—a kind of spasmodic eschatology. Only the double thrust of the question can be retained. Holistic criticism is not a process of accumulation whereby details are gathered and stored to construct with them the image of an author, but instead one in which the impossibility of assembling the fragments in a coherent whole can provide a glimpse of totality.

There is an ultimate meaning to Cortázar's mythology of writing that belies its negativity, a meaning that is performative rather than conceptual. What Theseus's self-reflexive quest shows is that literature, in the long run, cannot say anything about itself. The countermodernist position that decries literature's purity, its refusal to signify something other than itself, fails to recognize that, on the contrary, literature is always having to signify something else, and to implicate someone else. And indeed here we are reading, talking, writing about Cortázar, or better yet, reading, talking, writing Cortázar. Minotaur, Theseus, Johnny, Bruno—we as readers also drift into our own textual journeys, to turn reading once more into the ritual confrontation where you and I and we share for one moment, in each other, the illusion of meaning.

6. *Biografía de un cimarrón* and the Novel of the Cuban Revolution

"Hay cosas que yo no me explico de la vida. Todo eso que tiene que ver con la naturaleza para mí está muy oscuro, y lo de los dioses más. Ellos son los llamados a originar todos esos fenómenos que uno ve, que yo vide y que es positivo que han existido. Los dioses son caprichosos e inconformes. Por eso aquí han pasado tantas cosas raras." These are the opening lines of Miguel Barnet's *Biografía de un cimarrón*, confusedly, yet significantly, translated as *The Autobiography of a Runaway Slave.*[1] But who speaks here, the old runaway slave or the young Cuban anthropologist? Is the book a biography, as the original title proclaims, an autobiography, as the English title reads, or a documentary novel, as it is generally classified? I hope to show in what follows the pertinence of these questions with regard to Cuban literature by analyzing the documentary novel, one of the most popular forms of narrative to emerge in Cuba since the triumph of the Revolution. I also hope to show through such an analysis, which will focus mainly on Barnet's book, the role that Cuban literature of the Revolution plays today in the context of Latin American literature.

As is well known, the questions posed above are fundamental ones in anthropology. They are the questions that Claude Lévi-Strauss asks throughout *Tristes tropiques*, and they address fundamental concerns in the social sciences: How can I ever know the other, yet remain myself?[2]

In the literary realm the problem is quite similar: How can I reveal the other in my writing without turning that other into literature and thereby falsifying him or her? By what means, in other words, can I become disentangled from writing to produce a sincere and authentic account of the other and of myself? The question is not new, but as applied to a literature produced within a political and social revolution as radical as Cuba's, it acquires a specific relevance. It is in the struggle to transcend, to go beyond or remain outside of the literary that Cuban literature of the Revolution provides a corrosive, critical element to Latin American letters in general, akin to the influence that the Revolution has had in other spheres, the political, for instance. As we shall see, that move away from literature takes on various forms—the confessional mode, the journalistic reportage, the scientific report—all purporting to exist before the symptomatic elusiveness and ambiguity of literature have set in. I shall begin by sketching some of the basic problems faced by the Cuban narrative in the Revolution, using as example Edmundo's Desnoes's well-known *Inconsolable Memories*, then I shall turn to the documentary novel in general, and finally to Barnet and his *Biografía de un cimarrón.*

In a remarkably candid speech closing the First Congress of the Cuban Communist party in the spring of 1976, Fidel Castro spoke in passing about his own bourgeois origins and those of many members of the revolutionary government:

I know, comrades, that some of you were hurt when we analyzed some of our errors. I know that specifically some comrades were really hurt when we spoke about the germs of petty bourgeois spirit and chauvinism with which we used to be afflicted— those of us who had come to the ways of the Revolution by purely intellectual paths. But if many of us were not proletarian, if we were not exploited peasants, if our class background did not make us objectively revolutionaries, how else could we come to the Revolution if not by way of thought, of vocation, of human sensibility? Perhaps because we had some revolutionary genes. It is possible that in my case they come from my great-grandparents, who were exploited Galician peasants. It is possible. But this is what we have been talking about and it is true. We would not be able to state that the world is full of revolutionaries, but we can say that the world is full of petty bourgeois. And we can truly say that the world is plagued with people who through purely intellectual ways reach revolutionary positions, but who drag with them the burdens of their own social class and who carry those germs.[3]

Fidel Castro's musings about this somewhat uncomfortable topic reflect one of the prevailing themes in Cuban literature since 1959: conversion, more specifically, the conversion of liberal intellectuals to the ideology and practice of a Marxist-Leninist revolution. No matter what the genre, this theme appears insistently in Cuban literature after 1959. It can be found in Roberto Fernández Retamar's essay *Calibán* as well as in Manuel Cofiño López's novel *La última mujer y el próximo combate.*[4] The pervasiveness of this topic no doubt results from quite tangible historical circumstances and easily documentable sociological realities. With very few exceptions, Cuban writers belonged to the bourgeoisie, something that, given the nature of Cuba's prerevolutionary society, should not be surprising. In addition, the politico-historical tempo during the first years of the Revolution was very fast, with drastic changes in government policy taking place within very short time-spans, sometimes literally overnight. To be a revolutionary before the spring of 1961, when the Revolution was declared to be socialist, was one thing. It was another to be a revolutionary after that.

Conversion was a real phenomenon in Cuba, even as it became a literary topic, and a question immediately arises about the relationship between the historical fact and the literary trend. Is conversion a literary topic, or does it reflect the historical process? Also, has conversion been accompanied by or has it generated a new, distinctly revolutionary literature, or is conversion still a literary strategy that is part of what could broadly be called literary modernity?[5] Has the conversion of writers meant as well a radical conversion of literature? These questions are vexing because conversion, the desire to declare the beginning of a new age and the coming of a "new man," is a recurrent topic in Western literature and particularly in the modern tradition. Christian thought is permeated by a sense of theodicy, by the expectation of a providential upheaval that will radically transform humanity and the world.[6] History is the time between Genesis and Apocalypse, or between Genesis and the coming of the Messiah. Moreover, the peculiar form of conversion that most frequently appears in Cuban literature of the Revolution, the attempt to turn literature into the direct expression of a radical new reality and of a freshly discovered collective consciousness, is the most common in the postromantic period. The account of a conversion, in these terms, would no longer be literary, but a true account of something entirely new. The dilemma that Cuban literature of the Revolution faces, in short, is that to speak of a revolutionary literature in a modern context may very well be a pleonasm. The modern tradition is or proclaims itself to be revolutionary, so how can literary tradition be subverted to mark a new beginning without reasserting the tradition of subverting tradition? How can I become another without really remaining the same? Barnet's *Biografía de un cimarrón* and the documentary novel in general are at the very center of these complex issues.

Cuban critics have often urged writers to abandon the chiliastic scheme of modernity and write not about a revolution yet to come but about a revolution in the making; not about past history but about the present and about *presentness* (because of the writer's insistence on portraying the struggle against Batista).[7] The notorious Padilla affairs, particularly the 1968 episode, revolved around this issue, one that forced both the poet and his critics to play rôles handed down by the modern tradition. The critic's demand that literature be made a part of the ongoing political process could have been rendered with Wallace Stevens's lines to the effect that "poetry is the cry of its occasion / part of the res itself and not about it." Padilla, true to the paradoxical spirit of modernity, wanted to have it both ways: he asked to be "out of the game" (the title of his book) while bemoaning in a poem about the Bay of Pigs his fate as a "simple and silent witness." Edmundo Desnoes's protagonist in *Inconsolable Memories*, a novelist, has fixed for posterity the image of the Cuban writer paralyzed by these dilemmas.

If the call to produce a literature of and about the present was difficult for poets to answer, it was particularly so for novelists, because narrative *[handwritten marginalia: "cannot distinguish bet.) Trivial and significant events in his life"]*

appears to be bound to the feeling of belatedness. The poet can perhaps utter the "cry of his occasion," but the novelist must make that cry articulate. If Cuban poets such as Roberto Fernández Retamar declare themselves to be "transitional men," in order to skirt the rhetorically (and, for quite a few, humanly and politically) intolerable present, novelists are faced with the task of chronicling that transition.[8] The narrative records the past to make it present memory and thrives in the interplay between past and present and between individual and collective conscience. In Desnoes's novel the protagonist, Sergio, is suspended between the past upheaval of the Revolution (which sent his family into exile) and the impending holocaust threatened by the Missile Crisis. (In the film version by Tomás Gutiérrez Alea, we see at the end a dawn that looks like a nuclear explosion, and it is difficult to tell whether this is a new beginning or the final end, an end that would significantly merge with that of the film.)[9] Sergio is caught in a pure present in which he has lost his bearings and about which he feels he cannot write. Like Fabrizio del Dongo (in Stendhal's *La Chartreuse de Parme*), who was in Waterloo but could not experience while at the battle the momentousness of the event, Sergio is unable to distinguish between the trivial and the significant in his life; the present is too chaotic, fragmented, and partial. His situation is summed up in the line from Alain Resnais's *Hiroshima mon amour* that he often repeats: "Je voudrais avoir une inconsolable mémoire." Like the characters in the film, he can only envisage a telling event in the future, but is indifferent to the collective cataclysm about to take place before his very eyes. As each moment ushers in a new one, as each beginning is replaced by another, both collective and individual memory slip inexorably into oblivion.

As a writer, the protagonist has as his only recourse the inscription of the memory and its gradual fading—writing hovers on that point where memory slips away from the present to become literature, a code that is both memory and the gesture of its recovery. Once it becomes literature, memory may return to the present, but (already) only and always belatedly, having relinquished immediacy in the process. The present engenders a past that has been fragmented into epochs, a series of breaks—a system of spacings—that lead to the present again without being visibly and decisively connected to it.[10] One looks back upon life and sees it as a series of turning points, but cannot be sure which is the last of those breaks that links up with our current predicament—writing provides a fictive bridge whose last space shimmers in the distance without really touching the other side. That gap, that stubborn disconnectedness, is the detachment of writing (not only actual writing, but also virtual writing, that is, memory—the moment of absolute *objectivity* in which we perceive a text, even our text, as other, as text). Desnoes's protagonist remains in Cuba but does not convert to the cause of the Revolution, perhaps because of the ironic realization that the gesture will also become literary, yet another break that will be "consolable," that will not effectively remain a present, but will become instead one more space in that selfless text of memory and of writing.

Desnoes's 1965 novel contains the most productive dilemmas that the Cuban narrative has had to deal with in the revolutionary period. The Revolution is a radical break in history, the constitution of a new beginning, of a new present. But how can the present be chronicled? From what vantage point? And, if to answer the desire for immediacy, the writer must convert, shed the old man to put on the new, how can a past that no longer belongs to him be dealt with, how can he write about it without turning it into a literary theme? How in short, can the present and the author's presence be harmonized?

It would be naïve to expect a clear-cut solution to these questions, and more so to anticipate satisfactory answers on the rather abstract level on which I have formulated them. What we can expect to find is not a definitive resolution to these questions, but the residue of the repeated attempts to answer them. This we also learn from Desnoes's novel, for, in spite of the paralysis that besets the narrator-protagonist, we do have in the book itself the various texts that he has produced in response to his predicament. And what we find in that text is a fragmentation of the character into various selves who have tried to write the "authentic" account of different moments that do not merge, but are instead at odds with each other. The system of spacings that distinguishes those moments is hypostasized in the various "I's" of the narrator: the narrator-protagonist, who is the author of some short stories included at the end of one of the editions of the novel; Eddy, whom we suppose to be Edmundo Desnoes, and in the fiction is the author of a novel of questionable value; and, of course, Edmundo Desnoes, who signs the book that we read. This Desnoes would be a sort of master-author, who controls all others from a vantage point so far ahead of them that he can write *about* them, though we know that he too is a part of the fiction. This solution, needless to say, leaves us again on the side of belatedness and of literature; the text's swerve away from the literary turns out to be an assertion of its literary constitution.

If we now turn from *Inconsolable Memories* to the larger field of the Cuban narrative in the Revolution, we shall see that a similar, inconclusive struggle to bypass literature appears, both in the evolution of the trend that most persistently has attempted to move out of the problematic outlined, and in individual works in that trend. I am referring, of course, to the so-called *narrativa de testimonio*, roughly, the documentary novel; a literature that is both testimonial in the sense of being a witness account and a kind of memorial. This trend has been so pervasive since the beginning of the Revolution that Casa de las Américas instituted a literary prize for books of this kind.

Initially, the documentary novel does not differ greatly from journalism, and in fact some of its practitioners—Lisandro Otero, Norberto Fuentes, and many others—are journalists. This is not a coincidence. The desire to chronicle the present leads inevitably in the direction of journalism, and the two books published by Norberto Fuentes—*Condenados de condado* and *Cazabandido*—originated as newspaper articles. The journalistic origins of the documentary novel betray the desire to bypass literary entrapments, or to dissolve the literariness of the narrative by turning to its sources. Ian Watt has convincingly demonstrated the close relationship between the birth of journalism and the beginnings of the modern novel in eighteenth-century England, a phenomenon that is paralleled in Latin America, where the first novel, *El periquillo sarniento*, was written by a pioneer Mexican journalist, José Joaquín Fernández de Lizardi.[11] One might also remember that Cervantes plays with the notion that the *Quijote* is based on contemporary accounts of its action, which were kept in the archives of La Mancha. The epic, too, some theories maintain, arose from the collation of ballads that told of recent events. Journalism leads away from literature and aims at immediacy. A journalistic account is faithful to facts, not to rhetorical modes; it deals with real people and events, not with literary characters or incidents endowed with a written history. Journalism also tends to diffuse the question of authorship. Since facts determine content, the author becomes a neutral conductor, not the generator of the text. Journalism fosters the illusion that incidents write themselves into history.

Taken at a glance, then, the documentary novel appears to solve many of the riddles seen before. But if one looks more closely at the situation, it is not as simple as all that, for in practice the paradoxes resurfaced as the newspaper accounts became books and the books a literary tradition. Norberto Fuentes's two volumes about the campaigns against counter-revolutionary invaders were the object of debate and, to some degree, of dissatisfaction.[12] Besides, if at first the works produced within the new tradition remained close to journalism, variations soon arose. In other words, once a literary tradition was established, the dialectics of literary production were reconstituted (if, indeed, they were ever abolished). The process can be understood better if viewed globally.

Two trends can be distinguished in the tradition of the documentary novel. One could be called "epic testimony" and consists of the more or less contemporary account of military actions as given by participants in the armed struggle against Batista, or in the battles against counterrevolutionary invaders. This kind of book appeared more frequently, for obvious reasons, during the first years of the Revolution. Some of the better-known books in this trend are Che Guevara's *Pasajes de la guerra revolucionaria* (1963), Carlos Franqui's *Cuba: el libro de los doce* (1966), and Norberto Fuentes's *Condenados de condado* (1968) and *Cazabandido* (1970). This trend has continued in books such as *Aquí se habla de combatientes y de bandidos*, by Raúl González de Cascorro, winner of the 1975 Casa de las Américas prize for *narrativa de testimonio*. I call this trend "epic" not only because it deals with war, but because it institutes war as the beginning of history. That is to say, war becomes the cataclysm that sets off a new present. This trend is epic also in that it deals predominantly with action, rather than description, as a way of fostering the illusion of presentness.

The second trend is quite different and more recent. One could call it the account of a marginal witness, and it deals with much more remote history. Instead of military events, here we find the *petite histoire*, a sort of cultural history dealing with everyday life and folk traditions. One could mention as belonging to this trend books such as Miguel Barnet's *Canción de Rachel* (1969), Renée Méndez Capote's *Memorias de una cubanita que nació con el siglo* (1969), and *La abuela* (1973), by Captain Antonio Núñez Jiménez. The significant differences between the two trends will become much more evident if we look briefly at this last book and at González de Cascorro's *Aquí se habla de combatientes y de bandidos*.

González de Cascorro's book narrates the battles against counter-revolutionary bands in the province of Camagüey. Authorial intervention has been reduced to a minimum. The "Presentación" gives a brief, impersonal account of the emergence of counterrevolutionary bands, and a "Nota" at the end explains that the author utilized provincial archives for documents and transcripts of questionings to which the prisoners had been subjected. The core of the book consists of a series of brief statements by those involved. There is no clear plot line and no narrator: each utterance is preceded, as in a play, by the name of the participant. There is at the end a list of names that is very much like the cast in the program for a play. As in *Ulysses* the reader is able to reconstruct the sequence of events only as he or she learns to recognize each "voice." The book is a gallery of voices that, true to the title, talk about the confrontation between *"combatientes"* and *"bandidos."* The action exists as in a pure present (*aquí*), the pure present of theatrical performance, without protagonist and without the centering figure of the narrator. The insistence on speech underscores the desire for immediacy and presentness: the absence of an articulate narrative discourse emphasizes the illusion that this is unmediated action before writing.

Núñez Jiménez's *La abuela* consists of a series of interviews with the author's then ninety-four-year-old grandmother. In the prologue we read the following: "Grandparents are like books that speak. They tell the stories that live through them, collecting those that they heard from their parents and from the parents of their parents, in such a way that the children know, through their narrations, many things from the past that at times conventional books don't transmit. The grandparents teach the young about a fascinating world with much more spontaneity and freshness than that learned in some chronicles or histories written by professionals."[13] As in González de Cascorro's book, there is a privileging of voice ("talking books") over the written word, and therefore a desire to create the illusion of presence (not to mention the disdain for literature obvious in the preceding quotation, too). But the telling difference is that in *La abuela* Núñez Jiménez attempts to establish a genealogy of voices that endows that presence with a past, with an origin. Besides, *La abuela* deals not with action, but with description; it is an attempt to preserve an oral tradition, a collective memory. On a more thematic or even symbolic level it might be relevant that the grandmother in this book is an expert on caves, and some of her stories have to do with explorations in the entrails of the earth, as it were. It is perhaps no coincidence that the books in the second trend of the documentary novel tend to have female protagonists, whereas the first trend is peopled by men. The second, by turning back to origins, suggests a return to the womb, to a sort of stasis before birth and violence.

The appearance of the second trend of the documentary novel is a significant factor per se, for it clearly represents—even while enthroning voice—a move back from the present, a retreat to endow that present with a past. In other words, if we disregard the authors altogether and see the whole of the Cuban documentary novel as one continuous text, the second trend constitutes a gesture similar to the one made by the protagonist of *Inconsolable Memories*: presentness immediately calls forth a past with which it attempts to align the moment of writing, with memory-become-literature.

These two trends of the documentary novel combine in Miguel Barnet's *Biografía de un cimarrón*, which is perhaps a good reason to consider it the most enduring work of the new tradition. It grew out of a newspaper article that he had read about a nursing home with several residents over 100 years old.[14] His professional interest aroused, since he was then researching Afro-Cuban religions, Barnet went to the home. There he found Esteban Montejo, a marvelously loquacious and witty black, then about 105 years old. Born around 1860, Montejo had been a slave, a maroon, a laborer, a soldier in the wars of independence. Although he often expressed a very Voltairian skepticism, Montejo was full of information about Afro-Cuban religious practices. He remembered in great detail life in the slave barracks; his recollections of the wars of independence were vivid; and his perspective on events following independence demolished pious historical accounts. Most of all, however, he remembered his years in the wild, living in caves, always alert so as not to give himself away and be forced back to the sugar factories where he had labored.

Barnet grew increasingly interested in what Montejo had to say, and *Biografía de un cimarrón* began to take shape. The book, written in the first person, is an epic account by a very active participant in momentous military events; but it is also a detailed personal and cultural history of daily life as a slave in the sugar factories, as a maroon in the wild, as a soldier in the army of liberation, as a wage laborer in the republic that followed the first U.S. intervention. *Biografía de un cimarrón* aims at being both past and present, individual and collective. Esteban Montejo is history incarnate, or its living, breathing child. His voice in the present swells up from the darkest depths of time. He spans two epic beginnings: the War of Independence and the Revolution.

Biografía de un cimarrón shares with all the other books in the tradition of the documentary novel the explicit desire to bypass literature. All the strategies that we have observed before are here, the most poignant being the use of the first person, which is a way of dramatizing presence, and the age of the protagonist, who would establish a *living link* with the past. There is, moreover, Barnet's own expressed intention in the introduction: "We know that to make an informant speak in the book is, in a certain way, to create literature. But we don't intend to create a literary document, a novel" (p. 10). Even more than in the case of other books of this nature, the format deviates radically from literary practice. *Biografía de un cimarrón* consists of an "Introducción," in which Barnet explains his intentions and tells the story of how the book came to be written. This is followed by Montejo's life as told by himself, divided into three periods: slavery, the abolition of slavery, and the war of independence. A glossary of Cuban words and expressions used by Montejo in his narrative ends the book.

The book purports to be factual, the result of a series of interviews with an informant, strung as a first-person narrative for the sake of continuity and convenience. Yet, there is a peculiar literary propriety to Esteban Montejo's figure and to *Biografía de un cimarrón* in general. Born on 26 December, the feast of Saint Stephen, the Protomartyr, Esteban bears the name of two important literary protagonists: Joyce's Stephen Dedalus and Carpentier's Esteban in *Explosion in a Cathedral*. He shares more with them: their epic-like wanderings, their authorial propensities, their more or less obvious association with Christ (once removed, since they hark back to Saint Stephen, born the day after Christ's birthday; the first martyr after Him). Furthermore, according to Barnet, Montejo may be a corruption of the French *mont haut* (high mountain). It is the name of Esteban's mother, who was a descendant of Haitian slaves (his link with the past is matrilineal, thus sharing a feminine quality with the protagonists of the second trend of the documentary novel).

The Christian symbolism of the mountain is clear. What is not so clear is that *monte*, both "mountain" and "wild" or "bush," is charged with implications in Afro-Cuban religion and lore. There is, in fact, a famous book written by a Cuban anthropologist, Lydia Cabrera, called *El monte* (like Barnet, she was a disciple of the renowned Cuban anthropologist Fernando Ortiz). There can be no doubt that Cabrera's *El monte* is in many ways an antecedent of *Biografía de un cimarrón*. But what is relevant here is the significance of *el monte* in Afro-Cuban lore. Cabrera writes,

Belief in the spirituality of the woods [*monte*] persists among Cuban blacks with remarkable tenacity. The same ancestral divinities that inhabited the African jungles—powerful spirits who today, as at the time of the slave trade, are most feared and worshiped, and on whose hostility or benevolence depend every success or failure—dwell in the mountains of Cuba. The black who goes into the mountains, who penetrates fully into a thicket in the wild [*un corazón de monte*], does not doubt that he is establishing direct contact with supernatural forces that there, in their own domain, are all around him. Any given space in the woods is considered sacred because of the visible or invisible presence of what is considered holy. "The wild [*monte*] is sacred," because divinities reside, "dwell" there. "The saints are more in the wild than in heaven." It is the source of life: "We are children of the wild because our life began there; the saints are born in the wild and our religion is also born in the wild." So says Sandoval, my old herbalist, a descendant of Eggwdódos. "Everything can be found in the wild"—the foundations of the cosmos—"and one has to ask the wild for anything." "We are children of the wild," etc. For Cuban blacks the Wild is equivalent to the concept of the universal mother, source of life. "Earth and Wild [*monte*] are the same."[15]

Esteban's life as a maroon was spent in *el monte*—both high and deep, in caves far in the bush and in hills—so that in a sense he is the one who has been to the mountain and returned. He lives on the far side of all change, of all upheavals, because he has already endured the most difficult trials and is in possession of the special knowledge that such a journey confers on him. *El monte* inscribes Montejo within a textual memory, both African and Cuban. He can incarnate the child, the Messiah, and the old man– prophet: Jesus and Moses at once. Rather than the voice of history and change, Esteban appears as a sort of Ulysses or Aeneas about to tell a timeless story.

After the publication of his two documentary novels—*Biografía de un cimarrón* and *Canción de Rachel*—Barnet wrote a confessional essay that is a sort of poetics of the genre. In it he insists that the purpose of the author, whom he calls the *gestor*, of documentary novels, is not aesthetic, that the aim of this kind of narrative is "more functional, more practical. It should serve as a link in the long chain of a country's tradition. It should contribute to the articulation of a collective memory, a we not an I." Barnet also says that the documentary novel should contribute to the knowledge of a certain reality and "give that reality a historical sense [*sentido* as meaning and direction]." Barnet's appeal to collective memory and to history leads him to make a symbol of his protagonist in *Biografía de un cimarrón*:

Thus, Maroon, after a childhood as a slave . . . enters into a wild stage when he becomes a maroon. He is later a wage laborer and finally a *mambí* [an insurgent who fought against Spanish rule in the wars of independence]. In other words: a slave, a maroon, an indentured servant, a soldier in the wars of independence. Each one of those stages has left a deep imprint in the psychology of the Cuban, has helped to shape him, has given him a history. These are not marginal, isolated facts, but social commotions, collective events, epic events that can only be reconstructed through a historical memory. And what could be better than having a representative protagonist, a legitimate actor.

In the more autobiographical part of the essay, Barnet speaks about the nature of his relationship with Montejo:

Without meaning to I was searching for an identity, for a sincere confession. In this relationship between author and protagonist or researcher-informant one has to look for an unfolding [*desdoblamiento*], becoming the other by prying apart one's self. In other words, one must try to live one's life in order also to live another life, that of one's character. The gestor of the documentary novel lives a second life that is real, that transforms him in an essential way. . . . I said that there was a distancing. There is also a depersonalization. One is the other already and only by being so can one think like him, speak like him, feel deeply life's blows, communicated to one by the informant and feel them like one's own. There is the poetry, the mystery of this kind of work. And, clearly, that wide, open door that allows one to penetrate into the collective conscience, into the we. The dream of the gestor of the documentary novel, that thirst for expansion, for knowledge and identity, was also Malinowsky's, Ortiz's, Nina Rodríguez's, and that of the French novelists of the nineteenth century.[16]

The language of Barnet's remarkable essay betrays the same problems as *Inconsolable Memories*. He wants to convert, to become another, to write from within a memory that will be inconsolable, a memory that will finally give meaning, sense to the past by aligning it in significant fashion with the present, a memory that will not be consoled by the ambiguities of language and literature. That other from whom he wants to write is Montejo, who is in turn a tangible, irreducible link with history, the living word of history, the missing link of memory, a real Atlas who bears the present on his back.

The resilience of the dream that these desires be satisfied is what makes *Biografía de un cimarrón* such an appealing and important book within as well as beyond the context of Cuban literature. It is an illusion that those dreams are realized, an illusion that the text's own dialectics dissolves. Montejo's memories are not inconsolable. Montejo is no naïve Sancho and certainly not the Rousseau-inspired native who is going to save Barnet from the perplexities of writing; no Man Friday is he to be easily overpowered by the world's superior knowledge, finding solace in his mindless ignorance. The stream of his thought cannot be easily engulfed by a vast, sea-like collective conscience. In fact, what is truly significant about

Montejo, at least as the character in the book, is his resemblance to an author. What distinguishes him is his status as a maroon, a runaway. And as a runaway he did not join others in a maroon society, as generally happened, but remained alone in the wild for years, talking to no one, brooding about life, and acquiring the kind of self-knowledge granted only to introspective memorialists. Each flight into the bush is a flight into silence, into a sort of erasure that will allow one to convert, to start anew, to shed the trappings of society, to run naked back to Mother Earth.[17] Though he did have many relationships with women (he refers to them as "ambulatory marriages"), he recognized none of the children that his mistresses told him were his. He was a true skeptic who rarely established lasting affective or social bonds. When Montejo returned to society after abolition he was able to look on it not with the eyes of the future informant of Miguel Barnet, but as a sort of social anthropologist in his own right. He remarks at some point that he did not particularly like to sing and dance at religious rituals because he had grown used to looking at things from afar: "In my own case, it isn't that I didn't like dancing, it's that I've taken to looking at things from a distance" (p. 65). In many ways Esteban is as lonely and detached as the narrator-protagonist of *Inconsolable Memories*.

Esteban Montejo's ironic wisdom ultimately betrays Miguel Barnet. If the author wished to leap into immediacy through the figure of Montejo, Montejo offered him, from the other side of the mirror, the same perspective. Like Melquíades in *One Hundred Years of Solitude*, Montejo turns out to be the author of the book, but as such, he is led to assume all the perplexities of his position. The true symbiosis of Barnet and Montejo occurs not when one becomes the other, but when both turn out to have been the same all along, when the difference between them is discovered to be the conventional distinction necessary for the constitution of the text. The figures of Montejo and Barnet reenact the original novelistic dialogue between Dante and Vergil, Celestina and Calixto, Lazarillo and Vuestra Merced; between Cervantes and his friend of the 1605 prologue, between Don Quijote and Sancho, not, of course, Sancho the simpleton that the eighteenth century imagined, nor the folk hero of the Romantics, but Kafka's Sancho:

Without ever boasting of it, Sancho Panza succeeded in the course of years, by supplying a lot of romances of chivalry and adventure for the evening and night hours, in so diverting from him his demon, whom he later called Don Quixote, that his demon thereupon freely performed the maddest exploits, which, however, lacking a preordained object, which Sancho Panza himself was supposed to have been, did no one any harm. A free man, Sancho Panza philosophically followed Don Quixote on his crusades, perhaps out of a sense of responsibility, and thus enjoyed a great and profitable entertainment to the end of his days.[18]

The novel emerges from its own *cimarronaje* from literature always as that essential dialogue of telling and being told. The result is a tense dialogue between the characters. Difference is enacted, dramatized, personified in figures vying with each other to attain absolute power and abolish it. In that fundamental dialogue Montejo, not Barnet, gains the upper hand, through one last lunge at immediacy. For in this primal ritual of writing—in this playing out of a mythology of writing—it is the illiterate former slave who is in possession of a masterful wisdom, whereas Barnet is reduced to "taking down" what the other dictates. Montejo is the voice of authority, the dictator; Barnet is merely the scribe (the "editor," as the English version of the book reads).

But we know now that this is also an illusion, that Montejo's memory is a text, too, inscribed in the same problematic as that of the protagonist of *Inconsolable Memories*. If one were to fall prey completely to the illusions fostered (and fostering) *Biografía de un cimarrón*, one could hope that, once the results of the literacy campaign are more telling and the Montejos now in Cuba write their own biographies, these dialectics would dissolve. But if anything can be learned from the sort of reading that I have performed here it is that then they would no doubt have to invent their own Miguel Barnets.

There can be no question about the important functions performed by the documentary novel on that practical level to which Barnet alludes in his essay. It has, for instance, begun to rewrite Cuban history, to rescue the past from conventional, often distorted, accounts. As with much of what the Revolution has accomplished in this respect, this rewriting is primarily concerned with the history of slavery, and in this sense *Biografía de un cimarrón* must be seen in the context of books such as Manuel Moreno Fraginal's *El ingenio*, José Luciano Franco's *Los palenques de los negros cimarrones*, César Leante's *Los guerrilleros negros*, current research on the antislavery novel, and films such as *El otro Francisco* and *La última cena*. Within the Cuban literary tradition *Biografía de un cimarrón* in particular has established links between current writing and the Afro-Cuban movement and also constitutes a kind of rewriting of the so-called antislavery novels produced in Cuba during the nineteenth century.

But there is also a good deal to be learned from the documentary novel on what one could call a theoretical level. On the one hand it has shown that, indeed, radical change in literature is not compatible with visible changes in other domains; that, when pressed by sociopolitical phenomena, literature tends to seek refuge in its own foundations rather than simply give way to self-denying innovations. This, I hope, should be evident from our reading of *Biografía de un cimarrón* and the documentary novel. Not only has that reading shown us that in that tradition there is a series of gestures backward, toward the textual origins of the novel, but also, in the specific case of Barnet's book, a reduction to the basic, founding novelistic situation.

The import of this phenomenon in the broader context of the Latin American narrative can be gauged if we consider that what *Biografía de un cimarrón* accomplishes by this reduction is a return to what could be called the primal American literary scene. The formula entails a chronicler, possessed of writing, asking the native to unveil his or her secrets, and the native doing so, but only by gradually usurping the chronicler's place and turning the account of this confrontation into something quite different from what was originally intended. In other words, what Barnet replays in *Biografía de un cimarrón* is the *crónicas de la conquista*. But he shows that the Conquest, rather than being simply a takeover, was a dialogue by which the European also was denuded, his language contaminated, the foundations of his self-assurance undermined, his need of the native shown to be as great as the need he thought the native had of him. The tension of this power play within the text is indeed the forever-crumbling foundations of modern literature, as much the child of the "discovery" of America as any other manifestation of the "modern world."

It is in this sense, I think, that *Biografía de un cimarrón* and Cuban literature of the Revolution play an important role in Latin America, by showing not only the functional value of writing, but more importantly by forcing literature to stake out its own domain anew, its own *palenque*. Such a task is not given to a revolutionary literature that indulges in the ephemeral language of current politics or that is satisfied with the vapid jargon of the social sciences. It is, to the contrary, allotted only to the literature that in searing and uncompromising language seeks to rewrite the foundations of a culture.[19] Montejo/Barnet/Marnet/Bontejo have done at least that much.

7. Literature and Exile: Carpentier's "Right of Sanctuary"

> *and without making a sad tango out of being awash*
> *in the tide of remembrance, in the suitcase full of*
> *thousands upon thousands of chicks belonging to*
> *the sage of Alexandria, in the magician's briefcase*
> *that opens for the public, ladies and gentlemen,*
> *because the show begins every time you reach one of*
> *the stories, and will continue, I say, beyond the very*
> *limits of memory.*
>
> —Gabriel García Márquez

1

Not too many years ago a pessimistic and short-sighted critic proclaimed that Latin America was a novel without novelists. His gloomy assessment has been discredited by the work of a splendid group of contemporary novelists and the discovery of a rich narrative tradition going back to colonial times. Today the most frequent lament is that Latin America's is a literature with little criticism to speak of.[1]

I would say instead that, although there may be little independent critical thought in Latin America, there is no literature that enjoys a higher degree of reflection than Latin America's; that, in fact, literature is Latin America's mode of criticism. Such critical reflection encompasses not only literature and criticism, but philosophy, sociology, and politics as well. What I mean by critical reflection here is not merely an examination of literature, criticism, sociological reality, or political evolution, but a meditation on the why and the how of such criticism, on the prolegomena of such analytical activity. At Yale *One Hundred Years of Solitude* has been taught not only by professors of Latin American literature, but also (to our increasing alarm) by historians, sociologists, and political scientists. Borges is taught in courses on literary theory, and Carpentier and Fernando Ortiz can be found on the reading lists of professors of Afro-American studies. Octavio Paz's *The Labyrinth of Solitude* is taught by historians and sociologists, and Puig and Cortázar are known experts on film and on popular culture. Latin American literature may lack a body of original, independent critical reflection, but Latin American literature is in itself a rich source of criticism at the highest levels. It would be difficult to find a more penetrating analysis of the transition between the Enlightenment and romanticism, or a more systematic search for the origins of Latin American modernity than Carpentier's *Explosion in a Cathedral*. Carpentier himself was not a great critic or theoretician, yet his novels and stories are exceptional critical reflections, which display an intellectual daring often missing from his expository prose. Literature is the criticism and the philosophy of Latin America and, I suspect, of much of the postcolonial world.

In a curious way literature thus becomes again, like storytelling and the epic, a society's mode of reflection about the timeless questions facing it, a retreat from the facile answers officiously tendered by the mass media and the contingent and strategic solutions of politics. Latin America's major modern writers—Carpentier, Borges, Guimarães Rosa, Lezama, Vallejo, Guillén, Neruda, Paz, Roa Bastos, and García Márquez—are all agents of a ruthless, dizzying critical reassessment of tradition. The first and most sobering lesson one learns from reading Carpentier is that he gambled always for the highest possible stakes. *The Kingdom of This World, The Lost Steps,* and *Explosion in a Cathedral* were conceived with the most demanding issues of modernity at their foundation.

The most poignant question raised by modernity in Latin America was that of national or cultural identity, as well as of the link between such identity and literary production. The major literary figures of the nineteenth century (the founders of Latin American literature), Bello, Sarmiento, and Martí, conceived the issue in a rich metaphoric system linking humanity and culture to the land, to geography. Metaphors, drawn from nineteenth-century natural science, were mostly botanical or geological. From the times of the *cronistas de Indias*, American nature appeared to be the key to American differences, but most early historians were so imbued with scholastic thought that they could hardly conceive such a notion. Only Fernández de Oviedo came close to positing that the American natural world was a system apart from those known then. The romantics and their followers saw a different nature as a source for a different being, a distinct consciousness. Bello sang to agriculture in the torrid zone; Sarmiento spoke of the vast, barbaric pampas; Martí longed for the emergence of what he called a "natural man" in Latin America, and spoke of "grafting European tradition onto the trunk of Latin American culture" (instead of the other way around).[2] There were significant discrepancies between these writers, but for them culture was grounded (if I may be allowed the pleonasm) in the land, in local values and beliefs as different from Europe as nature, whose image literature would be.

But modern literature is not a set of platitudes; it is instead a relentless questioning of all pieties. Nineteenth-century truisms about the continuity of humanity and nature on the American continent are subjected by contemporary literature to a severe critique in the broadest possible sense of the term. This literature, which we could call postmodern, likes to parody and satirize such received notions, to show that, contrary to the assumption of a natural link between Americans and nature, the relationship is quite artificial, dependent on political and literary conventions. From a strictly political perspective, the importance of such a criticism—rendering visible the metaphoric nature of the definition of culture—lies in its ability to elucidate the ideological origin of the relationship between people and the American landscape. An all-encompassing concept of culture based on nature for its metaphoric cogency is a mechanism whereby the liberal imagination blurred class distinctions. From a literary point of view the critical gesture allows Latin American literature to declare its independence from a crude referentiality that hinders its ability for self-analysis. One of the topics most commonly used to engage in such an analysis of the modern tradition is exile, for it contains both a longing for a lost motherland as source and a sense of its irrevocable loss. If the land endows people with a special knowledge, exile would be a heightening of that knowledge through the ordeal of separation and return.

Given the pervasive, and even spectacular, character of exile in Latin American history and the notion that being American is in itself a form of exile, a correlation between Latin American writing and exile can all too quickly be established. An absurd reduction of this would run as follows: being Latin American is to be in exile from the metropolitan culture, not to mention that most important Latin American writers have, at one time or another, been exiles; therefore banishment and deracination are essential qualities of all Latin American writing. Moreover, since writing itself could be seen as a form of exile, Latin America's is the truest or most natural writing. Corroboration for this crude essentialist argument could be found by turning to the literature of the United States, where the names of Henry James, Ernest Hemingway, T. S. Eliot, Ezra Pound, and others would be invoked to show that indeed exile is a continental malaise, but one for which we must be grateful, because it is an important source of American writing.

The persuasiveness of such a self-serving argument is lessened once we turn to the broader context of modernity, for the topic of exile can be easily subsumed within the general theme of alienation that runs across all postromantic literature—the feeling of not belonging to one's place and time, of having been torn away from a better world and epoch. Because modern literature is permeated by this sense of loss and distance, because writing appears to be a secondary activity that can record only what is no longer there, the tendency would be instead to make an overall formulation equating writing and exile that would invalidate all claims Latin America could make for its uniqueness. On a less abstract, but more general, level Harry Levin has written in a seminal essay on the subject that "exile has been regarded as an occupational hazard for poets in particular ever since Plato denied them rights of citizenship in his republic."[3]

If to these already compelling overdeterminations one adds the evidence of contemporary linguistic and psychoanalytic theories, the bond between writing and exile seems inevitable. The signifier's flight away from the signified would be the primal voyage, of which all fictions are but mere reflections. Psychoanalytic lore would make us all exiles from our mothers, prey to the anxieties of an impossible return that we continually rehearse in awkward, yet repeated, sexual encounters, encounters whose pleasure can never match the oneness felt within the mother's womb.

But all of these generalizations are of little use and, unless qualified and refined, may easily lead to distortions, because, in historical terms, exiles are quite different from each other, despite their apparent similarity, for they are exiled in substantially dissimilar circumstances and from quite different regimes. Nicaraguan and Chilean exiles in the United States differ in many respects, first and foremost in political ideology; it would, therefore, be somewhat rash to declare that there is a link between Latin American literature and exile, or even between literature and the historical phenomenon of exiles. What can be safely said instead, it seems, is that exile is one of those founding tropes that literature invokes constantly as a part of its own constitution, a trope already present in the work of the great Garcilaso de la Vega, el Inca, who, from Spain, his father's country, wrote about the lost kingdom of his mother's people. It is against the background of this argument that I wish to read a short story by Carpentier, "Right of Sanctuary." It is in this story that Carpentier, in the midst of the agitation of the sixties, considers the issue of exile as a founding literary trope and in relation to political power in Latin America. "Right of Sanctuary" is one of the most political of his fictions, yet one of the most critical. The issue seems to be, in the end, whether the two are compatible. The story, which was published separately as a slim volume in 1972, has been added to recent editions of *War of Time*. It is in many ways also a critical synthesis of Carpentier's works.[4]

2

Exile is one of the more pervasive themes in Carpentier's work, in both his fiction and his expository writing. A list of exiles in Carpentier's novels and stories would be very long, so I shall mention only Ti Noel and all the slaves in *The Kingdom of This World*, who dream of a return to Africa, a Lost Paradise inhabited by gods and strong men, and the narrator-protagonist in

The Lost Steps, a Latin American who has been living in the United States for many years. The fact that Carpentier spent a good part of his life in France, where his family originated, makes the topic particularly poignant and suggestive when dealing with his works. Were Carpentier's own exiles journeys back to the source or away from it? Were his trips to Havana returns of the prodigal son or flights from home?

Carpentier was aware of the irony implicit in his situation as cultural attaché of the Cuban government in France, a country where he was obviously also at home and where no one would take him for a foreigner. A year before his death he told me that whenever he had to attend a formal official function he would go to the same Parisian establishment to rent a tuxedo. There, the old French tailor, after fitting him carefully, would stand back to admire his work and proclaim, "Vous allez bien représenter la France!" This dilemma is very visible in a set of articles Carpentier wrote in 1939, upon his return to Cuba after eleven years in France. The articles are suggestively entitled "La Habana vista por un turista cubano." In these articles, which I have studied at some length in *The Pilgrim at Home*, Carpentier figuratively strolls through his native city, discovering remarkable things that had passed unnoticed before he left but that he is capable of detecting now from the double perspective of a tourist in his own home.

What Carpentier is practicing is a "reading" of his city, the sign of which reading is the double temporal dimension and his own detachment; reading can take place only through the creation of this spacing, which is not so much the reflection of the space we occupy as an internal need of the process itself. Things merge into significant systems, but only by focusing on them through the isolation of detachment, of not being a part of them, of being an insider who is also an outsider—a *voyeur* of oneself. Carpentier's mature fiction is marked by this double vision, this need and fear of being at once the one and the other. There is throughout his recent works the apprehension that characters will merge, will collapse into one, or that they will all turn out to have been projections of one who needs to be different (foreign) in order to be himself or herself, and who must project another who resembles him or her, yet is not the same. In terms of everyday experience, the issue of distance and exile is related to the question that all of us ask when traveling to a faraway or exotic place: Are we still ourselves? Are we the same, or has the trip changed us completely, and how can language signify that difference? How can one *be* the same in two different places? Should my name not reflect this difference? Should I be called Roberto here in New Haven and something else elsewhere? This is, as Sharon Magnarelli demonstrated in a brilliant essay, a key issue in "The High Road of Saint James."[5] In that story Juan is always named for what he was, not for what he is . He is successively pilgrim, *indiano*, student, musician, but he is never what the adjective that describes him says he is in the present.[6]

All of Carpentier's exiles live in a timeless state—a sort of suspended animation—and seek to return home by means of two intimately related activities: love and reading. The role of the erotic is clear, particularly if we think of a story such as "Journey Back to the Source," where the old Marquis dies while making love to a young woman. The story, told backward, takes him back to his mother's womb. Through the various women they encounter, Carpentier's characters seek to return to the mother and to a sort of rebirth. In *The Lost Steps* there is a regression from Ruth to Mouche, to Rosario, leading back to a prenatal bliss that the narrator-protagonist cannot find. This regression runs parallel to his voyage from the modern world back to the jungle.

The role of reading is more complex. Away from home, from language, Carpentier's exiles reify their mother tongue, petrify it. The mother tongue dies the moment the exile leaves and ceases to hear it. To preserve it the exile reads, caressing language as if it were a dead body that could be brought back to life through a sort of ritual incantation. By means of this practice the exile hopes to recover his or her original self and shed the new, alien self, which has become a silent code that does not "belong" to him or her, a petrified body devoid of meaning, like the statue of Pauline Bonaparte that Solimán caresses in *The Kingdom of This World.*

In Carpentier's work exile has three elements. The first is timelessness. Exile as a temporal gap has no duration except within itself, and, as a result, events, things, and people, not subject to the dynamism of becoming, appear as scaled-down models of themselves. Although distance makes reading possible, it also distorts dimensions by reducing them. Carpentier's characters seek to remedy this situation through love and reading. Love mimics a return, a rebirth, a starting anew. Reading is an attempt to recover language, but instead makes language ever more artificial, more self-contained, less able to designate distinctions between the various elements in reality.

"Right of Sanctuary," though probably conceived around 1928 when the Pan-American Conference mentioned in the text took place in Havana, is a late work and as such a reassessment of the larger, earlier fictions that make up the core of Carpentier's works.[7] As with other fundamental topics in his own fiction, exile is, in a manner of speaking, deconstructed in this story. As suggested before, what "Right of Sanctuary" demystifies is the notion that there is a natural link between writing and exile. Exile itself, so the story seems to tell us, is a convention, a literary artifice that does not afford the kind of radical change with which fictions invest it. It does not furnish, in other words, a truly distinct perspective, nor can it be taken as a transcendental state that offers a special, privileged vision. Ultimately, every place and every moment is the same, except in writing, where signs set off one indistinguishable moment from the next, one place from another. In order to achieve this demystification, the story puts forth the topic of exile with all of the related elements seen before, exaggerating and distorting each.

Like *Reasons of State*, "Right of Sanctuary" is set in an archetypal Latin American country, a country that resembles Venezuela but that could also be Chile or Peru. With all of its symbols—shield, flag, uniforms—expressing cooperation, prosperity, and democratic ideals, the country appears like the invention of a Committee on Icons of the Organization of American States. The protagonist is the Secretary to the President and the Council of Ministers, a typical functionary of a corrupt government. His main occupation seems to be the procurement of whores for the pleasure of his superiors. When the President is deposed in a coup, the Secretary manages to gain sanctuary in the embassy of the neighboring country, with which there is a border dispute (a Galtieri *avant la lettre*, the dictator provokes the neighboring country to whip up nationalistic pride in his own and to deflect attention from internal repression). The Secretary remains in that other country for so long that he can eventually claim citizenship, the embassy being, technically, the territory of the foreign state. In addition, since to kill time the Secretary—now the Refugee—has been performing most of the duties of the ambassador, including making love to the ambassador's wife, he takes the citizenship of the embassy's country and is named ambassador to his original country. The story has the neat functioning of a baroque rhetorical figure: it is a *retruécano*, an inversion. The story ends as the former secretary presents his credentials to General Mabillán, the dictator, and they exchange some banter sotto voce.

These reversals of reversals—an exile, he returns from a place he never visited to a place he never left—all occur within a rather heavy-handed meditation on the passage of time and its relation to the signs that denote it. Each chapter is preceded by a brief indication of the day of the week in which the action takes place: the first says "Sunday," the second "Monday," but the third, once the protagonist is ensconced in the embassy, reads "Another Monday (it doesn't matter which)." The time of exile is a timeless gap, a kind of death. The story begins on a Sunday and ends on a Tuesday—exile, fiction, is lodged in that Monday that does not exist but that expands into countless days and years, as if a mad calculus took over in the designation of time. The days in the story are shuffled and expanded until the secretary becomes again a functionary. Once he presents his credentials, the week resumes a normal course.

Within the brackets of that fictional Monday, the Refugee begins to "read" the neighborhood around the embassy, much like Carpentier read Havana after his return from Paris. A tourist and a recluse in his own city, the Refugee reifies the capital, turns it into a system of signs that he reads and interprets; the city becomes an iconography. From a church behind the embassy he can hear and hence follow the liturgical activities—liturgy endows time with meaning, reducing it to a revolving system of fixed signs. In front of the embassy—perhaps the location of the church and these institutions is meaningful—the Refugee sees two stores. One, a hardware store, appears to him like a museum, an archeological, linear display of the history of mankind as seen through its instruments of labor: "I look across at the ironmongery and hardware store of the Brothers Gómez (founded in 1912, so one reads on the façade), and become absorbed in the dateless antiquity of the things sold in it. For the history of man's industry, from protohistoric times up to the electric light bulb, is illustrated by the objects and implements offered for sale by the Brothers Gómez." To the Refugee the store represents history, or better yet, it is the conventional, linear representation of history. To him as a reader, objects and time appear set off, differentiated, put in systematic order. The ironmongery has become writing, as conventional as the Latin he hears from the church.

From yet another window the Refugee can see

the toy department of the great American store. And there, immovable and always himself, through all the responses, lessons and liturgies that poured from the church, in spite of the archaism of the modern utensils in the Brothers Gómez ironmongery and hardware store, was Donald Duck. There he was, brought to life in pasteboard, with his orange feet, in a corner of the shopwindow, dominating a whole world of little railway trains on the move, of dressers with dishes of wax fruit, cowboy pistols, quivers full of arrows, and go-carts with colored beads on a rod. There he was, although he was sold and sold again a dozen times a day. Whenever a child asked for "that one," the one in the window, a woman's hand would seize him by his orange feet and soon afterward put another similar Donald Duck in his place. This perpetual substitution of one object by another identical to it, standing motionless on the same pedestal, made me think of Eternity. Perhaps God was relieved of his duties from time to time like this, by some superior power (the Mother of God? The mothers of the gods? Didn't Goethe say something on the subject?), who was custodian of his perennially. At the moment of change, when the Lord's Throne was empty, there would be railway disasters, airplanes would crash, transatlantic liners would sink, wars begin, and epidemics break out. (pp. 76-77)[8]

The time of exile is the time of Donald Duck and of the electric train going around and around—it is the time of scaled-down models, of artificial, mimetic systems, of endless and mindless substitutions and repetitions. What the Refugee longs for is the child's ability to fix upon an object and deem it sufficiently different and unique to be able to say, "That one." This wish he seeks to satisfy in his maniacal reading of everything—from books to labels to calendars—and through the seduction of the Ambassador's wife. But all this activity yields only repetition, not differentiation and uniqueness. Nothing appears to be singular enough to say, "That one."

Carpentier has skillfully woven together reading and love by ironically alluding to the canonical seduction-through-reading scene in Western literature. The Refugee seduces the "Ambassadress" by reading her lewd scenes from *Tirant lo Blanc*: " 'The Ambassadress' was amused by the sly humor of some passages in the book. She laughed even more over the chapter describing the dream of My Life's Delight, in which the princess said: 'Let me alone, Tirant, let me alone.' And, at the risk of seeming pedantic, it is true to say 'that day we read no more' " (p. 88). The line is from *Inferno* V, 138: "Quel giorno piu non vi leggemmo avante."

The suggestions of this allusion to the story of Paolo and Francesca are too many to exhaust here, but let me mention those directly concerned with the theme of exile.[9] On the one hand, there has been a change in the book the lovers read. Instead of Lancelot, we have here *Tirant lo Blanc*, a book of bawdy lovemaking and raucous humor. There is a clear demystification in this transformation—the love of Carpentier's couple is not the sublime love of Paolo and Francesca, but the more physical one of Tirant. Yet, what is most pertinent is that Paolo and Francesca, confined to Hell, suffer a fate quite like that of the Refugee and the Ambassador's wife. The two couples are sentenced to repetition within a timeless void. Paolo and Francesca, like two mechanical dolls, reenact once and again the seduction scene. The Refugee and the Ambassador's wife, caught in the artificial and ahistorical time of the embassy, also repeat the same gestures over and over. Like the condemned in Dante's *Inferno*, who can remember the past and foretell the future but are blind to the present, the Refugee and the Ambassador's wife live in an empty moment—the fictional present of toys, of writing, of lovemaking.

The irony in "Right of Sanctuary" is that the Secretary does manage a return, does come back to be "reborn" in another who is himself, yet not quite himself. Once he accomplishes this, however, he is gripped by the realization that, on the other side, things are not substantially different; hence the banter he exchanges at the end with the dictator. Whether he is Secretary or Ambassador is a matter of custom, of uniform, and home is an arbitrary distinction of places, a convention determined by Pan-American conferences and other such political rituals. What "Right of Sanctuary" seeks to demonstrate is that, on the level of writing, exile is a figure of speech, not a shortcut to vision: it is a figure much like the inversion that constitutes the plot of the story.

It is not without a great deal of irony that "Right of Sanctuary" should open with a quotation from the agreement drawn up by the Pan-American Conference that met in Havana in 1928, which set forth the rules for accepting political refugees in foreign embassies (that irony has been increased in recent times by historical events such as the flight of ten thousand refugees into the Peruvian Embassy in Havana). The irony points to the meaninglessness of such conferences, and more specifically, to the peculiar sham of Pan-Americanism as fostered by U.S. policy in Latin America as a means of concealing the purposes of interventionism in the twenties and thirties.[10] But more important, the irony is most devastating because in "Right of Sanctuary" Carpentier is demystifying the Americanist ideology that supported the work of a great many Latin American writers from the twenties on. Latin American culture appears in the story as the irrevocable mixture of heterogeneous codes typical of the modern city (advertisement, mass media, the myriad messages on city walls obeying no peculiar language and offering no special knowledge), together with an official iconography supporting the ideology of the state.

Much of the writing demystified in the story, writing that depended on a more primitivistic notion of culture, was, of course, done by Carpentier himself, and it should be quite clear that "Right of Sanctuary" is also a parody of some of Carpentier's own work, particularly of *Manhunt*. This self-parody, however, requires no previous knowledge of Carpentier's work, because its most immediate object is "Right of Sanctuary"; a text's critical reassessment of the tradition usually spirals back onto itself. We have seen how one of the main characteristics of exile as presented in the story and in Carpentier's works in general is a sense of timelessness and, within the atemporal gap, the creation of scaled-down models. Exile provokes a heightened desire to recapture the past, a desire that makes of that past—be it in the body of the mother or its substitutes, be it in writing—a model whose main activity is repetition. The electric train goes around and around the same track: it is a scaled-down representation of a train that presumably goes somewhere. The ironmongery becomes a museum in which the whole history of humankind is reduced to a special representation enclosure. Love in the timeless gap is reduced to its most basic, yet most perverse, form as the mindless repetition of movements and gestures—Paolo and Francesca are doomed to repeat their every gesture in the depths of the fifth circle of Dante's *Inferno*. Sanctuary as exile is time in a temple of toys, self-sufficient reproductions, minute hermeneutic machines, such as the erector set mentioned in the story, that allow one to construct discrete models.

But is this not the same process as the one through which "Right of Sanctuary" is written? The story not only depicts a scaled-down Latin American country, a reduced iconographic model of a banana republic, but even reduces time to the basic model for its demarcation: the days of the week. All of Latin America's space and time are compressed in "Right of Sanctuary." The whole of the history of the "Frontier Country," for instance, is a capsule history of an archetypal Latin American country, which reads like a project for *One Hundred Years of Solitude*:

Once the Frontier Country was discovered, the first batch of citizens began to arrive: governors, *encomenderos*, ruined noblemen, blackguardly Sevillian tuna merchants, all of them great manipulators of loaded dice, drinkers of old and new wine, and fornicators with the Indian women. Then came the second batch of arrivals: magistrates, shady lawyers, tax collectors, and auditors, who spent more than two centuries transforming the colony into a vast ranch, with cattle and corn plantations as far as the eye could see, except for a few plots growing Spanish vegetables. But one day—who can say how?—there appeared in the country a copy of the *Contrat social* by Rousseau, a citizen of Geneva (*federis aequo, dictamus leges*). And next was the *Emile*. The schoolboys, taught by a disciple of Rousseau, stopped studying books and took to carpentry and nature study, which consisted in dissecting coleoptera and lizards that had been thrown into the burrows of tarantulas. The more influential among the parents were furious; simpler souls asked when and on what ship the Savoyard would arrive. And then, as a last straw, came the French *Encyclopédie*. A Voltairian priest made his first, unexpected appearance in America. There followed the foundation of the Patriotic Council of the Friends of the Nation, based on liberal ideas. And one day the cry of "Liberty or Death!" was heard.

And so, under the aegis of the Heroes, a century was given over to military revolts, coups d'état, insurrections, marches on the capital, individual and collective rivalry, barbarous dictators and enlightened dictators. (pp. 81-82)

The characters in the story, like Sergeant Mouse, appear to be drawn from comic strips or from games like toy soldiers. Is writing not itself, then, a model of exile? Yes, but not so much as a result of a peculiar Latin American condition as of a peculiar Latin American stance. Exile is a founding literary myth, as it is a founding Latin American cultural construct, a strategic form of self-definition.

A significant element in this radical critique of the notion of exile and its relation to literature is the protagonist of "Right of Sanctuary." The story is not only an inversion in terms of its plot, it is also an inversion in terms of the tradition. "Right of Sanctuary" is a microdictator-novel in which the Secretary has become the protagonist, replacing the tyrant. In Asturias's *El señor presidente* (1946), the secretary is slain by the dictator. The dictator is the voice of authority, the telluric force that deflects writing, the latter threatening to undercut his authority. In the postmodern dictator novels, particularly in Augusto Roa Bastos's *Yo el Supremo*, the secretary has gained power, but that power, as opposed to the dictator's, is hampered by its own contradictions. Patiño, a little Oedipus, has swollen feet and is burdened by having memorized every scrap of paper in the Republic. His is the power of cutting, spacing, writing, a power incapable of erecting itself as authority. The Secretary in "Right of Sanctuary," whose instruments are "several dossiers that were able to be dealt with quickly" and "an inkpot surmounted by a Napoleonic eagle" (p. 64), and who is an obsessive reader, is caught up in a world of writing, a world of repetition, of differences set up with apparent arbitrariness, of gaps and frontiers. As a protagonist he cannot claim any kinship to nature, nor declare himself to be the product of tradition. He is a product of convention on the level of fiction, and of political expediency on the level of history. He rules over an unnatural world of comic-book characters, a fictional world much like that of Donald Duck.

With respect to the dictator-novel, the inversion present in "Right of Sanctuary" is analogous to the one that occurred in the French theater from the seventeenth to the eighteenth centuries, in which the servant eventually became the protagonist (the best example is the work of Beaumarchais). In the novel something similar happens as we move from the chivalric romance to the picaresque. The transition in all cases is toward humor. The world of the Secretary is humorous because the central figure stands not for authority but for the abdication of authority, not for an absolute knowledge but for fragmentation and criticism.[11]

Nineteenth-century ideology connecting humankind to nature is shown in Carpentier's mature fiction to be, instead, a set of conventions; it is, among other things, an attempt to bypass all mediations, all codes erected by social and political humankind to process and interpret its world. Postmodern literature, most prominently Carpentier's, demonstrates the artificiality of those codes, their conventionality.

One of those codes is, of course, literature. The theme of exile promises to offer a privileged vision containing the proximity and distance from the source, a kind of double exposure whose perfect analogy is literature. But "Right of Sanctuary" shows that literature and exile possess their own mediations: a persistent tendency to construct models whose finality appears to be to lay bare their own gyrations, to provide pleasure and solace in the absence of recuperable past, to suggest, perhaps, that all life is lived within a gap in which we can only understand models, never whatever it is they represent.

The analogy between literature and toys is all but inevitable and one that I am sure Carpentier would not have disavowed. There is a knowledge to be gained from literature, as there is from toys, a knowledge that has to do with people's creation of palpable models as access both to beauty and to wisdom. Some may outgrow toys, but literature, art, replace these as forms of representation that give substance to our ideas and desires. Literature's own peculiar game, however, is constantly to remind us of its conventionality, to afford once and again the pleasure of its own form of self-denial. Despite the political criticism present on a primary level in "Right of Sanctuary," beyond the preoccupation with the existence of a Latin American culture, the world that Carpentier's story opens up is not too dissimilar from that in Roland Barthes's *Le plaisir du texte*: a maternal refuge (sanctuary) filled with toys and texts.

The process by which "Right of Sanctuary" undercuts the claims of both politics and literature leads us to conclusions that are at odds with Carpentier's avowed commitment to political ideology in the sixties and seventies. His critique of Pan-Americanism—and also of the Alliance for

Progress—as fabrications to mask American imperialism is so radical that the story leads inevitably to the conclusion that all political activity consists of the generation of sign systems whose aim is to deceive rather than to enlighten, and much less to guide; to deflect attention rather than to focus it. There seems to be no real world, no original, no truth against which to measure the validity of these signs, and although literature seems to be capable of demystifying them, it too seems to be caught up in the same process of distortion and deflection. There seems to be no way out of this circle, and, like the toy train in the store, we go around and around. In this sense, literature is a sanctuary, an elaborate form of exile.

Although it may seem that the sort of demystifiction that "Right of Sanctuary" performs denies any specificity to Latin American literature, it seems to me to do the opposite. The critical element of the story sets forth a founding literary myth in Latin America—that of exile—and shows how this myth engenders literature through a process of contradiction and self-denial. Criticism of this sort is not only part of modern literature, it is modern literature itself.

"Meta-End," by Guillermo Cabrera Infante, Translated, with an Introduction, Commentary, and Notes

Introduction

Three Trapped Tigers was perhaps fated to exist as an evolving collection of fragments, in keeping with its own fragmented structure.[1] A brief history of the book soon reveals its vocation for multiplicity and metamorphosis. In 1965 a manuscript entitled *View of Dawn in the Tropics* was awarded the Seix-Barral prize for fiction in Barcelona. The prize, at the time the most prestigious in the Spanish-speaking world, had been won or was going to be won by the likes of Mario Vargas Llosa and Carlos Fuentes. It was a great launching for a young novelist, and the times were good for young Latin American novelists. Had it been published then, *View of Dawn in the Tropics* may or may not have become a celebrated novel, but it certainly would have changed the life of its author, and the recent history of Latin American literature would have been different.

The author of *View of Dawn in the Tropics* was a forty-year-old Cuban writer who not only had been active in the struggle against Batista, but had become an important cultural promoter after the triumph of the Revolution. He was editor of a lively literary journal, *Lunes de Revolución*, until the authorities closed it, traveled in Fidel Castro's retinue, and was influential in the cinema.[2] He was finally sent as cultural attaché to Brussels, perhaps because his iconoclasm made him dangerous to the emerging cultural bureaucracy. When he won the Seix-Barral prize, Cabrera Infante had published a collection of short stories, *Así en el paz como en la guerra* (1961), the first best-seller published after the Revolution in Cuba.

View of Dawn in the Tropics was not published save, in 1974, as a totally different book, which may contain parts of the first version. Yet the unpublished original was one of the reasons for the first of the well-known "Padilla Affairs," when the Cuban poet Heberto Padilla was reprimanded by the authorities for publishing counterrevolutionary poetry.[3] *View* had been withdrawn from publication by Cabrera Infante who, by this time, had decided not to return to Cuba. He proceeded to make substantial changes in the manuscript. According to his own testimony he excised some vignettes dealing with the war in the Sierra Maestra against Batista. The Spanish censor also made some cuts, dictated more by prudishness than by politics. The result was *Three Trapped Tigers*, published to much critical acclaim by Seix-Barral in 1967. Some of this acclaim came from Heberto Padilla, who wondered why an inferior novel like *Pasión de Urbino* by Lisandro Otero was drawing so much attention in Cuba while nothing was being said about *Three Trapped Tigers*, a far superior work. Otero, a faithful bureaucrat, had competed for the Seix-Barral prize with *Pasión de Urbino* the same year Cabrera Infante won it with *View of Dawn in the Tropics*.

In 1971 Cabrera Infante produced yet another version of *Three Trapped Tigers*, the English translation, written in collaboration with translators Donald Gardner and Suzanne Jill Levine.[4] Though the translation follows the original fairly closely, it is really a new version of the novel. An "Epilogue for Late(nt) Readers," which took the form of a commentary on the translation, was published in *Review 72*. The fragment I am using was first published by *Alacrán Azul*, a Cuban-exile magazine based in Miami, which ran for two issues (see commentary 1). There are, then, the following fragments and versions of *Three Trapped Tigers*: (1) the original manuscript, awarded the Seix-Barral prize, which was never published and had the title *View of Dawn in the Tropics*; (2) *Tres tristes tigres*, published in 1967; (3) *Three Trapped Tigers*, published in 1971; (4) the "Epilogue for Late(nt) Readers," published in 1972; (5) *View of Dawn in the Tropics*, the 1974 book, which incorporates some of the vignettes excised from the prize-winning manuscript; and (6) "Meta-Final," published in 1970. The textual fragmentariness of the book as a product, in its most tangible sense, reflects the fragmentariness of its inner structure, which is made up of various texts, ranging from transcriptions of tapes supposedly recorded by a character named Bustrófedon, to a woman's sessions with her psychiatrist, to dialogue, lists, drawings, and the like. This fragmentariness is, to be sure, part of the book's profound meditation on the nature of language, literature, and culture.

My translation does not pretend to be yet another fragment of the novel, nor a new ending to *Three Trapped Tigers*. The "Epilogue for Late(nt) Readers" is *Three Trapped Tigers*' "meta-end." Clearly, it cannot be a new ending for *Tres tristes tigres*, either, given that the Spanish version is already that. My translation aims at being both commentary and interpretation, as well as a more concrete deployment of the reading strategies presented in this book. Translation is interpretation, and interpretation is judgment.

I believe that "Meta-Final" is among the most important texts written in Latin America. In my view it is much more important than anything Cabrera Infante has written since, including his voluminous and meritorious *La Habana para un infante difunto* (1981).[5] This is not meant to diminish

Cabrera Infante. The promotion of a writer's career is a task for journalists. In my estimation, Cabrera Infante's claim to immortality was established by *Three Trapped Tigers* and by "Meta-Final." The latter ought to figure in all anthologies of Latin American literature. It is more important than a great deal of Borges, Carpentier, and Neruda.

"Meta-Final" does not need *Three Trapped Tigers*. This independence in the face of the larger text, which it cannot altogether make disappear, is one of its commentaries on literature: the language of literature creates its antecedent, its foundation. A valid reading of "Meta-Final" would certainly be one in which *Three Trapped Tigers* is considered a necessary fiction for the constitution of this finale, not a "real" book. In "Meta-Final," which is appropriately eschatological and scatological, language is written on the brink of its own extinction, and the past is an evocation that gains reality only as support for the present. Language is always, already beyond the end, a sort of permanent liminality. But my reading, which intends to be historical, will have to consider the reality of the fiction that *Three Trapped Tigers* is for "Meta-Final." Thus, although I will not summarize the plot, a summary that could conceivably be longer than the novel itself, I will furnish details here and in the notes to establish the relation between the two texts, a relation on which my interpretation wishes to inscribe itself.

"Meta-Final" is a Cervantean postscript in which the characters in *Three Trapped Tigers* confront one of the authors/narrators (Códac) to make a correction in the ending of the story, or, better, in one of the possible endings of the story. "Meta-Final" is, then, a dialogue in which a minor character, Walter Socarrás, Silvestre, Rine Leal, and one of the authors/narrators discuss what happened to Estrella, the obese black nightclub singer they admire and sometimes protect, who was reported to have died in Mexico. The correction is not really of the ending of *Three Trapped Tigers*, since the novel does not end with Estrella's death; it is an alternative ending to that strand of the narrative. As will be seen, endings proliferate once "Meta-Final" is considered.

Estrella is a "natural"; she has no training at all in music. She sings in nightclubs, after the show is over, without an orchestra background. During the day she is a maid in a well-to-do Havana household. Estrella is to the other characters in the novel what Johnny in Cortázar's "The Pursuer" is to the narrator. She is grotesque in physical appearance, yet her voice and tempo make any song she sings new and hers. Like Johnny, she is in touch with mysterious sources from which her music issues, sources of an absolute knowledge that cannot be expressed in language. Estrella is a compelling enigma to the trapped tigers, whose lives take place after dark, in the secret world of Havana nightlife before the Revolution.

Like Estrella, Silvestre, Arsenio, Rine, Cuba Venegas, Beba Longoria, and most other characters in the novel move beyond the confines of their social class. They are all from the lower classes and from the provinces and are trying to mask their origin in the social no-man's-land of Havana nightlife, where pretense is relatively easy.

Three Trapped Tigers is a bitter social novel, marked very deeply by the Cuban Revolution and no doubt by the proletarian background of the author (whose parents were among the earliest members of the Cuban Communist party). One of the Cabrera Infante's enduring achievements is to have captured in language what could only be called a class war. Many of the metamorphoses of language in the novel stem from the variegated backgrounds of the characters, and from their efforts to conceal them. There is pathos bordering on social melodrama in the plight of these characters, a constant in Cabrera Infante's work, which culminates in *La Habana para un infante difunto*. In "Meta-Final" this characteristic appears in the short biography of Walter Socarrás and the other musicians who play in Havana casinos (see commentary 10). But besides the clear sociopolitical criticism implied in this dynamic display of language, there is another level at which the fragmentation and metamorphoses of language in *Three Trapped Tigers* can be viewed, a level that could be called, for lack of a better name, "ontological."

Estrella is not the only enigma in *Three Trapped Tigers*; her counterpart is Bustrófedon, the character whose ability to distort and remake language is admired and imitated by all the others. Bustrófedon, who never appears in the novel, is, however, captured on tape by Arsenio. These tapes, which contain his parodies, are transcribed and included in the novel as "The Death of Trotsky as Described by Various Cuban Writers, Several Years after the Event—or Before." After his death it is discovered that Bustrófedon had a brain "lesion (he, poor guy, would have called it a lesson) since he was a kid, or earlier, from birth, or before he was even formed and that a bone (what do you think, Silvestre and Cué: an aneurysm, an embolism or a bubble in the humorous vein?), a knot in the spinal column, something like that, which pressed on his brain and made him say all those marvelous things and play with words so he ended his life as a new Adam, giving everything a name as though he really was inventing language" (p. 231). The pathologist's diagnosis explains that the disease "*in its last stages dissociated the cerebral function from the symbolism of thinking by means of speech*" (p. 232; emphasis in original).

If Estrella is in touch with the mysterious sources of language, with logos as melos, as music before articulation, Bustrófedon incarnates the differentiating power of language. In Bustrófedon language is distancing, splitting, fission, what Magnarelli has called the "writerly" in *Three Trapped Tigers*.[6] The writerly is, of course, not necessarily writing as such, but a representation of language's own constitution as spacing, a constitution whose visual image is writing; the orality of *Three Trapped Tigers* is obviously a deluded representation of this quality.

There is a profound sadness in the fact that Bustrófedon's joyful ability to deface language is made possible by a brain lesion. In a way, the explanation is in consonance with the material decay of bodies in the novel, not only Estrella's but also the bodies of the various women who hide their physical miseries with cosmetics. A shadow of naturalism lurks in the background of Cabrera Infante's work, where the body is often viewed in terms of its anatomical dysfunctions. But Bustrófedon's brain lesion is special because it is the source of language, that is to say, of a new language whose ability is to name is dependent on a founding negativity, the hypostasis of which is the lesion itself, the cut, or death, the final dysfunction, which releases the tapes to be transcribed and included in the text of the novel. We possess Bustrófedon's language because of the double negation of the lesion and his death. Logos as ontology in this play of language is the interval of dysfunction, the play of language announcing the dysfunction through its proclivity to malformation and error. Malformation and error are the gaps between the self and the world and between the self and its own intended representation in language. All the distortions of language in *Three Trapped Tigers* issue out of this double negation of lesion and death. The novel is sad because of the realization that logos as ontology is at best this marriage of error and death. The novel is a kind of wake for Bustrófedon, and in this sense it has a profound affinity with *Finnegan's Wake*. "Meta-Final" is a wake for Estrella, and this may very well be the reason why Cabrera Infante chose not to include it in the novel, wishing to avoid an excessive symmetry (see commentary 1). "Meta-Final" has much in common with "Big Mama's Funeral," though Cabrera Infante's text is superior.

Dictated, transcribed, spaced, broken, Bustrófedon's texts endure in the novel. Not so with Estrella's. Her dark powers endow her with an aura of absolute knowledge that is apparently beyond description—she is the specular counterimage of Moby Dick, a black negative counterposed to the whiteness of a whale, neither of which is "readable." Because she is black and a singer, there is an allegorical level at which Estrella could be seen as the embodiment of culture, of tradition, and of knowledge. She is a black star who guides not toward a lucid comprehension of fate, but instead toward an obscure destiny, toward a kind of occult wisdom (there are many Afro-Cuban cult symbols in the novel, which clearly allow for this interpretation).[7] On that level "Meta-Final" is a sort of funeral for the delusion of authority based on the telos, a telluric sapience before language itself. But in that death Estrella and the occult knowledge are not obliterated. She floats away after having inflicted wounds of her own, after having become, in the stasis of death, an instrument of rending, a projectile that penetrates and cuts apart. Her monstrous maternal self becomes a ramming projectile, an aggressive phallus, unsettling whatever calm or joy could be expected from life in the gap, from knowledge of the gap as a renewed source of authority.

In this, it seems to me, lies the richness and complexity of "Meta-Final."

The correction in "Meta-Final" alludes to the following passage in the novel. This section is narrated by Códac, the photographer:

[S]he even cut a record (I know: I bought it and *listened* to it), and after that she went to San Juan, P.R., and to Caracas and to Mexico City and everywhere she went people were talking about her voice more than listening to it. She went to Mexico against the advice of her private doctor (no, *not* Alex Bayer's private doctor) who told her the altitude would kill her and she went in spite of his advice and in spite of everything she overstayed herself until one evening she ate a huge dinner and the next morning she had acute indigestion and called a doctor and the indigestion became a heart attack and she spent three days in an oversize oxygen tent and on the fourth day she got worse and on the fifth day she died. There ensued a legal battle between the Mexican impresarios and their Cuban colleagues about the cost of transport to take her back to Cuba for burial and they wanted to ship her as general freight but came under special transport and then they wanted to put her in a frozen-goods container and have her sent the same way they fly lobsters to Miami and her faithful acolytes protested, outraged by this ultimate insult, but finally they had no other alternative than to leave her in Mexico to be buried there. (pp. 307-308)

Meta-Final/Meta-End

Meta-Final

Te equivocaste en un dellate en un detalle me dijo Walter Socarrás, socarrón, para añadir socorrido, corrido, corriendo, corrigiendo, te equisbotaste. Lo que éste quería decir es que no era verdad lo que dije de La Estrella, el tercero en decirme que no era verdad lo que dije pero él no hablaba de la mentira de su vida sino de su muerte. No de su muerte sino de la muerte de La Estrella. A lo que Silvestre replicó cómo es posible, hay vidas inauténticas pero todas las muertes son auténticas. Y ahí se paró, dándose cuenta demasiado tarde para su ser de que no daba pie porque le había dado pie al muy cabrón de Socarrás para que dijera socorriendo, No todas las muertes son auténticas, Silverio. Hay muertes ortodoxas.

Pero tenía razón Walter Socarrás, de verdadero nombre Gualterio Suárez, que es el marido de Gloria Pérez cuando ella se llama Cuba Venegas, ése que no se si ustedes saben que es director de orquesta o un conductor como dicen sus peores amigos queriendo decir que éste está mejor en una guagua de pie cobrando el pasaje que orquestando un pasaje parado sobre el podium o podio o poyo o como se llame esa tribuna de gestos, salvado en el último rollo por el Difunto quien solía decir solito que en definitiva ir en guagua de pie, con aquello de la velocidad, los tumbos y las maneras de ser de los guagüeros no es más que estar sobre un podium que camina. Lo cierto es que Dobleve Ese es arreglista y él mismo dice de sí mismo en el mismo disco de plomo de La Estrella para el que debía de haber una goma de borrar sonidos, escribió él de él: "Walter Socarrás reclama, al lanzar este disco, el puesto de el mejor arreglista de América." Discóbolo que le da la razón a Cerpentier (o a la Condesa de Marlín, no sé: tal vez a los dos) cuando dijo que los cubanos estaban todos grisés, diciendo así quizás en francés que Cuba es una isla rodeada (por todas partes) por un mal de genios o genios del mar. Aunque Silvestre cuando él se llama Isla dice que las islas siempre terminan por (o al menos tratar de) dominar al continente, como el líquido que contiene una botella. A lo que el Diphunto respondía citando, recitando a las islas del Maregeo, a esa isla de Cretinos, creta, a Sicilia, a Ingalaterra y ultimadamente-dijo El al Japón, conocido también como Nipón, Nihón o Imperio del Sol Na Siente.

Pero volviendo a dar vueltas a este disco o mejor a su envoltura o cuadratura del círculo donde se dicen o dice WalSoc cosas como éstas que hay que leerlas para creerlas y sic sic sic *La Cadena de avocaciones que llega a cada amante de la música del acento auténtico de Cuba, lo lleva al público una voz de mujer, la de La Estrella. La Reina, La Monarca absoluta de la música cubana en todas sus manifestaciones. En las modalidades y estilos dentro de un mismo ritmo, en la expresión definitiva, en el alarde acentuado de una realidad indiscutida, desde el ayer lejano al presente y, quizá en el futuro, hay una sola estrella: La Estrella* (del

Meta-End [1]

You blew it in a detail a detale[2] said Walter Socarrás, rascal Socarrás, only to add, correcting, succorer, ranting red: You blue it.[3] What the above mentioned meant to say is that what I said about Estrella wasn't true, being the third to tell me that what I said about Estrella wasn't true. He was not talking about the lie that her life was but where she lay in her death.[4] Not her death but Estrella's death. To which Silvestre replied how could that be, there may be inauthentic lives, but all deaths are authentic. And he stopped there realizing much too late for his selbst that he had gotteninto hot walters, giving Walter, the big fucker, succorer Socarrás, the chance to retort: Not all deaths are Authentic, Silver-io. There are orthodox deaths.[5]

But Walter Socarrás was right. Walter, whose real name is Gualterio Suárez, who is Gloria Pérez's husband when she was called Cuba Venegas. The one whom I don't know if you know is an orchestra leader, or a conductor, as his worst friends call him, meaning that the above mentioned is better suited for a bus, collecting fares, than orchestrating a suite standing on some podium, flatform, platform, rostrum or whatever you call that gestual tribunal, saved in the last reel by The Deceased, who used to say himself that to be standing in a bus, what with the speed, the near falls and the drivers' way of being is nothing more than being on a moving podium.[6] What's certain is that Doblew Es is a musical arranger and he himself says about himself in the same disc(us) of Estrella's for which there should be an eraser to erase sound, he wrote there about himself: "Walter Socarrás, upon releasing this record, claims his place as the best musical arranger in the Americas."[7] A discoballus who confirms Cerpentier (or the Countess of Marlin—I don't know which, perhaps both) when he said that all Cubans are grisés, meaning maybe in French that Cuba is an island surrounded (on all sides) by an ocean of geniuses, or sí-men.[8] Though Silvestre, when he calls himself Island says that islands wind up dominating (or trying to) the Continent, the way the liquid in a bottle does the bottle. To which The Dead One replied, citing, re-citing the islands of the Algian sea: Crete, island of cretins, Sí-Celia, Angleland, and finally Japan, also known as Nikon, or the Empty Ire of the Raisin Son.[9]

But turning to the turning record or better to its square cover, or squared circle, where it says or WallSock says things like this, that have to be read to be believed sic sic sic: *The string of beats that reaches every lover of music that has a true Cuban accent carries to the public the voice of a woman, Estrella's. The Queen, the Absolute Monarch of Cuban music, in all of its manifestations. In all the modulations and styles contained within a single beat, in the bold stress of an indisputable reality coming from a faraway yesterday to the present and maybe even to the future, there is only one Star: Estrella.* (Holy shit! This is more than poor Gualterio Suárez could

carajo! más que del pobre Gualterio Suárez que después de todo quizá no ha escrito esto porque interrogación lo permitiría Cuba cierra interrogación cierra paréntesis y punto y seguido Pero sí fue WSeguro quien escribió lo que sigue sobre sí sobre la cubierta encubierta del disco "En este álbum Walter Socarrás hace un alarde inusitado del perfecto dominio que tiene sobre las distintas combinaciones orquestales imaginablemente (*así mismo*!) posibles y traza pautas en la orquestación moderna" *mierda, trazar pautas en la orquestación*! "Así vemos como logra magníficas combinaciones de cuerdas y metales, quintetos de trombones con piano, bajo y ritmo" para terminar diciendo que comillas actualmente dirige la orquesta de un lujoso Casino habanero para la cual hace los arreglos orquestales además de hacer los arreglos orquestales para otro fastuoso Casino siempre con C mayúscula cierra comillas y cogiendo al todo por el culo de la parte hace de la orquesta casino (no confundir por favor con la Orquesta casino de la playa) y convierte o se convierte a sí mismo en sus notas nada musicales en Walter Socarrás el dealer que orquesta, además de que me cago! TODOS grisés. Hasta los casinos o Casinos. Cacasinos.

Estás equivocagado, me dijo Walter Socarrás en esa o esta ocasión. (¡O casino!) La Estrella no está enterrada en México, me dijo aunque no así sino con jota. No, le dije, le grité yo: ¿NO? no, me respondió él, no está enterrada en México con jota. Entonces dónde pregunté yo interrogante. Ella no está enterrada en Méjico ni en ninguna parte. ¡Como! dije yo preguntando con signo de exclamación doble, por delante y por detrás, la palabra cogida, como el general custer, entre flechas. ¿Ella no está muerta entonces?¡¿¡Que NO está muerta!?¡! me dijo él interrogante asombrado aunque no estaba asombrado ni interrogante sino más bien arrogante, abrogante, atorrante. Está más muerta que el mar muerto me dijo y se rió. Lo que después de todo no es tan mal acorde, me dijo, no señor. Aunque sería mejor hacerlo un acorde invertido, muerto el mar, así y en este caso un acorde perfecto o mayor si se dice muerta en el mar. Porque así es me dijo y me dijo mucho más.

La Estrella se murió de verdad en México y su secretario con el neceser hizo lo imposible por traerla a enterrar en Cuba, y ya se sabe lo que pasa cuando se hace lo imposible posible que todo termina en el caos. La cosa o el caos empezó cuando intentaron embalsamarla y unos amigos del amiguito de La Estrella buscaron al embalsamador adecuado, de nombre Inocente Adecuado, que era el que tenía más fama en México porque no era otro (es decir que era él mismo) que el que embalsamó el caballo de Zapata. Pero resulta ser que este embalsamador Adecuado era ahora una momia él mismo, un viejo viejo pero muy viejo que apenas si veía a quien embalsamar y tal vez hasta había empezado a autoembalsamarse, y como todos los embalsamadores estaba bastante tocado o tal vez todo lo contrario: es decir, intocable! Lo cierto es que este taxidermista mexicano tenía la teoría de que la mejor

do, after all maybe didn't even write this because Cuba wouldn't allow it interrogation point close parenthesis period. But for sure it was Wsure who wrote the following in the covered cover of the record: In this record Walter Socarrás boasts of his surprisingly perfect control of the various orchestral combinations imaginably (like that) possible and offers new keys to modern orchestration. *Shit, to offer new keys to modern orchestration.* Thus he accomplishes magnificent combinations of strings, metals, trombone quintets with piano, bass and percussion, and finishes up saying quote at present he conducts the orchestra of a plush Casino in Havana, for which he makes the orchestra arrangements in addition to making orchestra arrangements for another great Casino always in caps unquote and grabbing the whole by the parts makes the quasino-orchestra (not to be confused with Orchestra Casino on the beach)[10] quasinothing and himself in his not so musical benders Walter Socarrás, the dealer who orchestrates, on top of all of which I shit! ALL grisés. Even the quasinots, or casi-nots, cacasinaughts, quasinos.

You laid one, said Walter Socarrás on that occasion or on another (O quasinot!). Estrella is not buried in Mexico, he said, though not like that but with a j. No, said I yelling, no? No, he answered, she is not buried in Mexico with a jay. Then where, asked I interrogatingly. She is not buried in Mexico or anywhere else. What? said I, asking with a double exclamation point, a word caught from the front and the back, like General Custer between arrows. Isn't she dead then? That she is not dead?! said he interrogating astonished, though he was neither interrogating nor astonished but very arrogant, abrogating, abe-ranting. She is deader than the dead sea, he said and laughed. Which by the way is not disc-ordant at all, no siree. Though it might be better to make it an inverted chord, dead the sea, thus being in this case a whole or major chord, if said: she is dead in the sea. Because that's the way it is, he said, and said a lot more.[11]

Estrella really died in Mexico and her secretary carrying the toilet-case tried to do the impossible to have her buried in Cuba, and it's a known thing that when the impossible is made possible everything ends up in chaos.[12] The thing or chaos began when they tried to embalm her and a few friends of Estrella's little friend looked for a proper embalmer, named Innocent Proper,[13] who was none other (being himself) than t、 ʔ one who embalmed Zapata's horse. But as it happens this embalmer Proper was by now a mummy himself, an old, old man who could barely see who it was that he was embalming and had even begun to embalm himself, and who, like all embalmers had a touch of madness, or quite the contrary was untouchable.[14] The fact is that this Mejican taxidermist had the theory that the best way of

manera de embalsamar es la natural, que no es tan desatinado como suena o como se lee sino que es más, porque este doctor en taxidermia de Oaxaca dice o decía tal vez dice todavía (nunca se sabe cuando un embalsamador está del todo embalsamado), decía que la mejor tajidermia, así dijo, la hace la Madre Natura y ahí están los mamuts, dicen que dijo y los amigos del amiguito y el amiguito que no era otro que el necesario con su secreter se volvieron agitados para eludir el alud de mamuts, la estampida, antes de que el viejo tuviera tiempo de agregar "que aparecieron en Siberia." Y con esta confidencia más el suspiro aliviado de la concurrencia comenzó su conferencia con la inferencia de que era una teoría a tomar en consideración por la congregación. En una palabra (que es un decir: ya verán) su texis era embalsamar a la gente tal y como están, es decir, muertas, pero sin destriparlas ni limpiar sus vísceras (que el viejo pronunciaba viseras) ni formolizarlas pero teniendo cuidado de colocarlas en una tartera de zinc ad hoc y echándoles encima celofán derretido pero no derretido al calor sino al frío, licuado, dijo el viejo, y con este plástico hacer un molde transparente rodeando al cadáver por todas partes menos por una que se llama tarta. Isla incorrupta en un mar de plástico, dijo el viejo. Sí, dijo un amigo entre los amigos, como la Bella Durmiente. Y para qué lo dijo porque el sectario recordó a La Estrella antes de haberla olvidado y se cubrió los ojos con una manita, así, como diciendo Que no quiero verla pero dijo Ay no! locual el viejo momificante puso punto final a su charla diciendo, Y eso es lo que cuesta, hijito, un ojo de la cara! Ahí no estaba el punto final de la charla sino un poco más adelante cuando el viejo dijo su precio, este taxidermista poniendo el taxis por delante de la dermia y ver que nadie tenía dinero suficiente siquiera para iniciar el proceso que después de todo era absoluta y totalmente experimental en el sentido de que, como decía el Difundido, es perimental toda teoría sin prajis. (Entre paréntesis) si los amigos de La Estrella no tenían dinero La Estrella misma no tenía mucho tiempo y ya se sabe que time is money como money is time y lo que es peor todavía y terrible: *time is time!*

De manera que, la momia aconsejó que después de todo él estaba por lo positivo, que era aquí lo natural y que tan bueno como el hielo plástico era el hielo verdadero y si no se podía conseguir hielo glaciar o siberiano el hielo aunque fuera seco hielo era y mejor que nada o que la Nada. Acto seguido le dio dos inyecciones de caballo (zapatista) de formol a La Estrella que estuvo allí de cuerpo presente todo el tiempo y recomendó (el viejo taxidérmico) que aceptaran la oferta de enviarla por mar, que después de todo el mar es salado y la sal cura. Además de ser el transporte marítimo mucho más barato, dijo. Y luego habló de la calma oceánica, del yodo, del aire puro y de cómo se gana perspectiva cuando uno se rodea de horizonte y se hace isla. Terminó. Pero antes, una mención comercial. Son diez pesos. Digo dólares, al cambio actual. Por la consulta. Ustedes la pasen bien.

embalming was the natural way, which is not as wild as it sounds or reads but more so, because this doctor in taxidermy from Oaxaca says or used to say, or perhaps says until now (one never knows when an embalmer is all embalmed), said, says that the best tajidermy, he said it like that, is done by Mother Nature and there are the mammoths to prove it, they say that he said and the friends of the little friend and the little friend who none other than the toilet-case with the secrets went into a frenzy to avoid the mountain of mammoths, the stampede of mammoths, before the old man had the chance to conclude "which were discovered in Siberia."[15] After confiding this and a sigh of relief from the audience the lecture began, inferring that his theory was worth considering by the gathering. In one word (which is just a manner of speaking as you will soon find out) his thexis was to embalm people just as they are, which is to say dead, but without disemboweling them or cleaning out their viscera (which the old man pronounced visors) or putting them in formaldehyde, but making sure of placing them on a long ad hoc pan and pouring on them molten cellophane, but molten not by fire but by cold, liquidized, said the old man, and with this plastic making a transparent mold covering the body on all parts except for the part for making tarts. Incorruptible island in a sea of plastic, said the old man. Yes, said a friend among friends, like Sleeping Beauty. And why did he have to go and say that, because the sectarian remembered Estrella as she was before he forgot her and covering his eyes like this with his little hand, as if saying I don't want to see it said Oh, no! withwhich the loquant mummy came to the end of his talk saying, And that's the price, sonny, an arm and a leg! That wasn't really the end of the talk, which came a bit ahead of that when the old man stated his price, this taxidermist put the tax(i) before the hearse, and when he saw that no one had enough money to begin the process, which after all was absolutely experimental in the sense that, as The Departed put it, all theory without prajis is perimental.[16] (in parentheses), if Estrella's friends didn't have any money, Estrella herself didn't have much time, and since *time is money* and *money is time*, the worst part of it is that *time is time*.

So the mummy advised that, after all, he was in favor of whatever was positive, which in this case was the natural way itself, and that real ice was just as good as plastic ice and if one couldn't get ice off a glacier or Siberian ice, even dry ice was better than nothing or Nothingness. Right away he gave two formidable formaldehyde injections to Estrella, big enough for a (Zapatista) horse, for she had been there all this time in body if not in soul and recommended (the old taxidermist) that they accept the offer to send her by ship because the sea is salty and cures. In addition to being cheaper to ship by ship, said he. Then he spoke of iodized air, of pure air, and of how one gets a proper perspective when surrounded by the horizon and becomes an island. He finished. But before a commercial message. It's ten pesos. I mean dollars at the going rate. For the visit. And have a good day.

El secresectario de La Estrella la embarcó por tren hasta Veracruz donde la caja o como dice el Gran Be no un ataúd, un cataratafalco, el esféretro, donde sería embarcado rumbo a La Habana. La CompañíaNacionaldeTransporte Ese‚A había quedado en que en la aduana mexicana después que abrieran la caja para la inspección (ya ustedes saben: plata posible, el Sagrado Patrimonio Artístico de la Nación Azteca siendo saqueado seguro, mariguana que fumar) se le pondría más hieloseco, antes de cerrarlo claro está. Y en Ver-a-Cruz abrieron y cerraron el, el, el cajón sin más problema que el pequeño, casi insignificante, deleznable olvido de un adjetivo que, a quién se la va a ocurrir joven que haga daño que falte dígame usted. Es decir que enviaron a un mandadero a echarle hieloseco dentro y éste y compró hielo a secas en el bar de enfrente y lo regó bien por todas partes de la isla de acero macabro que tenía adentro la perla negra barrueca. Fue cuando le preguntaron (no a la perlada sino al pelado) si era hieloseco que dijo, Qué seco niqué seco. Pero tiene que ser hieloseco! Seco o mojado, joven todo es hielo, y siguió echando el hielo, si bien frappé, alrededor del estuche de metal que encerraba la suma mortal de La Estrella. Luego cerró la caja y dijo que ya podían embarcarla gritando, Arriba con La Escarchada!

No sé si ustedes saben que cuando se dice que hace calor en Veracruz quiere decir que la olla del golfo hierve bajo el sol y que de la selva viene un vaho tórrido que convierte al puerto en agua a baño de maría. Ese día hizo calor en Veracruz y el barco estuvo atracado desde por la mañana con el ataúd con la Estrella encerrado en la bodega, una caja con hielo dentro de una marmita en agua a baño de maría cociéndose a fuego violento en la olla del golfo calentada a vaho selvático.

El barco zarpó a las quince dos puntos cero cero horas. Dos horas mar afuera el hedor se sentía en todo el barco cubriendo todas las zonas de la rosa de los vientos fétidos y supieron que el barco era el centro universal de la peste. En sus entrañas encontraron la caja chorreando agua pútrida, soltando vapor hediondo, chirriando mefítica. El médico de a bordo declaró que no llegaría a La Habana y si llegaba el ataúd no llegaba el barco. La disyuntiva impresionó al capitán quien haciendo uso de sus prerrogativas navales rompió en pedazos el manifiesto de carga fúnebre y ordenó lo único posible, echarle el muerto a otro. En este caso al agua.

Izaron con gran trabajo la caja a cubierta y la dejaron sobre el puente mientras, en deferencia a su condición de mujer (la del cadáver no del féretro), buscaban una bandera cubana, con respeto a su condición de tal, con que cubrirla (la caja no el cadáver), acciones que fueron gestos innecesarios o sentimentales porque dentro de la caja no había un ciudadano cubano ni una mujer sino una increíble masa de carroña al vapor. Casi como quien dice carne asada. Para añadir al absurdo ocurrió que nadie a bordo sabía cómo era una bandera cubana, cosa nada extraña en un barco canadiense fletado por un armador griego que navega bajo bandera

Estrella's secretsectary traveled by train to Veracruz to meet the box, or as The Great B says, not a coffin but a mountain, a mammothphagus, a spherophagus, a sark oafagus, from where it would be shipped to Havana.[17] TheNationalFreightCo.Ink had agreed that at the Mexican border, after opening The Box for inspection (silver, you know, The Sacred Artistic Patrimony of the Aztec Nation being sacked, a little maryjane), they would put in more dry ice, before closing it, of course.[18] And Invert-a-Cruise they opened the closed the, the, The Great Crate with no problem but for a minor insignificant trifling omission of an adjective which, after all, young man, who was going to think that its absence was going to cause any harm. That is to say that they sent a messenger boy to pour the dry ice and he went to the bar across the street and bought plain ice and spread it on all sides of the macabre iron island containing the baroque black pearl.[19] That's when they asked (not the pearly one but the plucked one) if it was dry ice. What do you mean dry? But it has to be dry ice! Dry or wet, young man, ice is ice, and he went on pouring the ice, though at least frappé, around the metal container with Estrella's mortal addipositions. Then he closed the lid and pronounced her fit to ship by shouting, Up with The Glacée.

I don't know if you know that when they say that it's hot in Veracruz, it means that the Gulf's pot is boiling under the sun and the jungle is letting out a steaming vapor that turns the pot into a double boiler. That day it was hot in Veracruz and the ship was moored since morning with Estrella's coffin in its hold, a box with ice in a stewpot boiling in a double boiler, cooking at furious heat in the cauldron of the Gulf heated by the steaming vapor of the jungle.

The ship weighed anchor at fifteen dash hundred hours. After two hours at sea the stench was all over the ship, covering all points of the stinking comp-ass and it was discovered that the ship itself was the source of the smell. In its entrails they found the box dripping putrid water, letting out fetid vapors, screeching noxiously.[20] The ship's doctor declared that the box would not make it to Havana, and if the coffin arrived the ship wouldn't. The dilemma so impressed the captain that taking recourse to his naval prerogatives he tore up the manifest for the funereal freight and gave the only possible order, to pass off the load to someone else. In this case it was to the water.

They laboriously hoisted the box onto the deck and left it on the bridge while, in deference to her being a woman (the body not the box), they looked for a Cuban flag with which to cover it (the box not the body), in deference to her citizenship, all unnecessary or sentimental gestures because in the box there was nothing but an incredible mass of steaming, rotten meat. Almost roast beef. To add a touch of the grotesque to the absurd, no one on board knew what the Cuban flag looked like, not an odd thing to happen in a Canadian ship rented by a Greek shipping magnate, sailing under the

panameña con una tripulación compuesta de mexicanos, argentinos, un gallego, un liberiano, la morralla de siete continentes y cinco mares (o es al revés? la morralla de cinco mares y siete continentes?) más el capitán, polaco exilado y un polizón de Pernambuco nacido en la isla de Malta que nadie detectó hasta llegar el barco a Madeira. Finalmente, el capitán decidió o dictó que la bandera de Havana, así dijo, debía ser color habano ya que ese era el nombre y el color de un buen cigarro, y de la bodega trajeron un pedazo de lana color chocolate sucio en que envolvieron el ataúd, de acuerdo con la tradición marina. Pero todavía no lo echaron a mar.

Antes de hacerlo decidieron buscar lastre. Qué lastre ni qué lastre! dijo uno de los mexicanos o el otro. No están viendo nomás que no hay cristiano que levante ese fardo! Se val fondo, dijo, predijo, al mero fondo que se va como van las arengas al mal! Le hicieron caso, siempre se hace caso al hiperbólico: en todo caso mucho más caso que al parabólico. Toda la tripulación, menos el capitán, el timonel y el polizón, tuvo que dar una mano y luego la otra para levantar el ataúd, mientras el mexicano decía, declaraba, gritaba, Quéles dije, quéles dije! Quéles dije, quéles dije! Quéles dije! Quéles dije!, varias veces y finalmente exclamó: Qué les dije! justo antes de tropezar con un cabo, caer hacia delante, empujar al cocinero gallego en su caída que en la propia se aferró la caja al tiempo que también caía (como todos los cocineros gallegos cuando son empujados por detrás mientras llevan en andas un ataúd pesado a bordo de un barco de carga para echarlo a la mar porque hiede) hacia delante, logrando en su gestión cayente tumbar al primer andero y ambos servir de propulsor al cuerpo inerte convirtiéndolo gracias al impulso en proyectil y hacer que saliera disparado sobre cubierta mientras los demás anderos, en acción tardía, agarraban primero aire hueco y finalmente lienzo vacío y todavía color habano entre las manos, mirando inútiles cómo la bala de lata envuelta en madera, el balón cuadrado, el misil inverso caía de regreso a la cubierta, cepillaba las planchas de hierro, se deslizaba libre y rompía la varanda del puente para volver a ser cohete segundos antes de decidir convertirse en torpedo y zambullir en arco de trayectoria y caer al agua con un ruido de barrigazo tan alto como la columna de doce metros de altura por cuatro de ancho que levantó agua, rocío y salitre hasta las caras aliviadas del peso y la responsabilidad de los anderos y su capitán mientras el marinero mexicano, en pie de nuevo y asomándose al agua, gritaba otra vez Quéles dije, hijos de la, quéles dije! Ay Chihuagua!

Ya se iban a ocupar sus puestos los miembros de la tripulación, a reparar el puente algunos, el capitán a fumar su pipa, el cocinero al caldero, cuando el silencio abrupto del mexicano entre dos Quélesdije! Qué les di-je! les hizo volver la cabeza y luego los cuerpos respectivos hacia donde estaba éste mirando con la boca abierta debajo del arco de sus bigotes mexicanos. O séase, hacia el arco abierto debajo del barco. Vieron, como el mexicano, un

Panamanian flag, with a crew made up of Mexicans, Argentines, one Galician, a Liberian, the scum of seven continents and five seas (or is it the other way around, five continents and seven seas?), plus the captain, an expatriate Pole, and a stowaway from Pernambuco, born in Malta, who was not discovered until the ship reached Madeira. Finally, the captain decided or dictated that the flag of Havana, that's how he put it, should be the color of Havanas, they being good cigars, and they brought up from the hold a piece of chocolate-colored wool in which they wrapped the coffin, according to naval tradition.[21] But they still didn't throw it in the water.

Before doing so they looked around for ballast. What do you mean ballast, said one or the other Mexican. Can't they see that there's no man alive who can lift that load. It'll go to the bottom, said or predicted he, to the very bottom like a red herring that has mis(lead).[22] They listened to him, hyperbell being louder than parabell.[23] The whole crew, except for the captain, the helmsman and the stowaway, lent a hand and then both to lift the coffin, while the Mexican said, declared, shouted: What'dsay, What'dsay! several times. He finally exclaimed: What did I say!, just as he stumbled on a rope, fell forward, pushing the Galician cook as he went, who clutched the box as he too went (and as all Galician cooks go when pushed from behind while carrying a heavy casket on board a cargo ship to throw it in the sea because it stinks) forward, managing while on his falling mission to knock over the first beer bearer, both becoming prime movers of the inert body, making it, thanks to their momentum, into a projectile that shot through the deck as the other bearers, with belated reflexes grabbed first empty air and finally empty shroud, Havana cigar color still in their hands, looking futilely at how the tin bullet wrapped in wood, the square ball, the inverted missile fell back on deck, scraped the iron planks, skidded free, breaking the rail on the bridge, becoming again for a few seconds a missile before deciding to turn torpedo, plunging into the sea in a parabola trajectory, slapping the water with a splash as loud as the twelve by four meter column of water that shot up, spraying salt water on the faces, now relieved of weight and responsibility, of the pallbearers and their captain, as the Mexican sailor, on his feet again a leaning out over the water shouted again What'dItellyou, sons of bitches, What'dItellyou, ay Chihuahua![24]

The crew was on their way back to their stations, some to repair the bridge, the captain to smoke his pipe, the cook back to his pots, when the abrupt silence of the Mexican between two of his What'dItellyou   What'dItellyou made them turn their faces and later their respective bodies toward where he was looking, with gaping mouth under the rainbow of his Mexican moustache. That is to say toward the arch that opening out from the ship out. They saw, like the

poco después, un poco más, surgir primero un extremo oscuro y agorero y después todo el féretro como un submarino de madera, como un pez muerto y obsceno y no es verdad que bien narro? preguntó Socarrás, socarrando, mirando a Silvestre. Nadie le respondió ni nadie tuvo tiempo de hacerlo porque enseguida *explicó*, otrorrinelaringólogo, que evidentemente, así dijo, con el agua del hielo hecha vapor dentro del vapor se había hinchado la madera y ahora el estuche del féretro técnicamente era impermeable, navegante y flotaba. Es decir, dijo, era una nave del tiempo exterior.

Los mexicanos Quélesdije y su carnal y un estibador liberiano vieron en el ataúd flotante un castigo si no del cielo por lo menos del mar insultado, un seguro signo de mal agüero, la señal de la profecía y decidieron por su cuenta (y riegos) que había que hundir aquel navío satélite que insistía en navegar junto a su rampa de lanzamiento. Sin consultar con nadie empezaron a tirarle varias cosas, todas lanzables: un pedazo de varanda del puente roto hecha flecha, lanzas de trozos de madera del mismo origen, un zapato de baqueta, un huarache, un chorro de insultos, varias balas de saliva y finalmente su desesperación individual y colectiva y su odio ciego y mudo. Finalmente, álguien los socorrió trayendo una escopeta con que dispararle una, dos, varias descargas. Pero las balas (de plomo) o caían cerca o muy lejos y no daban nunca en blanco tan visible y oscuro o daban todas en diana si el blanco era el mar. Por fin un plomo pegó en el paquebote y rebotó hacia el agua, la madera no solo hecha impermeable sino también impenetrable. El capitán contagiado (ese no era su nombre, completo, era capitán Josef Teodor Achabowski, nacido en Korzeniev en la Ucrania Rusa, entonces bajo dominio polaco, el 3 de diciembre de 1857, por lo que contaría, mediante ábaco, con 101 años de edad, según el nuevo calendario. Su padre, un terrateniente de literarios gustos, fue exilado al norte de Prusia por participar en los movimientos por la independencia rusa del yugo polaco. Los padres de Achabowski murieron antes de que éste naciera, por lo que fue dado a luz por sus abuelos. Después de navegar muchos años por las aguas que rodean los continentes, decidió españolizar y apocopar su nombre por lo que era conocido ahora o antes, es decir en el momento en que ocurre esta historia como el Capitán José Acá o Pepe el Poloco, pero esa es otra historia) decidió ordenar bajar un bote cuando vio a los tres en cuestión descendiendo en otro bote y dejó su orden sin efecto o con efecto retroactivo. Los mexicanos y el liberiano embarcaron con las hachas de incendio en mano y luego de alguna indecisión decidieron depositarlas en el fondo de la embarcación para remar, cuidando de que no quedaran filo abajo. Como el barco tuvo que aminorar la marcha para arriar el bote, cuando éste tocó agua ya el féretro les llevaba algunos largos de ventaja hacia la proa y se vieron obligados a remar duro y contra el viento, logrando con su pericia y esfuerzo disminuir la ventaja del ataúd bogante. Ya le estaban dando alcance a éste cuando un golpe de mar, el cambio de viento, la

Mexican, one ominous and dark end of the casket coming out of the water, then the whole thing, like a wooden submarine, like a dead, obscene fish, and don't I narrate well? asked rascally Socarrás looking at Silvestre. No one answered, but that's because nobody had a chance before anotherhine-landerlogologist[25] who said, clearly, the water from the ice turned to steam while in the steamer and the wood had swollen, making the casket technically waterproof, seaworthy and floating. That is to say, it was a vessel of visible time.

The Mexicans, What'dItellyou, his brother and a Liberian longshoreman, saw the floating casket as a punishment, if not from heaven, at least from the offended sea, a sure sign of prophecy, an ill omen, and decided on their own account (and their own risk) that the satellite ship, insisting on traveling next to its own launching pad, had to be sunk.[26] Without consulting anyone they began to throw throwable things at it: a piece of railing from the broken bridge in the form of an arrow, lances made of wood from the same source, a leather strapped shoe, a huarache, a stream of insults, several shots of spit, a stream of insults and finally their collective and individual desperation and blind and mute rage. Finally someone came to their aid carrying a rifle with which they shot the casket several times. But the (leaden) shots either fell short or beyond missing such a visible and dark mark, or instead all hit the bull's eye, if the eye was the whole of the sea.[27] A bullet finally hit the liner and bounced back into the sea, the wood having become not only waterproof but also impenetrable. Stricken, the captain (that was not his name, his whole name was captain Josef Teodor Achabowski, born in Kerznief in the Russian Ukraine, then under Polish rule, on December 3, 1857, making him then, if we count Achabowski's age with abacus, 101 years old, according to the new calendar. His father, a landowner with literary leanings, was exiled to North Prussia for having participated in Russian movements of liberation against the Polish yoke.[28] Achabowski's parents died before he was born and his grandparents had to give birth to him. After sailing for many years through the waters that surround the continents, he decided to Hispanicize and shorten his name, which is the reason for his being known now or before, that is to say, at the time that this story takes place, as Captain José Acá, or Skip Acá, or Pepe the Poloco, but that's another story), decided to lower a boat when he saw the three in question going down in another boat, and so left the order moot or with retroactive power. The Mexicans and the Liberian embarked fire axes in hand and after some indecision decided to put them on the bottom, edges up, to be able to row.[29] Since the ship had slowed down to lower the boat, when the latter touched the water the casket was a few lengths ahead in the direction of the prow and they had to row very hard and against the wind, managing to diminish the lead of the floating coffin. They were already catching up to it when a wave and then a change of wind, the ship's own

estela del barco, la corriente, el trópico de cáncer o el azar (o todas esas
cosas juntas) hicieron que el ataúd barloventeara bruscamente, se volteara
en redondo y embistiera al bote, abriéndole un boquete de tamaño regular
antes de que nadie pudiera evitar el choque de los cuerpos y mucho menos
descargar un golpe de hacha salvador o bueno para paralizar al agresor, y
fue el bote el que hizo agua, se inclinó y se iba a pique entre el silencio del
mar y los marinos. Silencio que duró poco porque otra embestida del ataúd
con un chirrido como un chillido triunfal la popa del bote que se hundía al
mismo tiempo que los dos mexicanos nadaban con furia hacia el barco y el
liberiano chapoteaba, tragaba agua, parecía que se ahogaba y finalmente
nada también hasta el barco ansiosamente. Los otros marineros no pudieron
hacer otra cosa que recogerlos a los tres con cabos y salvavidas mientras el
capitán Acá ordenaba, Llámenme a Ismaelillo el médico de abordo antes de
volverse a ver alejándose a La Estrella en su tumba flotante que para él era
un destino envidiable: el insumergible, el navío perfecto, el anti-Titanic o
tal vez fuera el mito: un María Celeste de carne y hueso y madera, la
holandesa errante, y fascinado la miró primero a ojo limpio de lobo de mar,
después con ojos de marino, después con ojos sucios de llanto, después con
su catalejo, después con su catarata y vio cómo la Nao se hacía
Nada: primero fue ballena de madera y grasa, luego pez fúnebre, después
cresta de ola negra, luego mosca de los ojos hasta que se la tragó la distancia
y se perdió en el mar, en nuestra eternidad Silvestre, navegando viajando
flotando en el Gulf Stream a 13 nudos por hora con rumbo nor-noroeste.

Eso fue lo que me nos contó Walter Ego antes de anunciar lo inevitable,
que no era el anti-climax sino el clima, Y por ahí debe andar todavía,
dándole la vuelta al globo, y añadió, Un matías pérez marino. Bueno, dijo
Silvestre, una posdata es una forma de epitafio. O viceversa. Lo que es es un
retoque dije yo. O séase, dijo Silvestre, permiso para un leve sobreasalto.
Casar la verdad con el final. O como diría el Huno, un epitalaffo.

Pero el verdadero epitafio, la epifanía, la epifonema, la epístola, el
epígrafe, el epigrama o la epítasis no la dijo el epifito ni el Epígono, sino
menda. Cité, re-cité: Sicus Vita Finis Ita. Solo que realmente pronuncié *Sí
Cubita Finisita*.

Gibara-La Habana-Bruselas-Madrid-Londres, 1929-1969

wake, the current, the Tropic of Cancer, chance (or everything together) made the casket beat about abruptly, turn around windward and charge the boat, opening a regular size hole in it before anyone could avoid the collision and much less hit the coffin with a saving axe, good at least to paralyze the aggressor, and it was instead the boat that made water, listed and began to sink in the midst of the sea and the sailors' silence. A silence that didn't last very long because a second charge of the casket scraped the bow with a triumphant shriek and the boat sank at the same time that the two Mexicans swam furiously toward the ship and the Liberian splashed around, swallowed water, seemed to drown, and finally swims to the ship anxiously.[30] The other sailors could do nothing more than pick them off the sea with ropes and life preservers as Captain Acá ordered, Call Me Ishmael,[31] the ship's doctor, before seeing Estrella fade away in her floating tomb, which for him was an enviable destiny: the unsinkable, perfect ship, the anti-Titanic. Or perhaps a myth: a María Celeste of flesh, bones and wood, a Flying Dutchman. He looked at her with the naked eye of a sea wolf, later with mariner's eyes, later with eyes dirtied by tears, later with binoculars, later with cataracts and saw how the boat turned to naught, to nothing, to nothingness. First it was a whale of wood and grease, later a funereal fish, then blackcap on a black wave, then fly in the horizon until the distance swallowed her up and she was lost in the sea, in our eternity, Silvestre, sailing, traveling, floating on the Gulf Stream at 13 knots per hour in a North by North West direction.

That's what Walter Ego told us before announcing the inevitable, which was not an anticlimax but the climate, the atmosphere, And she must still be there, going around the world, and added, a seagoing Matías Pérez.[32] Well, Silvestre added, a postscript as epitaph. Or vice versa. It's merely a detail, a finishing touch, I added. That is to say, said Silvestre with a slight jolt. A marriage of Truth and The End. Or, as The Huan would say, an epitalaph.

But the true epitaph, the epiphany, the epiphoneme, the epistle, the epigraph, epigraph or epitasis was not uttered by the epiphyte nor the Epigone but by me. I cited, or re-cited: Sicus Vita Finis Ita.[33] Only that I pronounced it *Sí, Cubita is Finita.*

Gibara-Havana-Brussels-Madrid-London, 1929-1969

Commentary

1. How can there be an end beyond the end? How can there be a *meta-*end?[8] Cabrera Infante is playing here with the near synonymy in Spanish of "meta" and "end." As a prefix, "meta" has the same meaning in English as in Spanish. But by itself "meta" means "goal," "end," "finality," the accomplishment of an initial intention. "Meta" also means, quite literally, "the finish line." Therefore "Meta-Final" has a variety of meanings and rhetorical functions. Taken in relation to *Three Trapped Tigers*, "Meta-Final" is what Cabrera Infante says that it is in a note accompanying the text in *Alacrán Azul* (Miami, vol. 1, no. 1 [1970]:6):

The novelistic fragment that I am sending you is the end of *Three Trapped Tigers*. I never included it in the book because there was already too much symmetry to add this parody. By chance, a trunk that I had left in Brussels, containing many notes and fragments of mine, arrived recently. There I found this piece. I have only made a clean copy for you, adding a new spelling here, a malapropism there, a dosage of anacolutha and the title, which is possibly the only new thing. I like the text now in its clean copy, with its ferocious humor and its twisted homage to Monk Lewis, Melville, and Conrad.[9]

If we consider "Meta-Final" as the product of this intention, the title is doubly appropriate. Not only is it an end beyond the end, but the repetition of "end," "meta," and *"final,"* reflects this double ending. Seen in this fashion, one could also read the difference between "meta" and *"final"* as an adjectival addition. The end is not only a termination, but the accomplishment of goal; it is a happy coupling of eschatology and narratology, or as Bustrófedon is reported to have said, a "marriage of Truth and End." Thus "Meta-Final" would not be the pleonasm that it appears to be, but merely a refinement and a qualification. In this sense, there is also a general appropriateness to the text, since it is a sort of wake for Estrella: "Meta-Final" is about Estrella *in morte*, about her final destination, as it were.

There is still, however, a degree of incorrectness in the rhetorical coupling of "meta" and *"final."* It is pleonastic. Even so, as pleonasm, the title seems appropriate. If we look at the text in light of what Cabrera Infante says, it is, in fact, an excess, an appendage, an end beyond the end.

Still, how can there be two endings? Either the previous ending was not one, or this one is not the ending. What is an ending? Does the ending determine the plot of the story, is it the product of necessity, as Aristotle wrote in his *Poetics*? *Three Trapped Tigers* is not tragedy, and its ending is anything but necessary. Rather, it is abrupt and arbitrary, disconnected from the "action" of the novel. It is as much a *meta-end* as a "Meta-Final." In fact there is no proper ending to *Three Trapped Tigers*, as there is no proper ending to "Meta-Final" itself. The new ending suggested by Walter Socarrás is not accepted as such by the narrator. And is the note sent by Cabrera Infante to *Alacrán Azul* yet another ending?

"Meta-Final" alerts us to all these possibilities, but more than anything it warns us not to take ends as *metas*, as goals. The text, the title—which is itself another end beyond the end—invites us to interpret what it says as the opposite of what it says. In addition, "Meta-Final" performs the repetition that it warns us about, not only as a title, but also as a story. "Meta" and *"final"* can mean the same thing, yet the end provided by the story cannot be the real *meta*, the true finish line, for the narrator does not seem to accept the correction, and the text itself continues to provide further ends in the title, the author's note, and so on.

There is yet another end to "Meta-Final" that I have not considered. The annotation "Gibara-Havana-Brussels-Madrid-London, 1929-1969," not the end of the text, is the final word. The only way to interpret this "signature" is to look outside the text. Gibara is the town where Cabrera Infante was born and the other cities mentioned mark off his itinerary as cultural attaché and later as exile. What do the dates mean, then? At first glance they appear to suggest that the composition of the story has run parallel to the author's life. If so, and in consonance with the funeral theme of the story, the cities and the dates are a kind of epitaph, the most common sort of *meta-text* that acts as a *meta-end*. Although we know that as epitaph "Meta-Final" is improper—Cabrera Infante is fortunately very much alive, even if he likes to portray himself as an *infante difunto*—it does fit in as epitaph with the metaphysical considerations of the story. It is further appropriate if we take into account another biographical fact: *Three Trapped Tigers* is directly connected to Cabrera Infante's exile from Cuba. "Meta-Final" is, therefore, a kind of epitaph for the man left behind, for the life lived before. In fact, seen from this angle, the whole story takes on the form of an allegory of exile. Estrella's dead body floats on forever, permanently separated from the land, not only from the Cuba to which her remains could not finally return, but from the earth itself in which she is never interred. Reading "Meta-Final," a biographer of Cabrera Infante would also have to take into account that the writer's final break with the Revolution and his last trip to Cuba were made in 1967 to attend his mother's funeral.

"Meta-Final" invokes, then, death, eschatology, the question of intentionality, and, above all, the matter of ending. The title is a warning not only about the presence of such themes, but about the very manner in which language is going to deploy them.

"Meta-Final" loses a great deal in translation because "meta" has no other meaning in English as an independent word. To have translated it as "goal" would have probably brought about a greater loss without much gain.

2. If ending is problematic, so is beginning.[10] How does fiction begin? Does the beginning determine the plot? Instead of a single beginning, which suggests that there is a necessary bond between starting and intentionality, the text offers a repetition, an error. No single, determining instance sets off the text. In addition, the first sentence, by repeating "in a detail," performs what it says. As with "Meta-Final," however, this is an error that is paradoxically appropriate, or perhaps more than appropriate, for it not only designates error but is erring. This exaggerated appropriateness extends to the entire story, which is, after all, a correction of a presumed error, but it also may err. The beginning of "Meta-Final" announces its theme—error—and displays it as a warning for the mechanics of language in the rest of the text. It is a language that will fall short or go too far in its referential relationships and whose only appropriateness is to be gauged in relation to its own functioning. Even there, though, the failure of the mechanism to perform properly is what sets language in motion, as is the case in the relationship between "meta" and "*final*."

3. I have had to transpose the whole linguistic game with Socarrás because it is impossible in English to play off anything resembling *socorrido*, helped, helpful, and so on. I have settled for a repetition of the *r* sound because both the derivational play with *socarrás-socorrido* and the persistence of the *r*'s are part of the self-negation of the beginning-as-beginning. Instead of a single start, there is always already repetition. I have translated "you blue it" to transpose the repetition to the level of sound, with a difference in the graphic representation, a homonymy, to remain within the mechanics of repetition inaugurated by the start, and also to play "blue" off against the "red" in the previous line. The language of "Meta-Final," we soon discover, is generated by the tendency of language in general to repeat and yet differ, a hypostasis of which is writing itself. It is an economy of gain and loss that is akin to translation, not because language is a translation of the world, but because within language meaning issues out of transformations based on difference.

It would have been difficult to translate into English "*te equisbotaste*," a portmanteau word consisting of "*equis*," the word to designate the *x*, and "*botaste*," "you threw away." The latter in Cuba also means that one did something outstanding, including making a very noticeable error, which would be the case here. The *x* could stand here for crossing out the error, or simply marking it, and the supplemental *s*—"*equisbotaste*" plays off "*equivocaste*"—is also a sort of affectation common among uneducated people in Cuba, who often overcompensate for their tendency to aspirate sibilant sounds. Walter Socarrás is simply mocking the narrator, who tries to neutralize his aggression by giving us his biography and occasionally assimilating him as Walter Ego. In other words, the narrator is not taken in by the dialogic setting; he reveals its conventionality as a device to attach to the performance of language figures who will give referential validity to the pronouns.

4. The original does not have the sort of play that I have introduced here between "lay" and "lie," but it does contain an effort at precision, filling in the antecedent for *su*, which I thought could be conveyed by the misleading homonymy often leading to error in English. This correction falls within the theme of error and correction present in the story. Efforts to correct are often thwarted and lead to further error.

5. The Auténtico and Ortodoxo parties played an important role in Cuban politics after the 1933 revolution, but the pun here involves also Sartrean notions that were very much in vogue in Cuban intellectual circles through the fifties and sixties, when Sartre even visited the island. The Sartrean notions refer to "Meta-Final," too. Silvestre's précis that all deaths are authentic, whereas lives may not be would give this text about Estrella's death an authenticity lacking in *Three Trapped Tigers*, where her life is told. I have added the pun "hot-walters" to make up for the loss of a very subtle one in the original. "*Dar pie*," which means "to give a chance," links up with "*socorriendo*," which means to "come to the aid," but which, broken up, contains the verb "*correr*," "to run." By lending Walter a foot, Silvestre allows him to run. Translating is not simply a process of transposing, but of supplying elements to make up for lacks that emerge in recasting a text; it is a radical form of correction. It is also a kind of error. In this sense, there is a clear parallel between "Meta-Final" as text and the act of translation.

The allusions to Sartre in this passage are not the only ones. At the very end Estrella becomes "Nothingness" and the musicians in casinos are almost nothing. Though asystematic, the presence of these philosophical terms engages the text in a dialogue with philosophy, particularly in the humor with which they are dealt. The story being told and the textual performance of language in it bring to the fore, in dramatic fashion, a radical incompatibility between being and language and that may in fact be the way in which their congruence is made manifest.

6. The change from Gualterio to Walter is an instance of how Cabrera Infante's characters pretend to be what they are not, a fact that is related to the question of authenticity mentioned in the previous note. The Deceased is, of course, Bustrófedon, and his quip on the meaning of podium is more suggestive than it appears at first sight. To be in a moving podium as one conducts may allude to being as a nonfixed, dynamic condition, a performance in time.

7. Walter, who is attempting to usurp the authority of the narrator, turns out to be, appropriately, an *arranger*, meaning, of course, someone who alters (walters?) a musical score to tailor it for a specific performance. Walter is an image of the writer akin to that of the secretary in the dictator-novels, and indeed his work as a writer is criticized by the narrator farther on

in the text. Like Patiño and his heir in *Yo el Supremo*, he seizes power from the figure of authority to rearrange and rewrite.

8. The Countess of Marlin is La Condesa de Merlín, née María de la Merced Santa Cruz y Montalvo (1789-1852), who published in 1844 *La Havane*, par Madame la Comtesse Merlin. Carpentier—*serpent*ier, Cerpentier in the text—despite his French background, published only one story in French. Cabrera Infante includes a parody of Carpentier in *Three Trapped Tigers* and is generally critical of the author of *The Lost Steps*, who remained faithful to the Cuban Revolution until his death. Carpentier's presence in Cabrera Infante's work is strong, which perhaps explains the latter's hostility. There is a connection between "Meta-Final" and Carpentier's "Manhunt," as explained in note 7 of this chapter.

"Grisés" in the text involves a significant pun: it can mean "with gray matter," that is, "intelligent," "sharp," but also gray in the sense that Cubans are a combination of black and white.

I have added the play "semen-sí-men" to make up for the loss of the "mal de genios o genios del mar" game, which involves a number of linguistic and rhetorical operations. The pronunciation of the *l* for *r* is common of lower-class Spanish in the Caribbean and southern Spain. *"Mal de genios"* can mean here *"mar de genios,"* a sea of geniuses, which is certainly why the antithesis with *"genios del mar"* works. But *"mal de genios"* can also mean to suffer from too many geniuses; that is, that Cuba is in the clutches of men who think they are geniuses but are instead a plague. The political intention of the line allows me to insert "sí-men" as a political joke, meaning of course, that Cuba is full of "yes-men."

9. Insularity is an important theme in Hispanic Caribbean literature, but has also been a topic of Western literature since the Greeks. In "Meta-Final" it is of particular importance because Estrella's posthumous voyage is a return to Cuba, and she herself is referred to as an island. Silvestre's reported quip here concerning islands that attempt to take over continents is a game about the relationship between inside and outside, because *"continente"* also means that which contains. The problem of containers is crucial in the story: Estrella's body is crated, then put inside a ship, but escapes it to become itself a ship, which will then attack its/her former container. The names of the islands deformed by Bustrófedon had to be deformed in a different way in English, as was "maregeo," Aegean Sea. In "Sol Na Siente" Cabrera Infante is again taking advantage of popular forms of speech, *"na"* for *"nada,"* and homonymies, *"na siente"* for *naciente*.

10. The Orquesta Casino de la Playa, formed in 1937, was popular in Cuba in the forties and fifties. There was also a Conjunto Casino, one of whose members, Agustín Ribot, may or may not have inspired the Ribot in *Three Trapped Tigers*.[11] But the important detail here is that casino has been broken up to mean *"casi no,"* "almost nothing." Walter and the other

musicians are "almost-nothings."

11. In reporting Walter's correction, the narrator evokes the confusion of his dialogue with him, a confusion that involves a clash between spelling (writing) and speech (voice); Mexico is pronounced in Spanish as if it were spelled with a *j*. I have added the pun "with a jay" to make up for the partial loss of this game in English. Walter's correction takes on a musical character toward the end of the paragraph, but "no es tan mal acorde" as applied to the previous sentence is awkward and difficult to interpret. I have included "disc-ordant" to refer back to the previous game on disc and record. Repetition, meaningless or not, is one of the characteristics of "Meta-Final" from the very beginning.

Walter's news that Estrella is not buried in Mexico, and in fact is not buried at all, is quite suggestive, given her aura as a kind of Orphic voice issuing from the earth. She does not return to the earth, but floats forever on the sea, a floating island, a Floating Signifier, unmoored by referentiality and all cultural codes. With Estrella gone, language's congruity is gone, hence the pulverization that it suffers at the hands of the narrator and the frantic efforts of the characters, first to preserve Estrella's body and later to retrieve it.

12. The presence of this secretary is of particular interest because he stands in relation to Estrella like Barnet to Montejo and Patiño and his heirs to Supremo. The secretary begins the arrangements for embalming Estrella's body, which reflects his grasp of Estrella as a special entity, not as sound, in the same way that other secretaries turn the dictator's speech to writing. Writing and embalming are here parallel activities; embalming will turn Estrella's body into an island surrounded by plastic, instead of returning her to the earth.

13. Adecuado, the embalmer, gets his name as a twist within language that turns an adjective into a noun, a quality into a substance, thus his name in English: Proper. Proper, however, despite being not only Proper but Innocent, is anything but appropriate and naïve. His "natural" way of embalming is not natural at all: he wants to cover Estrella's body with molten cellophane. Together with the secretary and Walter, Proper stands as a sort of writer. His mythological counterpart is Toth, accountant of dead souls and god of writing.[12]

14. "*Estar tocado*" in Cuba means to be mad. Here the English "touch of madness" allows me to preserve the joke involving "untouchable."

15. Because he is dealing in dead bodies, Proper's price is quite appropriately a part of the body. The figure in Spanish, "an eye out of your face," which denotes a prohibitive price, finds a near-equivalent in "an arm and a leg." Translation works nearer to rhetoric than to grammar. The parts of the body are interchangeable from language to language, the rate of exchange here being a Spanish eye for an English arm and a leg. The line

before, "I don't want to see it," is taken from Federico García Lorca's "Llanto por la muerte de Ignacio Sánchez Mejía." The secretary, who pronounces the line from the elegy, is a textual storehouse, like Patiño.

16. The continued games with x and j lead to this rather awkward "*es perimental*," which I have rendered with the equally awkward "is perimental." In neither language does "perimental" exist as a word. Yet, there is a rigorous propriety to the sentence if we accept the neologism to mean "outside" or "around" the mind, as in "perimeter." What the Departed meant was that all theory that is not put into practice belongs to the periphery of the mind. In translation an approximation to propriety can often be attained by the improper use of language.

17. Estrella's casket is a key object in the story. The most suggestive name that it is given in this series of transformations is "*esféretro*," a combination of sphere (*esfera*) and "*féretro*" (casket), which I have rendered as "sperophagus," combining "sphere" and "sarcophagus." The notion of roundness here connotes circularity and closure, the latter becoming a tangible reality in the story when Estrella's coffin becomes watertight and bulletproof.

18. "*Mariguana que fumar*" is a line from a well-known Mexican song from the time of the Revolution. I was unable to find a comparable line in English and settled on "maryjane" as a circumlocution.

19. The omission of an adjective sets in motion the decay of Estrella's body in the casket. "Meta-Final" is engendered through an economy of omission and addition. Here, with uncanny precision, the omission is a negation. "Dry" is an adjective that subtracts a "natural" quality from ice. This omission of an omission activates, as it were, Estrella's body, which eventually becomes, within the enclosure, a projectile, among other things. The text is engendered around the negation of a negation, a negation with respect to the referentiality of language, and another with respect to the propriety of the inner correspondences of language itself.

"*Barrueca*" is an archaic form of "*barroco*," and the misshapen pearl that was so designated may have originated the concept of the baroque, as Severo Sarduy has explained.[13] There is a clear resemblance between Estrella, some of Sarduy's characters in *Maitreya*, and García Márquez's characters; they are conceived within a logic of supplementariness that is hypostasized in their enormous, swollen bodies. It is not, it seems to me, fortuitous that these characters should be women. As women they are representations of nature, within the conventional ideology of Latin American literature, and by being authoritative they reveal the connection between authority and the concept of nature in that ideology. Of course, there is an obvious contradiction in their being at the same time female and authoritative, which the texts exploit and expose. By being deformed and outsized, however, they point to the supplemental character of their authority, built, as it were, on an absence, a lack or fissure opened at the very spot where the metaphor joining nature and language joins the two terms.

20. Estrella, whose singing voice was so melodious and deep that it seemed to issue from the most profound telluric depths, has now begun to utter prelinguistic noises. *"Chirriando mefítica* / Screeching noxiously" is a synesthesia involving sound and smell, an irreducible combination, which nevertheless highlights the meaninglessness, and at the same time dissemination, of Estrella's new utterances.

21. The "international" composition of the crew and its ignorance of the color of the Cuban flag clash with its intention to base the burial ritual on a nationalistic iconography. By creating a flag with the color of Havana cigars, the text plays with the motivation of signs showing not their arbitrariness but their contingency. The captain appropriately dictates his order. He is a budding dictator.

22. A very difficult pun, which I have translated with a very awkward equivalent. "Como van las arengas al mal" means "in the same way that harangues wind up being evil," or, more generally, that oratorical agitation leads to demagoguery. But *"arenque,"* which can be heard underneath *"arenga"* because *"mal"* can also evoke *"mar,"* "sea" (given the tendency to turn *r*'s to *l*'s), produces the somewhat garbled, but distinguishable, meaning: "like herrings that return to the sea." In other words, everything to its origin (except Estrella in this story). Since harangues that become demagoguery are misleading, and since a red herring, being precisely an *"arenque,"* also means a subterfuge "to distract or divert notice from the relevant problem," I have rendered the phrase "like a red herring that has mis(lead)," adding the lead for ballast, given that I could not exchange liquid consonants in English.

23. I have added "bell" here to parable and hyperbole to make up for some of the texture lost in the previous sentences, where the *"nomás"* and the *"mero"* identify the speakers as Mexicans, given that these are words common to Mexican speech. It also seems to me that "Meta-Final" is both a hyperbole and a parable. The hyperbolic nature of the text, the escalating exaggerations, fit in the supplemental logic in which both the text and Estrella are conceived. The parabolic is just as clear: at the end the characters, particularly the narrator, try to come up with an allegorical reading of the story that can sum it all up. The misquoted Latin phrase at the end plays the role of the *sententia* at the end of parables stating their meaning. Furthermore, a parable is a story with a supplement; the reading added within the story stating its meaning that functions as a "meta-ending."

24. The metamorphoses of Estrella's casket in this latter part of the story are quite remarkable. On the other hand, they turn her into a sort of permanent foetus, floating forever in prenatal waters, and on the other, into

a missile, a submarine, an inverted Moby Dick. The changes that start with the decay of Estrella's body as a result of the absence of the adjective "dry" transform her into a series of contrary allegorical representations. She is an end/beginning, a round/square, a corpse/foetus, a black/Moby Dick, a vagina/phallus, a black point set against the infinite background of time and sea.

25. "*Otrorrinealaringólogo*" is the name given here to Rine Leal, one of the trapped tigers, who happens to be a real theater critic in Havana. The "*laringólogo*" part alludes to the larynx, to speaking, and the "*rin*" sound to the Rhine. I have rendered this name "anotherhinelanderlogologist" to preserve this allusion to German philosophy and its considerations of the link between language and being taken up in "Meta-Final."

26. Estrella's casket as satellite reintroduces the synecdoche of the island and the continent, of the fragment and the whole, of the end and the body of the text. Estrella's aggression against the ship that contained her marks the relation between the whole and the part as being a hostile one in which the fragment, or end, stands in opposition to that which gave it a context, and therefore a meaning by containing it. There is at bottom here an Oedipal scene reduced to the clash between two material objects, one of which issued from the other. Estrella's casket breaks up the ship as it comes out of it, and later beats about to ram it. The casket is going to make its mark, its wound, by attacking the ship. But all that it manages to sink is yet another fragment off the ship, the boat put out to counterattack it. There is no telling blow against the source; instead there is one against the representation, the phantom of the source, the smaller boat, which sinks. The split is but one of a series, not a blow against the Origin, the father, which is defended by elusive images of itself.

27. The pun here involves the fact that "*blanco*" means not only "white," but also "target" or "bull's eye." The pun takes the shape of an oxymoron: Estrella's casket is a "*blanco*," "white," "target," very visible and obscure. The white/black opposition partakes of the allusions to Moby Dick, it seems to me, and the theme of the thirst for absolute knowledge that besets the characters since *Three Trapped Tigers*. The text plays on the notion of absolute knowledge, a knowledge here represented by good aim, against the notion of infinity implicit in the sea, all of which becomes the target. I have tried to render this game in English using the homonyms "whole" and "hole" to create the undecidable pairing off of a contained, bordered space (hole), with a conception of boundlessness.

28. Achabowski's name evokes, for the Spanish speaker, "*acabose*," finished or ended, or, for Cubans, "*el acabose*," which in the island means a sort of melée that catastrophically brings about the end of something. The captain's name is appropriate for the subject of the story, perhaps in the same way as the embalmer's. The short biography of Achabowski is a good

example of how Cabrera Infante plays off accepted narrative structures and our uncritical association of temporality in the narrative with time. The Polish yoke/joke pun is not in the original, of course (in Cuba Spaniards are the butt of such class humor), though there is certainly a political meaning in this inversion of the relationship between Poland and the Soviet Union.

29. A difficult passage to understand, which perhaps alludes to the very question of decidability in reading. By putting the axes edge-up, the sailors are careful not to pierce the bottom of the boat, but by doing so, they turn them against themselves. The passage is either a triviality or brings up the issue of allegorical versus literal reading. One allegorical reading could be that it is impossible to ward off danger without at the same time risking harm. A literal reading, if such is at all possible, would be that they are willing to risk cutting themselves to avoid sinking their own boat, choosing, therefore the lesser of two evils. A self-conscious reading can go two ways: either it is impossible to make all fragments of a story cohere or be dependent on some sort of supralogical scheme derived from the real world, or reading must allow for these undecidable instances, represented by such counterposed choices.

30. There is an abrupt change in tense from the imperfect to the present that appears to be a move to show the conventionality of tenses in the narrative. The change to the present tense has a jarring effect in the original that I think I have preserved in the English version.

31. The allusion to the beginning of *Moby Dick* is but one of several allusions to Melville's book. In the original Ishmael is called Ismaelillo, bringing in yet another literary reference. Ismaelillo was the name of José Martí's son, and it is the title of the book that the Cuban poet dedicated to the boy. In the translation I had to make a decision—thus, a reduction— between these two allusions, which coexist in the original. I could have added an allusion to the English by putting "Reed" in parentheses after "Ishmael," but thought that the Afro-American writer's name would not be as recognizable to the English-language reader as "Ismaelillo" would be to the Spanish-speaking reader. Perhaps a better solution might have been to translate "Llámenme a Ismaelillo" as "Call me *Usmail*," thereby alluding to the novel by the Puerto Rican Pedro Juan Soto.

32. Matías Pérez was a Cuban balloonist who went up once and was never heard from again. He is invoked in Cuban speech when alluding to someone who has disappeared suddenly and perhaps involuntarily.

33. I have been unable to find the source of this (mis)quotation, which should read "sicut vitae finis ita," "thus is the end of life." The garbled quotation, in general agreement with the tendency to error in "Meta-Final," is further deformed in the original to sound in Spanish like, "Yes, dear little Cuba is finished." I have tried to reproduce this in English by simply putting "is" in a normal position and turning "*finisita*" into "finita," which the

English reader should recognize.

The "true epitaph," which attempts to put an end to all of these endings, tilts the story in the direction of parable. The epitaph is to be taken as the meaning of the preceding text, forcing us to turn Estrella into a sort of allegory of Cuba; "Meta-Final" would then be a political allegory. But given the polemical nature of "Meta-Final," one could also take this statement by the narrator as a last effort to regain power over the other characters, after the correction made by Walter.

Notes

Preamble

The epigraphs preceding the Acknowledgments are from *El artista latinoamericano y su identidad*, ed. Damián Bayón (Caracas: Monte Avila, 1977), p. 22; and the foreword to Carol Jacobs's *The Dissimulating Harmony: The Image of Interpretation in Nietzsche, Rilke, Artaud, and Benjamin* (Baltimore, Md.: Johns Hopkins University Press, 1978), p. xi. The epigraph to the Preamble is from "Seis ensayos en busca de nuestra expresión," *Obra crítica* (Mexico City: Fondo de Cultura Económica, 1960), p. 244, my translation.

1. Carlos Pérez Cavero, "Julio Cortázar y la literatura revolucionaria" [interview], *El Viejo Topo*, no. 59 (August 1981), pp. 48-49; my translation.

2. Michael Ryan, *Marxism and Deconstruction* (Baltimore, Md.: Johns Hopkins University Press, 1982).

3. See my "Carpentier, crítico de la literatura hispanoamericana: Asturias y Borges," *Sin Nombre* 12, no. 2 (1981):7-27.

Chapter 1: The Case of the Speaking Statue: *Ariel* and the Magisterial Rhetoric of the Latin American Essay

1. My conception of how this class exercised hegemonic power, and, indeed, what this class was, parallels the analysis offered by Richard M. Morse in "La cultura política iberoamericana," *Vuelta* (Mexico), no. 58 (1981), pp. 4-16. Morse writes,

Lo que se plantea respecto de la independencia iberoamericana no es, pues, una esquizofrenia de la *intelligentsia*, atrapada entre una cosmovisión ibérica y otra anglofrancesa. Se trata más bien de que ninguna de ellas, así como tampoco ninguna mezcla de ambas, se tradujo en una ideología "hegemónica" que suscitara aceptación, o ni siquiera una aquiescencia no coercitiva, en sociedades: 1) cuyas identidades nacionales eran artificiales, b) donde no había un poder soberano legitimado, c) cuya articulación interna carecía de vértebras, de cuyas relaciones económicas con el mundo exterior, dictaban una imprecisa combinación de concesiones externas y liberalizaciones internas. Este dilema no se planteó sin previo aviso a los pensadores de los mil ochocientos veintes o los mil ochocientos treintas, ni tampoco la "emancipación mental" de estos ocurrió de un día para otro. (p. 4)

And also,

Por hegemonía no queremos decir aquí simplemente una ideología de clase, dominante y doctrinal, un concepto uniforme del mundo impuesto a toda una sociedad. En esto seguimos a Laclau al subrayar que una ideología hegemónica ofrece, primero, un conjunto aceptado de principios, con los cuales pueden armarse varios mensajes, y, segundo, un marco consensualmente reconocido dentro del cual es posible articular esos mensajes—para reconciliarlos o neutralizarlos—en una manera que favorezca sin interrumpir *la dominación de los dominadores*. "Articular" implica la necesidad de dar acomodo no sólo a las simples contradicciones e interpelaciones que surgen de los dominados, sino también a las planteadas por grupos de los mismos dominadores. (p. 5)

2. Martin S. Stabb, *In Quest of Identity: Patterns in the Spanish American Essay of Ideas, 1890-1960* (Chapel Hill: University of North Carolina Press, 1967); Peter Earle and Robert Mead, *Historia del ensayo hispanoamericano* (Mexico City: Ediciones de Andrea, 1973). Though less directly concerned with the essay, there are two excellent books about the history of ideas in Latin America: W. Rex Crawford, *A Century of Latin-American Thought* (1944; reprint, Cambridge, Mass.: Harvard University Press, 1967); and Harold Eugene Davis, *Latin American Thought: A Historical Introduction* (1972; reprint, New York: The Free Press, 1974).

3. Antonio Cândido writes,

In the era we are calling of "pleasant consciousness of backwardness," the writer participated in the ideology of the Enlightenment, according to which education automatically carries with it all the benefits which make for the humanization of man and the progress of society. At the beginning education was proclaimed for the *citizens*, a minority from whose rank were recruited those who participated in economic and political advantages; afterward it was proclaimed for the people, which was envisioned vaguely and from a distance, more as a liberal concept than as a reality. Brazilian Emperor Pedro II said that he would have preferred to be a professor, which indicates an attitude similar to that of Sarmiento, according to which the domination of civilization over barbarity presupposed a latent urbanization, based on education. In Andrés Bello's continental vocation it is possible to distinguish the political vision from the pedagogical project, and in the more recent group of the Atheneum of Caracas, resistance to the tyranny of Gómez was identified with the spread of enlightenment and the creation of a literature impregnated by myths of redemptive education, all projected onto the figure of Rómulo Gallegos, first president of a reborn republic. ("Literature and Underdevelopment," in *Latin America in Its Literature*, ed. César Fernández Moreno; tr. Mary G. Berg [New York: Holmes & Meier, 1980], pp. 168-169; I have tinkered with the translation)

4. For all details concerning Rodó's life and works, the reader should consult Emir Rodríguez Monegal's introduction to the *Obras completas* (Madrid: Aguilar, 1967). For the text of *Ariel* I have based my translation on that of F. J. Stimson, published by Houghton Mifflin in 1922, but have made numerous changes.

5. Ciriaco Morón Arroyo, *Sentido y forma de La Celestina* (Madrid: Ediciones Cátedra, 1974).

6. I am quoting from Reyes's *Obras completas* (Mexico City: Fondo de Cultura Económica, 1960; originally published 1942), indicating volume and page number. Translations are mine.

7. "True, the Conquest deprived these cultures [*decapitó esas culturas*] of their religion, their art, their science (where any existed), and their writing (in the case of the Aztecs and the Mayas); but many local traditions survived in daily and domestic life" (Pedro Henríquez Ureña, *A Concise History of Latin American Culture*, tr. Gilbert Chase [New York: Praeger, 1966], p. 25). The original was published in 1947 by Fondo de Cultura Económica in Mexico as *La Cultura en la América hispánica*.

8. Severo Sarduy, *Barroco* (Buenos Aires: Editorial Sudamericana, 1974). Peter G. Earle writes in a piece on the contemporary essay that recent critical trends have tended to make the Latin American essay wither: "But if the power of the imagination is more than a game and reality truly transcends language, the structuralists had from the beginning embarked on a course that was arbitrary and suicidal; it required a progressive elimination of individuality (and personality) and led to a truncated cosmology. The essay has been unable to assimilate these restrictions. It has not made, together with the major genres, the conceptual leap from language as a manifestation of reality to reality as a manifestation of language" ("On the Contemporary Displacement of the Hispanic American Essay," *Hispanic Review* 46 [1978]:330). My answer to Earle's observation is, besides my analysis of Sarduy in the body of the text, that the essay changes in form, and that from the very beginning it has systematically called into question both individuality and personality, as may be observed in *Ariel*.

Chapter 2: *Doña Bárbara* Writes the Plain

1. In the thirties and forties this agreement crystallized into editorial and research institutions such as the Instituto de Filología in Buenos Aires, and the Fondo de Cultura Económica in Mexico City.

2. In the preface to the first history of Latin American literature, which was written by a North American, we read the following:

But shall we call Spanish-American writings literature? A professor in Argentina wished a few years ago to establish a course for students in Spanish-American literature. The plan was opposed by Bartolomé Mitre, ex-President of the republic and himself a poet and historian of the first rank, on the ground that such a thing did not exist. (Alfred Coester, *The Literary History of Spanish America* [New York: Macmillan Co., 1916; reprint, 1921], pp. vii-viii)

3. The most serious Latin American work devoted to the dissemination of Marxist criticism is that by Adolfo Sánchez Vásquez, *Estética y marxismo*, 2 vols. (Mexico City: Ediciones Era, 1970).

4. Emir Rodríguez Monegal, "Borges and *la nouvelle critique*," *Diacritics* 2, no. 2 (1972):27-34.

5. Of note are Octavio Paz's *Claude Lévi-Strauss o el nuevo festín de Esopo* (Mexico City: Joaquín Mortiz, 1967), and Sarduy's *Escrito sobre un cuerpo* (Buenos Aires: Editorial Sudamericana, 1969), and *Barroco* (Buenos Aires: Editorial Sudamericana, 1974).

6. Jitrik's most valuable contribution is *Las contradicciones del modernismo* (Mexico City: El Colegio de México, 1979).

7. Paz, "Palabras al Simposio," in *El artista latinoamericano y su identidad cultural*, ed. Damián Bayón (Caracas: Monte Avila, 1977), p. 23, my translation.

8. Ibid.

9. Ibid., p. 22.

10. The work that best explores this historical juncture is a novel, Alejo Carpentier's *El siglo de las luces* [*Explosion in a Cathedral*]. For details on how this novel may be read in this way, see the last chapter of my *Alejo Carpentier: The Pilgrim at Home* (Ithaca, N.Y.: Cornell University Press, 1977). Carpentier's novel provides a view of the Latin American Enlightenment and romanticism that is

quite at odds with Paz's. It seems to me that Carpentier suggests that the great issues debated at the dawn of modernity were concrete, living dilemmas in the New World, and that Latin American *philosophes* and romantics must be studied in actions as much as in thought.

11. "The nation can be reduced to the class capable of *conceiving* it, of speaking about it, of drawing its perimeter" (Alfred Melon, "Alrededor del concepto de identidad nacional," *La Gaceta de Cuba*, no. 177 [1979], p. 15).

12. It is this dilemma that produces the split between structuralism and French existentialism, represented, of course, by Sartre. I cannot reproduce here the heated debate that this split has generated, but one of its principal texts is the last chapter of *La pensée sauvage* by Lévi-Strauss.

13. I am alluding, of course, to the work of Lévi-Strauss, but this idea is really basic to all modern anthropology, present in figures like Frazer, Mauss, and Malinowsky.

14. This split was implicit, contradictorily, in Lévi-Strauss's work, but it is in the work of Jacques Derrida, especially in *La grammatologie*, that it has been studied in detail.

15. Paz, *Children of the Mire: Modern Poetry from Romanticism to the Avant-Garde*, tr. Rachel Phillips (Cambridge, Mass.: Harvard University Press, 1974).

16. All of the recent essays by Fernández Retamar to which I allude, along with *Calibán*, have been collected in *Calibán y otros ensayos: nuestra América y el mundo* (Havana: Editorial Arte y Literatura, 1979).

17. I have outlined the prolegomenon of this critical rereading in "Roberto Fernández Retamar: An Introduction," *Diacritics* 8, no. 4 (1978):70-75.

18. Included in *Tientos y diferencias*. I will cite from the (unauthorized) Arca edition (Montevideo, 1967).

19. "In order to be able to ignore the tremendous reality that was asserting itself in Eastern Europe, some began to speak of the future of 'Our America' in the language of soothsayers and prophets, proclaiming that what the dreamers at the turn of the century envisioned was much closer than even they had suggested" (ibid., p. 81). The irony of this allusion to the Russian Revolution is that Carpentier was among those who ignored its effects for many years.

20. In *Discusión* (1932), but quoted here from *Obras completas* (Buenos Aires: Emecé, 1974), p. 267.

21. *The New Republic* (9 April 1977), p. 27.

22. With Juan Goytisolo, Fuentes has shown interest in Castro's theories on the triple origin—Judaic, Arabic, Christian—of Spanish culture; they both follow Castro in explaining in this way the problematic specificity of Spanish literature. Fuentes has added to this what appears to be a rather hurried reading of Derrida, without discovering a secret confluence: there is a Hebrew concept of textuality, of commentary, promoted in Derrida, which is akin to that of Borges and Cervantes. But to attempt such a project on the basis of a vague concept of culture, of a determining origin of present phenomena, is a totally anti-Derridian mystification, which Fuentes can allow himself in *Terra Nostra*, but which, in *Cervantes o la crítica de la lectura* (Mexico City: Joaquín Mortiz, 1976), simply does not work as criticism. See also Fuentes's review of the English version of Goytisolo's novel *Reivindicación del Conde Don Julián* in the *New York Times Book Review* (5 May 1974), pp. 5-7, and chap. 4 in this book.

23. Guillermo Sucre, "Poesía hispanoamericana y conciencia de lenguaje," *Eco*, no. 200 (1978), p. 611.

24. Carlos Rincón, "El cambio actual de la noción de literatura en Latinoamérica," *Eco*, no. 196 (1978), p. 390.

25. Irlemar Chiampi, "A imagem de América," *Língua e Literatura* (Universidade de São Paulo) 6 (1977):84.

26. Melon, "Alrededor del concepto," p. 17.

27. Pedro Henríquez Ureña, *Literary Currents in Hispanic America* (Cambridge, Mass.: Harvard University Press, 1946), p. 99.

28. José Martí, *Páginas escogidas*, ed. Alfonso M. Escudero (Madrid: Austral, 1971), p. 120.

29. Ibid., p. 122.

30. Antonio Cândido, "Literature and Underdevelopment," in *Latin America in Its Literature*, ed. César Fernández Moreno; trans. Mary G. Berg (New York: Holmes & Meier, 1980), p. 264.

31. Philip E. Ritterbush, "Organic Form: Aesthetics and Objectivity in the Study of Form in the Life Sciences," in *Organic Form: The Life of an Idea*, ed. G. S. Rousseau (Boston: Routledge & Kegan Paul, 1972), pp. 38-39. This book also contains important essays by G. N. Giordano Orsini and William K. Wimsatt, along with a useful bibliography on the topic. See also "Genealogy, Growth, and Other Metaphors," by Robert Nisbet, *New Literary History* 3 (1970):351-363.

32. José J. Arrom, *Certidumbre de América,* 2d ed. (Madrid: Gredos, 1971), pp. 167-172.

33. Lukács, *Studies in European Realism*, tr. Edith Bone (London: Hillway, 1950), p. 11.

34. D. L. Shaw, *Gallegos: Doña Bárbara* (London: Grant & Cutler, 1972), p.7.

35. This is precisely what Alejo Carpentier proposes in his "Novelas de América," *El Nacional* (Caracas) (15 June 1951), p. 14.

36. There is a vivid portrait of Gallegos and his literary ideology in Lowell Dunam, *Rómulo Gallegos: An Oklahoma Encounter and the Writing of the Last Novel* (Norman: University of Oklahoma Press, 1974).

37. On these aspects of allegory, see Paul de Man, "The Rhetoric of Temporality,'" in *Interpretation: Theory and Practice*, ed. Charles Singleton (Baltimore, Md.: Johns Hopkins University Press, 1969), pp. 173-209.

38. I use the edition of *Doña Bárbara* published by Fondo de Cultura Económica (1954; reprint, 1971), but quote from the translation by Robert Malloy (New York: Peter Smith, 1931; reprint, 1948).

39. I base this on Jacques Derrida's well-known essay "La Pharmacie de Platon," in *La dissemination* (Paris: Seuil, 1975). There is an excellent English version by Barbara Johnson, *Dissemination* (Chicago: University of Chicago Press, 1981).

40. I am quoting and slightly correcting the translation from Gabriel García Márquez, *No One Writes to the Colonel and Other Stories*, tr. J. S. Bernstein (New York: Harper Colophon Books, 1968; reprint, 1979). The quotations are from pp. 158 and 161, respectively. For the original I am using *Los funerales de la Mamá Grande* (Buenos Aires: Editorial Sudamericana, 1962; reprint, 1967).

41. I quote from Severo Sarduy, *Cobra*, tr. Suzanne Jill Levine (New York: E. P. Dutton, 1975), and use for the original, *Cobra* (Buenos Aires: Sudamericana, 1972).

Chapter 3: The Dictatorship of Rhetoric / The Rhetoric of Dictatorship
Portions of this chapter appeared as "The Dictatorship of Rhetoric/The Rhetoric of Dictatorship: Carpentier, García Márquez, and Roa Bastos," in *Latin American Research Review* 15, no. 3 (1980).

1. "Finally, Batista's own laziness and weakness damaged morale more than anything else: the president played canasta when he should have been making war plans; as his press secretary put it in exile, 'Canasta was a great ally of Fidel Castro' " (Hugh Thomas, *Cuba: The Pursuit of Freedom* [New York: Harper & Row, 1971], p. 1041).

2. The bibliography of *caudillismo* and dictatorship in general is immense. There is a useful introduction to this problem by José E. Iturriaga, *El tirano en la América Latina*, Jornadas 15 (Mexico City: El Colegio de México, n.d. [appears to be from the forties]), as well as Ariel Peralta's *El cesarismo en América Latina*, 2d ed. (Santiago, Chile: Editorial Orbe, 1966). By far the most authoritative and enlightening work on the subject is Juan Linz's remarkable "Totalitarian and Authoritative Regimes," *Handbook of Political Science* 3 (Reading, Mass.: Addison-Wesley, 1975), pp. 175-411.

3. In a well-documented article (the best on this topic, in my view), Bernardo Subercaseaux mentions quite a few dictator-novels. He cites the following as the origins of the modern tradition:

The theme of the dictator was not new [when *Tirano Banderas* appeared in 1925]. José Mármol, following the formula of the historical novel as practiced by Walter Scott, had dealt with it in *Amalia*, 1851. The Peruvian Mercedes Cabello de Carbonera had focused on the origins of Leguía's dictatorship in her novel *El conspirador* (1892). The Venezuelan Pedro María Morantes had published *El cabito* in 1909, a sort of diatribe against Cipriano Castro's dictatorship. Rufino Blanco-Fombona, another Venezuelan, published in 1923 *La máscara heroica*, a novel whose setting was Venezuela under the dictatorship of Juan Vicente Gómez. ("*Tirano banderas* en la narrativa hispanoamericana [la novela del dictador 1926-1976]," *Anales de la Universidad de Cuenca* [Ecuador], no. 33 [1978], p. 58)

One must agree with Subercaseaux that *Amalia*, with *Facundo*, however, is the beginning of the subgenre, though Echeverría's "El matadero" was probably written fifteen years earlier, as Aída Cometta Manzoni has pointed out in "El dictador en la narrativa latinoamericana," *Revista Nacional de Cultura* (Caracas), no. 234 (1978), p. 90.

Besides those already mentioned, there are already quite a few studies of the dictator-novel. Bernardo Fouques's "La autopsia del poder según Roa Bastos, Carpentier y García Márquez," *Cuadernos Americanos* 38 (1979):83-111, has some interesting observations, though its main point, having to do with the presence of the corpse of the dictator in the texts, is difficult to grasp. Santiago Portuondo Zúñiga's "Cinco novelas y un tirano," *Santiago* (Santiago de Cuba), no. 30 (1978), pp. 47-75, is strong on the historical background and proposes a chronological division (not of the novel but of dictatorships) that is useful, but the treatment of the novels (*Tirano Banderas, El señor presidente, El gran Burundún Burundá ha muerto, The Autumn of the Patriarch,* and *Reasons of State*) is not too detailed or convincing. Brian J. Mallet's "Dictadura e identidad en la novela latinoamericana," *Arbor* (Madrid), nos. 393-394 (1978), pp. 60-64, contains many perceptive

comments. Angel Rama's *Los dictadores latinoamericanos* (Mexico City
de Cultura Económica, 1976) does not seem to have a thesis that one could retain or
refute. Rama fails to notice that what the recent dictator-novel demonstrates is
precisely the delusion on the part of both the politician and the writer of thinking
themselves at a center from which they can authoritatively construct or govern a
totality. Giuseppe Bellini's comprehensive *Il mondo alucinante. Da Asturias a
García Márquez. Studi sul romanzo ispano-americano della dittatura* (Milan:
Cisalpino-Goliardica, 1976) contains more reliable information than Rama's
monograph; it is perhaps the best general overview available. Among the various
useful facts in Bellini's book is the following, which gives us the anecdotal origin of
various recent dictator-novels: "Gabriel García Márquez has revealed the existence
of a projected collected volume entitled *Los padres de las patrias*, due to Carlos
Fuentes's initiative, which was frustrated almost at once by the appearance of books
by individual authors like Carpentier and Roa Bastos" (p. 10). Luis Pancorbo's
"Tres tristes tiranos," *Revista de Occidente*, 3ra época, no. 19 (1977), pp. 12-16, is
just a review. Mario Benedetti's "El recurso del supremo patriarca," *Casa de las
Américas*, no. 98 (1976), pp. 12-23, is also a review, but much better and with a bit of
interesting information. Though Benedetti's evaluations are based on somewhat
dated notions of novelistic technique, I agree with his very high opinion of Roa
Bastos's *Yo el Supremo*. I disagree, however, with his somewhat lukewarm reception
of *Reasons of State*, above all when he bases his opinion on the mistaken notion that
the picaresque is a minor genre. Angela B. Dellepiane is more thorough in "Tres
novelas de la dictadura: *El recurso del método, El otoño del patriarca, Yo el
Supremo*," *Caravelle (Cahiers du Monde Hispanique et Luso-Brésilien)*, no. 29
(1977), pp. 99-105. In "La novela de la dictadura: nuevas estructuras narrativas,"
Revista de Crítica Literaria Latinoamericana (Lima) 5, no. 9 (1979):99-105,
Martha Paley Francescato calls attention to *El gran solitario de palacio* (1971), by
the Mexican René Avilés Fabila. Domingo Miliani's exhaustive semiotic presentation is useful, though his conclusions are disappointingly facile in "El dictador, objeto
narrativo en dos novelas hispanoamericanas: *Yo el supremo* y *El recurso del
método*," *Actas. Simposio Internacional de Estudios Hispánicos*, ed. Mátyas
Horányi (Budapest: Akadémiai Kaidó, 1978), pp. 463-490.

4. Aída Cometta Manzoni has already noted that

the truth of the matter is that this political character, which appears as a typical product is not
American, because it is Spain that brings it here in the dawn of our history. If we take a look at
our Conquest and colonization we will discover the *caudillo* and the dictator among many of the
traits of Cortés and Alvarado, Pizarro and Almagro, Lope de Aguirre and Orellana, and among
many other Spaniards who came to the continent looking for adventures and wealth. All of them
dominated by power and terror conquered powerful empires and peoples by the superiority of
their weapons and the cruelty of their behavior. Many times they fought for leadership among
themselves, as in Pizarro's case. ("El dictador," p. 90; my translation)

The Spaniards, however, did not bring the *caudillo* to America but developed the
type here, when they came into contact with the peculiar sociohistorical conditions of
colonial America. In terms of the dictator-novels or dictator-book the important
pairings are Cortés-López de Gómara, Columbus-Bartolomé de las Casas, or
Cortés-Bernal Díaz, that is to say, between the powerful political leader and the
writer or editor who composes his biography or "corrects" it. The paradigmatic

couple would in this case be Cortés-López de Gómara. The latter's work prefigures uncannily the most recent dictator-novels.

5. Bellini writes, "With Sarmiento's, the character of the dictator begins to have its own consistency within Latin American literature. The figure of the tyrant becomes a protagonist, *de cuerpo entero*, and in the trajectory leading up to the twentieth century, it represents a significant evolution" (*Il mondo alucinante*, p. 7). I would say "definitive" rather than "significant."

6. See *The Breakdown of Democratic Regimes: Latin America*, ed. Juan Linz and Alfred Stepan (Baltimore, Md.: Johns Hopkins University Press, 1978).

7. Américo Castro, *La realidad histórica de España*, 3d ed. (Mexico City: Porrúa, 1966).

8. R. Menéndez Pidal, *La epopeya castellana a través de la literatura española*, 2d ed. (Madrid: Espasa-Calpe, 1959).

9. José Carlos Mariátegui, *7 ensayos de interpretación de la realidad peruana* (Lima: Biblioteca Amanta, 1928; reprint, 1968), pp. 57-58.

10. Hegel, *The Philosophy of History*, intro. C. J. Friedrich (New York: Dover, 1956), p. 30.

11. "But indisputably, Sarmiento's key find is to identify Facundo with a conglomerate of ethnopsychological, social, geographic, and political qualities. He is a myth, in fact, a negative myth of the barbaric forces" (Ezequiel Martínez Estrada, *Los invariantes históricos en el Facundo* [Buenos Aires: Casa Pardo, 1974], p. 23). By "literary myth" I mean a story or figure that literature conceives to speak about itself and inquire about its own foundation, given that literature cannot really speak about itself except by speaking about something else.

12. Domingo Faustino Sarmiento, *Facundo o civilización y barbarie en las pampas argentinas*, text, prologue, and appendices established by Raúl Moglia (Buenos Aires: Ediciones Peuser, 1955),p. 201, my translation.

13. I am, of course, alluding to Lukács, *The Theory of the Novel*, tr. Anna Bostock (Cambridge, Mass.: M.I.T. Press, 1920; reprint, 1971), perhaps in a somewhat simplistic fashion. In a sense Lukács knows that the hero of the novel is the ironic, all-knowing novelist, even when his total knowledge is precisely about the impossibility of knowledge:

The writer's irony is a negative mysticism to be found in times without a god. It is an attitude of *docta ignorantia* towards meaning, a portrayal of the kindly and malicious workings of the demons, a refusal to comprehend more than the mere fact of these workings; and in it there is the deep certainty, expressible only by form-giving, that through not-desiring-to-know and not-being-able-to-know he has truly encountered, glimpsed and grasped the ultimate, true substance, the present, non-existent God. This is why irony is the objectivity of the novel. (p. 90)

The latest Latin American writing deconstructs irony by finally moving away from the romantic conceit of *authority*.

14. Unamuno, "Cómo se hace una novela," *Obras completas*, vol. 10 (Barcelona: Vergara, 1958), p. 861, my translation.

15. A good though somewhat limiting history of this may be found in Joachim Weintraub, *The Value of the Individual: Self and Circumstance in Autobiography* (Chicago: University of Chicago Press, 1978). An exemplary exposition of the relation of the self to literary creation is contained in Paul de Man's "Ludwig Binswanger and the Sublimation of the Self," in *Blindness and Insight: Essays in the*

Rhetoric of Contemporary Criticism (New York: Oxford University Press, 1971), pp. 36-50. For a brief though clarifying synthesis of some current notions of the self and their relation to writing, see Sylvere Lotringer, "The 'Subject' on Trial," *Semiotext(e)* 1, no. 3. (1975):3-8; and Julia Kristeva's "The Subject in Signifying Practice," ibid, pp. 19-26.

16. A significant detail here is that Cara de Angel, the dictator's secretary in *El señor presidente*, is slain by the tyrant in a very crucial scene in the book. As should be obvious, secretaries are much more powerful in recent dictator-novels. They survive the dictator and threaten to take his place.

17. Some of the documentation for what I say here may be found in my *Alejo Carpentier: The Pilgrim at Home* (Ithaca, N.Y.: Cornell University Press, 1977), pp. 256-274.

18. In ibid. I studied the impact that the *Revista de Occidente* and Ortega y Gasset's publishing ventures in general had on Carpentier and other writers who began their work in the twenties and thirties. Vico was one of the thinkers very much in vogue during the period, and a rather useful gloss of his philosophy was published then that could very well have been Carpentier's introduction to the author of *The New Science* (Richard Peters, *La estructura de la historia universal en Juan Bautista Vico*, tr. J. Pérez Bances [Madrid: Revista de Occidente, 1930]).

19. Alejo Carpentier, *Reasons of State,* tr. Frances Partridge (New York: Alfred A. Knopf, 1976), p. 9. The translation reads fine but contains one crucial error: on page 197 it says " 'Santicló' who brought toys to children *three days before* the Three Magi." It should, of course, say *thirteen* days. The importance of the number lies in Carpentier's manipulation of the liturgical year, particularly of the time of Advent.

20. Considering the "erudite" nature of Carpentier's fiction, I was surprised to find that most readers in Cuba considered *Reasons of State* his most accessible novel, because they could recognize many of the incidents narrated.

21. Carpentier had written two dictator-works before *Reasons of State*: *The Kingdom of This World* and "Right of Sanctuary." *The Kingdom of This World* (1949) was a fantasy of order, a secret order, wrought by the author of the prologue (see my "Isla a su vuelo fugitiva: Carpentier y el realismo mágico," *Revista Iberoamericana* 40, no. 86 [1974]:9-64). I discuss "Right of Sanctuary" elsewhere in the present volume. "Right of Sanctuary" should be seen as a fiction beyond *Yo el Supremo*. Here the Secretary, a figure of the writer, changes countries and returns to his own as ambassador from the country he is at present inhabiting. S. Jiménez Fajardo's "Carpentier's *El derecho de asilo*: A Game Theory," *Journal of Spanish Studies-Twentieth Century* 6 (1978):193-206, is an intelligent reading of the story. Note that *El derecho de asilo*, published originally as a small book in Spanish, has been incorporated into the English translation of *War of Time* as a story.

22. Isabel Vergara has analyzed the interplay between the history of Colombia and biblical and Christian lore in "Mito e historia en *El otoño del patriarca*" (M.A. thesis, Cornell University, 1977). There are also interesting observations about the Bible and the novel in Katalin Kulin, *"El otoño del patriarca*: tema y mensaje," Horányi, *Actas*, esp. pp. 429-430.

23. González Echevarría, "Big Mama's Wake," *Diacritics* 4, no. 4 (1974):8-17. There is, it seems to me, a clear relationship between Carpentier's dream of order in

ingdom of This World and its deconstruction in his dictator-novel *Reasons of* and García Márquez's *One Hundred Years of Solitude* and *The Autumn of the Patriarch*. On the idea of order in *One Hundred Years of Solitude*, see my "With Borges in Macondo," *Diacritics* 2, no. 1 (1972):57-60. Raymond L. Williams has written an illuminating structural analysis of *The Autumn of the Patriarch*, "The Dynamic Structure of García Márquez's *El otoño del patriarca*," *Symposium* 32 (1978):56-75.

24. In the history of this treatment, the most decisive separation appears at the moment when, at the same time as the science of nature, the determination of absolute presence is constituted as self-presence, as subjectivity. It is the moment of the great rationalisms of the seventeenth century. From then on, the condemnation of fallen and finite writing will take another form, within which we still live: it is non-self-presence that will be denounced. Thus the exemplariness of the "Rousseauist" moment . . . begins to be explained. Rousseau repeats the Platonic gesture by referring to another model of presence: self-presence in the senses, in the sensible cogito, which simultaneously carries in itself the inscription of divine law. On the one hand, *representative*, fallen, secondary, instituted writing, writing in the literal and strict sense, is condemned in *The Essay on the Origin of Languages* (it "enervates" speech; to "judge genius' from books is like "painting a man's portrait from his corpse," etc.). Writing in the common sense is the dead letter, it is the carrier of death. It exhausts life. On the other hand, on the face of the same proposition, writing in the metaphoric sense, natural, divine, and living writing is venerated; it is equal in dignity to the origin of value, to the voice of conscience as divine law, to the heart, to sentiment, and so forth. . . . Natural writing is immediately united to the voice and to breath. Its nature is not grammatological but pneumatological. (Jacques Derrida, *Of Grammatology*, tr. Gayatri Chakravorti Spivak [Baltimore, Md.: Johns Hopkins University Press, 1976], pp. 16-17)

A more detailed account of the philosophical and mythological "repression" of writing at the expense of voice may be found in Derrida's "La pharmacie de Platon," a text that first appeared in *Tel Quel* (nos. 32 and 33) and was later collected in *La dissemination* (Paris: Seuil, 1975).

25. All translations from *Yo el Supremo* are my own. I found useful for its background and details *Comentarios sobre Yo el Supremo* (Asunción, Paraguay: Ediciones Club del Libro, no. 1, 1975), by Beatriz Alcalá de González Oddone, Ramiro Domínguez, Adriano Irala Burgos, and Josefina Plá. The best criticism on the novel is found in *Seminario sobre Yo el Supremo de Augusto Roa Bastos* (Poitiers: Publications du Centre de Recherches Latino-Americaines de l'Université de Poitiers, 1976), and in *Textos sobre el texto* (2° seminario sobre *Yo el Supremo* de Augusto Roa Bastos), ibid., 1980. There are three other important pieces on the novel: Luis María Ferrer Agüero's "La relación autor-personaje en *Yo el Supremo* de Augusto Roa Bastos," Horányi, *Actas*, pp. 491-500; Alain Sicard's "*Yo el supremo* de Augusto Roa Bastos: le mythe et l'histoire," in *Hommage des hispanistes français a Noel Salomon* (Barcelona: Editorial Luna, 1979), pp. 783-792; Sharon E. Ugalde, "The Mythical Origins of *El Supremo*," *Journal of Spanish Studies: Twentieth Century* 8 (1980):293-305. Hugo Rodríguez Alcalá has also written an important article on a story by Roa Bastos, "Official Truth and 'True' Truth: Augusto Roa Bastos' 'Borrador de un informe,' " *Studies in Short Fiction* 8, no. 1 (1971):141-154. The Cuban edition of *Yo el Supremo* (Havana: Casa de Las Américas, 1979) contains useful, if tendentious, background information on Dr. Francia and a chronology.

26. Oedipus means "swollen feet," according to Lévi-Strauss in his now famous

essay "The Structural Study of Myth" (*Structural Anthropology*, tr. Claire Jacobson and Brooke Grundfest Schoepf [New York: Anchor Books, 1967], pp. 202-228). The problem with the feet, Lévi-Strauss argues, has to do with "a universal characteristic of men born from the Earth that at the moment they emerge from the depths they cannot walk or they walk clumsily" (p. 212).

27. There can be no better definition of text than *Yo el Supremo* itself, but Roland Barthes's "From Work to Text" offers a more conventional characterization, from which I quote:

The text . . . practices the infinite deferment of the signified, is dilatory; its field is that of the signifier and the signifier must not be conceived of as "the first stage of meaning," its material vestibule, but, in complete opposition to this, as its *deferred action*. . . . The logic regulating the Text is not comprehensive (define "what the work means") but metonymic; the activity of associations, contiguities, carryings-over coincides with a liberation of the symbolic energy (lacking it, man would die); the work—in the best of cases—is *moderately* symbolic (its symbolic runs out, comes to a halt); the Text is *radically* symbolic." (*Image. Music. Text*, tr. Stephen Heath [New York: Hill and Wang, 1977], pp. 158-159)

28. Guillermo Cabrera Infante, *Vista del amanecer en el trópico* (Barcelona: Seix Barral, 1974); tr. Suzanne Jill Levine as *View of Dawn in the Tropics* (New York: Harper and Row, 1978).

29. Melodrama is one of the characteristics of Cabrera Infante's work, particularly in his early stories, collected in *Así en la paz como en la guerra*. It is also a very important element in *Three Trapped Tigers*, though in this book melodramatic situations are diffused by breaking down the narrative sequence and mixing several strands of the plot.

30. Mallet, "Dictadura e identidad," p. 65.

31. Borges is one of the quoted sources of Derrida's "La pharmacie de Platon," as he is of so much of current French criticism (see Emir Rodríguez Monegal's "Borges and *la nouvelle critique*," *Diacritics* 2, no. 2 [1972]:27-34). For Borges's influence on García Márquez, see my "With Borges in Macondo." The relation between Derrida's and Borges's texts should be studied in detail. One can anticipate that, besides Borges's influence on Derrida, there is also a coincidence in their sources, to wit, both Borges and Derrida refuse to read Western tradition as the product of only Greco-Roman antiquity, choosing instead to make manifest the productive marginal and polemical contribution of the Semitic world (both Arabic and Hebraic). If Derrida seems so akin to the Hispanic tradition, it is obviously because of the strong Semitic element in Spanish history. "La pharmacie de Platon" had a franchise in Fernando de Rojas's *Celestina*, and nearly all of the important Kabalists were from Spain. Carpentier also pays homage to this tradition in *Explosion in a Cathedral*, a text that can be read as a Kabalistic allegory, as I endeavored to show in the last chapter of *The Pilgrim at Home*.

Chapter 4: *Terra Nostra*: Theory and Practice

Portions of this chapter appeared as "Terra Nostra: Theory and Practice," in *Carlos Fuentes: A Critical View*, edited by Robert Brody and Charles Rossman, University of Texas Press, 1982.

1. Alejo Carpentier, "Problemática de la actual novela latinoamericana," in *Tientos y diferencias* (Montevideo, Uruguay: Arca, 1967), p. 7.

2. In his famous prologue to *The Kingdom of this World* (1949), Carpentier

speaks with admiration of Unamuno. He alludes to the Spanish thinker in many other instances, and as recently as 1980, in an article published only a few months before his death ("La difícil pureza idiomática," *Revolución y Cultura*, no. 89 [January 1980], pp. 16-18). Latin American writers have felt closer to Unamuno than to other Spanish thinkers because, being Basque, he felt marginal to Spain in a way similar to that of his colleagues from across the Atlantic (see my "Borges, Carpentier y Ortega: dos textos olvidados," *Revista Iberoamericana* 42 [1977]:697-704).

3. I have traced these ideas and their relation to Latin America in the first two chapters of *Alejo Carpentier: The Pilgrim at Home* (Ithaca, N.Y.: Cornell University Press, 1977), pp. 15-96.

4. Carlos Fuentes, *Cervantes o la crítica de la lectura* (Mexico City: Joaquín Mortiz, 1976), p. 36; my translation.

5. Ibid., p. 111.

6. Carpentier's *El recurso del método* is the best "study" that we have of how modernismo, though utilizing a philological thrust that is concerned with the origins of language, turns those "natural" origins into artifice, making nature and its display a museum. I have analyzed these ideas in "Modernidad, modernismo y nueva narrativa: *El recurso del método*," *Revista Interamericana de Bibliografía/Inter-American Review of Bibliography* 30 (1980):157-163.

7. Fuentes, *Cervantes o la crítica de la lectura*, p. 36.

8. Miguel Ugarte has studied competently Goytisolo's debt to Castro in "Juan Goytisolo: Unruly Disciple of Américo Castro," *Journal of Spanish Studies: Twentieth Century* 7 (1979):353-364. Fuentes himself has written about this issue in his review of Goytisolo's *Count Julian* (*New York Times Book Review*, [5 May 1974], pp. 5-7).

9. Fuentes, *Cervantes o la crítica de la lectura*, p. 109.

10. Lucille Kerr, "The Paradox of Power and Mystery: Carlos Fuentes; *Terra Nostra*," *PMLA* 95 (1980):98-99.

11. *Terra Nostra*, tr. Margaret Sayers Peden (New York: Farrar, Straus, Giroux, 1975), p. 485. The Spanish-language version is also from 1975.

12. In a long review of Octavio Paz's *The Other Mexico: Critique of the Pyramid*, Fuentes writes,

Octavio Paz was struck by the continuity of a power structure, masked by different ideologies, serving equally well the needs of Indian theocracy, Spanish colonialism, and modern *desarrollismo*, development for development's sake. . . . When Paz pulls apart the final curtain of his drama, we are facing the unmentionable, the skeletons in the closet of our subconscious national life. His stage becomes a bare space where naked figures sing, weep, crawl next to a blood-stained wall, or dance in a festival that will soon be crushed by a violent physical intrusion. The light on that deepest of stages is the light of time: past, present and future. The figures chant a line from a poem by Octavio Paz: "Time hungers for incarnation. . . . " How to link power and society democratically in Mexico? The first step, says Paz, is critical freedom. Only in an open critical atmosphere can the true problems of Mexico be defined and discussed, and the conflicting history of Mexico, hungering for incarnation, come out into the open. *The Other Mexico* is a critique of what the Mexican revolution achieved and failed to achieve, as well as a modest but far-ranging proposal for a new revolution: for a peaceful reform of our conscience and purpose. ("Mexico and Its Demons," *New York Review of Books* [20 September 1973], p. 16)

In *Cervantes o la crítica de la lectura* Fuentes seeks a parallel solution, but in the execution of *Terra Nostra* the demon reappears to reinstate violence.

13. Fuentes's debt to Frances Yates's *The Art of Memory* is great, particularly in the chapter entitled "Teatro de la memoria," which is a synthesis of Yates's book. But the fundamental issues raised by Yates's research are already present in at least two of Borges's stories: "The Garden of Forking Paths" and "Funes el memorioso."

14. Jorge Luis Borges, *Ficciones*, ed. Anthony Kerrigan (New York: Grove Press, 1962), p. 98.

15. I am indebted here, of course, to Edward W. Said's *Orientalism* (New York: Vintage, 1978). See also my "Modernidad, modernismo y nueva narrativa."

16. *Terra Nostra*, trans., p. 762; Spanish-language version, p. 766.

Chapter 5: *Los reyes*: Cortázar's Mythology of Writing

An earlier version of this chapter appeared in *The Final Island: The Fiction of Julio Cortázar*, edited by Jaime Alazraki and Ivar Ivask. Copyright 1976 and 1978 by the University of Oklahoma Press.

1. See Eugenio Donato, "*Structuralism*: The Aftermath," *Sub-Stance*, no. 7 (Fall 1973), pp. 9-26. Neither Anglo-American "new criticism" nor French structuralism really ever abandoned the notion of authorship. It is always found, albeit relegated to a self-consciously marginal position, as a rhetorical license that is tolerated but not questioned. It is only in what Donato calls the "aftermath of structuralism" that the notion of authorship has been subjected to a radical critique.

2. Roland Barthes, *Critique et vérité* (Paris: Seuil, 1966), pp. 60-61; my translation.

3. José Ortega y Gassett, *The Dehumanization of Art and Other Essays on Art, Culture and Literature* (Princeton, N.J.: Princeton University Press, 1968), pp. 31-32.

4. Michel Foucault, *The Order of Things: An Archaeology of the Human Sciences* (New York: Pantheon, 1970), pp. 217-221.

5. Jean Hyppolite, *Genesis and Structure of Hegel's Phenomenology of the Spirit*, tr. Samuel Cherniak, John Heckman (Evanston, Ill.: Northwestern University Press, 1974), p. 160.

6. See Borges's commentary in *The Book of Imaginary Beings*, tr., rev., and enl. Norman Thomas di Giovanni (New York: Discus, 1970), pp. 158-159.

7. Alfred MacAdam, *El individuo y el otro: Crítica a los cuentos de Julio Cortázar* (New York: La Librería, 1971), p. 34.

8. Cortázar, *Los reyes* (Buenos Aires: Sudamericana, 1970), p. 73.

9. Ibid., p. 49; my translation.

10. The title may come from fragment 28 of Heraclitus: "There is exchange of all things for fire and of fire for all things, as there is of wares for gold and of gold for wares" (Philip Wheelwright, *Heraclitus* [New York: Atheneum, 1971], p. 37).

11. Plutarch, *The Lives of the Noble Grecians and Romans*, tr. John Dryden, ed., Arthur Hugh Clough (New York: Modern Library, 1932), p. 11.

12. Cortázar, *All Fires the Fire and Other Stories*, tr. Suzanne Jill Levine (New York: Pantheon, 1973), pp. 116-117.

13. Cortázar, *Blow-Up and Other Stories*, tr. Paul Blackburn (New York: Collier, 1968), p. 169. Subsequent page numbers refer to this edition.

14. Cortázar, *Las armas secretas* (Buenos Aires: Sudamericana, 1964), p. 108.

15. Sarduy, *Cobra* (Buenos Aires: Editorial Sudamericana, 1972), p. 229.

16. Cortázar, *Hopscotch*, tr. Gregory Rabassa (New York: Signet, 1967), p. 436. Cortázar takes this excerpt from *Noches áticas*, tr. Francisco Navarro y Calvo (Madrid: Biblioteca Clásica, 1893), vol. 1, p. 202. The relevance of Gellius's book in relation to Cortázar's novel is greater than might be suspected. In his preface Gellius says the following about the composition of his book:

In the arrangement of the material I have adopted the same haphazard order that I had previously followed in collecting it. For whenever I had taken in hand any Greek or Latin book, or had heard anything worth remembering, I used to jot down whatever took my fancy, of any and every kind, without any definite plan or order; and such notes I would lay away as an aid to my memory, like a kind of literary storehouse, so that when the need arose of a word or a subject which I chanced for the moment to have forgotten, and the books from which I had taken it were not at hand, I could readily find it and produce it. (*The Attic Nights of Aulus Gellius*, tr. John C. Rolfe [Cambridge, Mass.: Harvard University Press, 1970], p. xxvii)

Cortázar has of course followed this same method of composition in the "dispensable" chapters of *Hopscotch*, as well as in *Libro de Manuel*. In fact, just as Ludmilla composes the *Libro* for Manuel's future enlightenment, so did Gellius assemble his "in order that like recreation might be provided for my children, when they should have some respite from business affairs and could unbend and divert their minds."

17. For further commentary on *The Birth of Tragedy* and "The Pursuer," see Djelal Kadir, "A Mythical Re-enactment: Cortázar's *El perseguidor*," *Latin American Literary Review* 2 (1973):63-73.

Chapter 6: *Biografía de un cimarrón* and the Novel of the Cuban Revolution
Portions of this chapter appeared as "Biografía de un cimarrón and the Novel of the Cuban Revolution," in *Novel: A Forum on Fiction,* volume 13, no. 3 (Spring 1980).

1. "There are some things about life I don't understand. Everything about Nature is obscure to me, and about the gods more so still. The gods are capricious and wilful, and they are the cause of many strange things which I have seen for myself." (Miguel Barnet, *Biografía de un cimarrón* [Havana: Academia de Ciencias de Cuba, Instituto de Etnología y Folklore, 1966], p. 15; my translation). All quotations in the text are from this edition. The translation appears as *The Autobiography of a Runaway Slave*, ed. Miguel Barnet, tr. Jocasta Innes (London: Bodley Head, 1966). The first American edition was published by Pantheon Books, New York, in 1968. Given the inadequacy of the title as translated, I shall use the Spanish title. Translations are my own.

Barnet was born in 1940, in Havana, to a well-to-do family, and educated in American schools until the Revolution. He is the author of three poetry collections (the last contains most of the previous two): *La piedra fina y el pavorreal* (Havana: Unión Nacional de Escritores y Artistas de Cuba, 1963); *Isla de güijes* (Havana: El Puente, 1964); and *La sagrada familia* (Havana: Casa de las Américas, 1967). Barnet's other documentary novel, *Canción de Rachel*, first appeared in Havana (Instituto del Libro) in 1969, though it was issued that same year in Barcelona by Editorial Galerna. There is a 1970 edition from Buenos Aires that claims to be the first and is issued as *La* [*sic*] *canción de Rachel*. Barnet has collaborated with various Cuban journals, most notably *La Gaceta de Cuba* and *Unión*.

2. Claude Lévi-Strauss, *The Scope of Anthropology*, tr. Sherry Ortner Paul and Robert A. Paul (London: Jonathan Cape, 1967).

3. Fidel Castro, "Discurso de clausura," *Casa de las Américas*, no. 95 (1976), p. 47; my translation.

4. In *Calibán*, first published in *Casa de las Américas* in 1971 (no. 68) and later separately in many other editions, Fernández Retamar, invoking a topic of modern confessional literature, the remembrance of childhood readings (present in, among many other works, Sartre's *Les mots*), establishes a distinction between a naïve self before the Revolution, and one who has been awakened to the evils of colonialism after it. In Fernández Retamar's case, the book being read is Sarmiento's *Facundo*. *La última mujer y el próximo combate* centers on the revelation of the true personality of a revolutionary who was formerly a well-heeled bourgeois but who has become a proletarian hero.

5. The historian, in his function as historian, can remain quite remote from the collective acts he records; his language and the events that the language denotes are clearly distinct entities. But the writer's language is to some degree the product of his own action; he is both the historian and the agent of his own language. The ambivalence of writing is such that it can be considered both an act and an interpretative process that follows after an act with which it cannot coincide. As such, it both affirms and denies its own nature or specificity. Unlike the historian, the writer remains so closely involved with action that he can never free himself of the temptation to destroy whatever stands between him and his deed, especially the temporal distance that makes him dependent on an earlier past. The appeal of modernity haunts all literature. It is revealed in numberless images and emblems that appear at all periods—in the obsession with the *tabula rasa*, with new beginnings—that finds recurrent expression in all forms of writing. No true account of literary language can bypass this persistent temptation of literature to fulfill itself in a single moment. The temptation of immediacy is constitutive of a literary consciousness and has to be included in a definition of the specificity of literature. (Paul de Man, "Literary History and Literary Modernity," in *Blindness and Insight: Essays in the Rhetoric of Contemporary Criticism* [New York: Oxford University Press, 1971], p. 152)

6. The Greeks . . . thought that even the gods could not change the past; but Christ did change it, rewrote it, and in a new way fulfilled it. In the same way the End changes all, and produces, in what in relation to it is the past, these seasons, *kairoi*, historical moments of intemporal significance. The divine plot is the pattern of *kairoi* in relation to the End. Not only the Greeks but the Hebrews lacked this antithesis; for Hebrew . . . had no word for *chronos*, and so no contrast between time which is simply "one damn thing after another" and time as concentrated in *kairoi*. It is the New Testament that lays the foundation for both the modern sense of epoch . . . and the modern distinction between times; the coming of God's time (*kairos*), the fulfilling of the time (*kairos*—Mark i.15), the signs of the times (Matt. xvi.2,3) as against passing time, *chronos*. The notion of fulfillment is essential; the *kairos* transforms the past, validates Old Testament types and prophecies, establishes concord with origins as well as ends. (Frank Kermode, *The Sense of an Ending: Studies in the Theory of Fiction* [New York: Oxford University Press, 1967; reprint, 1973] pp. 47-48)

M. H. Abrams, writing on the same phenomenon as expressed in nineteenth-century romantic thought, says,

The doctrine of an absolute revolution has not an empirical but, ultimately, a theological basis; its certainty is a faith in Providence—a Providence converted into its secular equivalent of an immanent teleology, or dialectical necessity, or the scientific laws compelling historical events; and its prototype is the deeply ingrained and pervasive expectation in the Western world, guaranteed by an infallible text, of an abrupt, cataclysmic, and all-inclusive change which, after an indispensable preliminary of fierce destructiveness, will result in the perfection of an earthly paradise for a redeemed mankind. Its roots, that is to say, are in the Biblical scheme of apocalyptic history. (*Natural Super-naturalism: Tradition and Revolution in Romantic Literature* [New York: W. W. Norton, 1973], p. 63)

7. The most notorious spokesman for this official view of what literature ought to be was Leopoldo Avila, "Sobre algunas corrientes de la crítica y la literatura en Cuba," originally published in *Verde Olivo* (Havana) 9, no. 47 (1968):14-18, but also available today in *El caso Padilla: Literatura y revolución en Cuba*, ed. Lourdes Casal (Miami: Ediciones Universal, 1970[?]), pp. 34-41. In 1968 Heberto Padilla's book of poems, *Fuera del juego*, was published with a prologue by the Writer's Union condemning the poet for his counterrevolutionary ideology. In 1971 Padilla was jailed briefly for alleged counterrevolutionary activities. Many European and Latin American intellectuals protested, and a veritable crisis ensued. Since then Padilla, with many other Cuban writers, has chosen exile over increasingly Sovietized Cuba.

8. Roberto Fernández Retmar, "Usted tenía razón, Tallet: somos hombres de transición," in *A quien pueda interesar (poesía 1958-1970)* (Mexico City: Siglo XXI, 1970), pp. 114-117.

9. For Desnoes's novel I am using the Joaquín Mortiz edition of 1975; the first edition was published in Havana in 1965. The novel was translated into English by the author as *Inconsolable Memories*, foreword by Jack Gelber (New York: New American Library, 1967). The English version of the filmscript and photographs may be found in *Memories of Underdevelopment: The Revolutionary Films of Cuba*, ed. Michael Myerson (New York: Grossman, 1973), pp. 39-107. The best criticism of both the novel and the film is contained in the three articles published by Henry Fernández, David Grossvogel, and Emir Rodríguez Monegal as "3 on 2: Desnoes-Gutiérrez Alea," *Diacritics* 4, no. 4 (1974):51-64.

10. For connectedness to exist there would have to be what Kermode calls a "fiction of concord" (*Sense of an Ending*, pp. 35-64). Such fictions are usually allegorical.

11. Ian Watt, *The Rise of the Novel* (Berkeley & Los Angeles: University of California Press, 1957).

12. In "Entrevista con Norberto Fuentes" (*Areíto* [New York] 2, no. 4 [1976]:46-48), Fuentes speaks in some detail about the composition of his books. He has not published a book of fiction since the two discussed here.

13. Antonio Núñez Jiménez, *La abuela (narraciones)* (Lima: Campodórnico Ediciones, 1973), p. 15: "Los abuelos son como libros que hablan. Cuentan las historias por ellos vividas, agregando las que oyeron de sus padres y de los padres de sus padres, de modo que a los nietos toca conocer, a través de sus narraciones, muchas cosas del pasado que a veces los libros convencionales no transmiten. Los abuelos enseñan a sus nietos un mundo fascinante con mucha más espontaneidad y frescura que el aprendido en algunas crónicas o historias escritas por profesionales."

14. Barnet explains this in a rather detailed account of the composition of *Biografía*, pp. 7-12.

15. Lydia Cabrera, *El monte (Igbo-Finda-Ewe Orisha-Vititi-Nfinda). Notas sobre las religiones, la magia, las supersticiones y el folklore de los negros criollos y del pueblo de Cuba* (Miami: Ediciones Universal, 1954; reprint, 1975), p. 13. I am translating *monte* as "woods," "mountain," and "wild," but the word has all those meanings simultaneously in Spanish. All the quotations are of Cabrera's informants.

16. The quotations are from Barnet, "La novela testimonio: socio-literatura," *Unión* (Havana) 6, no. 4 (1969):99-122. This essay has been appended to a 1970, Barcelona edition (Esleta) of *Canción de Rachel*.

17. In Cuba the maroons formed what were known as *palenques*, clandestine communities hidden in the wild. For details, see José Luciano Franco, *Los palenques de los negros cimarrones* (Havana: Departamento de Orientación Revolucionaria del Comité Central del Partido Comunista de Cuba, 1973); and also *Maroon Societies: Rebel Slave Communities in the Americas*, ed. Richard Price (New York: Anchor Books, 1973).

18. Quoted in Walter Benjamin, *Illuminations*, ed. Hanna Arendt (New York: Schocken Books, 1969), p. 139.

19. Raquel Chang-Rodríguez has already alluded to this "founding" aspect of Barnet's work in "Sobre *La Canción de Raquel*, novela-testimonio," *Revista Iberoamericana* 44, nos. 102-103 (1978):133-138.

Chapter 7: Literature and Exile: Carpentier's "Right of Sanctuary"

The epigraph to this chapter is from García Márquez's prologue to *¡Exilio!* by Lisandro Chávez Alfaro et al. (Mexico City: Tinta Libre, 1977), p. 10.

1. Octavio Paz, "Palabras al simposio," in *El artista latinoamericano y su identidad*, ed. Damián Bayón (Caracas: Monte Avila, 1977), p. 23.

2. José Martí, "Nuestra América," in *Páginas escogidas*, ed. Alfonso M. Escudero (Madrid: Espasa Calpe, 1953; reprint, 1971), pp. 117-124.

3. Harry Levin, "Literature and Exile," in *Essays in Comparative Literature*, ed. Herbert Dieckmann (St. Louis: Washington University Studies, 1961), p. 5. The bibliography of exile in relation to Spanish-language literature is immense, beginning with the classic study by Vicente Llorens, *Liberales y románticos: una emigración española en Inglaterra, 1823-1834*, 2d ed. (Madrid: Castalia, 1968). Paul Ilie's *Literature and Inner Exile: Authoritarian Spain, 1939-1975* (Baltimore, Md.: Johns Hopkins University Press, 1980), is a valuable thematic study, but limited by its exclusion of Latin American writers, more a quirk of American Hispanism than a reflection on the work of Spanish-language writers. A recent issue of *Review* (Center for Inter-American Relations), no. 30 (1981), contains provocative essays by Angel Rama, Julio Cortázar, Augusto Roa Bastos, and Fernando Alegría on the questions raised by exile. The organizers of the issue, however, left out Cuban exile writers, which resulted in an acrimonious controversy.

4. For the original I am using the first edition, *El derecho de asilo* (Barcelona: Editorial Lumen, 1972). Quotations in the text are from "Right of Sanctuary," in *War of Time*, tr. Frances Partridge (New York: Alfred A. Knopf, 1970), pp. 59-101. I have profited from S. Jiménez Fajardo's astute reading of "Right of Sanctuary" in his "Carpentier's *El derecho de asilo*: A Game Theory," *Journal of Spanish Studies-Twentieth Century* 6 (1978):193-206, and above all by Eduardo G. González's *Alejo Carpentier: el tiempo del hombre* (Caracas: Monte Avila, 1978).

5. Sharon Magnarelli, " 'El camino de Santiago' de Alejo Carpentier y la picaresca," *Revista Iberoamericana* 40 (1974):65-86.

6. *Indiano* is what Spaniards who returned from Latin America were called. They became a literary type.

7. Carpentier went into exile in 1928, fleeing from Gerardo Machado's dictatorship in Cuba. It is, of course, ironic that the first Pan-American Conference should have taken place in a Havana torn by the repression of Machado and the struggles against him organized mostly by the students. When the 1948 conference took place in Bogotá, Carpentier was in Caracas. During this conference the *bogotazo* took place. The 1954 conference was held in Caracas while Carpentier was living there. By the time he published "Right of Sanctuary," Cuba had been expelled from the Organization of American States at the Punta del Este Conference.

8. A landmark study of American influence in Latin America through popular culture, particularly comics, was published in 1971 (*Para leer al Pato Donald*, Ediciones Universitarias de Valparaíso), by Ariel Dorfman and Armand Mattelart (*How to Read Donald Duck. Imperialist Ideology in the Disney Comic*, tr. David Kunkle [New York: International General, 1975]). The most interesting part of the study, in my view, is the analysis of kinship structures in Donald Duck's world, which turn out to be unnatural in the sense that there is no clear genealogy. Carpentier's critique is broader and at the same time less virulent. He seems to be saying, on one level, that Latin American traditional institutions are being replaced by American ones, and that these banalize life by turning it into a sort of toy kingdom. Yet at the same time he is showing that the elements of these institutions contain the same sort of codification as the old one and that they can be used to think about the world and criticize it in the same way. The analysis by Dorfman and Mattelart would seem to confirm this.

9. I am indebted in my reading of the Paolo and Francesca episode to Renato Poggioli, "Paolo and Francesca," in *Dante: A Collection of Critical Essays,* ed. John Freccero (Englewood Cliffs, N.J.: Prentice-Hall, 1965), pp. 61-77.

10. There are allusions in the story not only to Pan-Americanism but also to the Alliance for Progress (1928, incidentally, was the year of the first international flight by the fledgling Pan American Airways. It took place between Key West and Havana, and the airplane, a Ford Trimotor, was named the "General Machado").

11. I am indebted in my analysis of the secretary to Jacques Derrida's "Plato's Pharmacy," in *Dissemination*, tr. Barbara Johnson (Chicago: University of Chicago Press, 1981), pp. 61-172.

"Meta-End"

The translation and annotations of "Meta-End" appeared in *Latin American Literary Review* 8, no. 16 (Spring-Summer 1980).

1. There are perceptive comments on the fragmentariness of *Three Trapped Tigers* in Alfred J. MacAdam's "Guillermo Cabrera Infante: The Vast Fragment," in his *Modern Latin American Narratives: The Dreams of Reason* (Chicago: University of Chicago Press, 1977), pp. 61-68.

2. For details, see the chronology of his life published by Cabrera Infante as "(C)ave Attemptor! A Chronology of GCI (After Laurence Sterne's)," in *Review 72* (Center for Inter-American Relations, New York) (Winter 1971/Spring 1972), pp.

5-9. This chronology, along with much useful material, appears in Spanish in the collective volume edited by Julián Ríos, *G. Cabrera Infante* (Madrid: Espiral, 1974).

3. The texts relative to the Padilla affairs were collected by Lourdes Casal in *El caso Padilla* (Miami: Ediciones Universal, 1970).

4. Cabrera Infante, *Three Trapped Tigers*, tr. Donald Gardner and Suzanne Jill Levine, in collaboration with the author (New York: Harper & Row, 1971). All quotations in the text are from this edition. Of the original I am using the second edition, published in 1968 by Seix Barral in Barcelona.

5. Cabrera Infante has also published *Un oficio del siglo veinte*, a collection of movie reviews. *Exorcismos de esti(l)o*, and *O* are both collages of variegated texts.

6. Sharon Magnarelli, "The 'Writerly' in *Tres tristes tigres*," in *The Analysis of Hispanic Texts: Current Trends and Methodology*, ed. Lisa E. Davis and Isabel C. Tarán (New York: Bilingual Press, 1976), pp. 320-335. The best analysis of the language of Cabrera Infante's novel is Stephanie Merrim's "Language in *Tres tristes tigres*," *Latin American Literary Review* 8, no. 16 (1980):96-117.

7. There is a strong connection between Estrella and one of Carpentier's better-known works, "Manhunt" (1956), the work parodied in *Three Trapped Tigers*. In that story a political activist is pursued by his former associates, whom he has betrayed to the police. He runs into a concert hall where Beethoven's *Eroica* is being played. The music, which he gradually begins to recognize, reminds him of the house where he was hiding under the protection of his former wet-nurse, a very old black. By the time the protagonist has arrived at the theater, she is dead and her body is being kept on ice at her wake. A younger mulatto woman, the prostitute Estrella, also offers refuge to the activist. The link between music and this dead black mother-figure and the Estrella in *Three Trapped Tigers*, whose name was possibly derived from the young black mother-substitute, is, to my mind, significant beyond establishing Cabrera Infante's indebtedness to Carpentier. In my view there is, in the set black-mother/music/ice, a contradictory conception of culture and tradition as melodic, prearticulate, of the origin, yet dead, frozen, keeping its issue out of its hieratic materiality. The relevant passage in "Manhunt" is in *Noonday* 2 (1959):143.

8. I have, to be sure, profited in my discussion of "Meta-Final" from Frank Kermode's excellent *The Sense of an Ending: Studies in the Theory of Fiction* (New York: Oxford University Press, 1966).

9. Cabrera Infante once told me that the initial idea for "Meta-Final" came from his reading a piece in a popular magazine about how Monk Lewis's body was transported back to England by ship.

10. Edward W. Said's *Beginnings* (New York: Basic Books, 1975) has no doubt influenced my observations here, as have Derrida's various meditations on beginnings of texts.

11. Helio Orovio, *Diccionario de la música cubana biográfico y técnico* (Havana: Editorial Letras Cubanas, 1981), p. 172.

12. Jacques Derrida, *Dissemination*, tr. Barbara Johnson (Chicago: University of Chicago Press, 1981), p. 84.

13. Severo Sarduy, *Barroco* (Buenos Aires: Editorial Sudamericana, 1974), p. 3.

Index